VIOLENCE AGAINST WOMEN

VIOLENCE AGAINST WOMEN
Dynamics of Conjugal Relations

MADHURIMA

GYAN

GYAN PUBLISHING HOUSE

NEW DELHI-110002

VIOLENCE AGAINST WOMEN
Dynamics of Conjugal Relations

(Women's Studies, Sociology)

ISBN: 81-212-0527-1

Published in 1996 in India by
Gyan Publishing House
5, Ansari Road
New Delhi 110 002

Laser Typeset at Rawat Computer Center, New Delhi-2
Printed at Mehra Offset Press, New Delhi-2

Dedicated to my beloved father

Late Prof. Amarjit Mahajan

Contents

	List of Tables		9
	Preface		11
	Acknowledgements		13
CHAPTER	1.	Introduction	15
	2.	Incidence of Violence	59
	3.	Correlates of Physical Violence	79
	4.	Coping Behaviour	109
	5.	Case Studies	129
	6.	Abusive Marital Relationship : An Overview	185
APPENDIX	I.	Social Class	199
	II.	Traditional Sex Based Roles	205
	III.	Value Orientation: Violence in the Family	209
	IV.	Objective Dependency	213
	V.	Subjective Dependency	215
	VI.	Total Dependency	217
	VII.	Interview Schedule	221
		Bibliography	229
		Index	263

List of Tables

2.1	Difference of opinion between the spouses	61
2.2	Difference of opinion leading to arguments	61
2.3	Issues on which spouses had arguments	62
2.4	Incidence of quarrel	63
2.5	Which of the spouse initiated quarrel	63
2.6	Instigators attributed to wife	64
2.7	Instigators attributed to husband	65
2.8	Withdrawal used by the spouses	67
2.9	The frequency of withdrawal	67
2.10	Psychological form of violence used by the spouses	69
2.11	The frequency of psychological violence	69
2.12	Verbal violence used by spouses	69
2.13	The frequency of verbal violence	70
2.14	Physical violence used by spouses	72
2.15	The frequency of physical violence	72
2.16	The frequency with which the spouses use different forms of violence against each other	75-76
3.1	Wife's age at marriage and physical violence	80
3.2	Wife's present age and physical violence	82
3.3	Children and violence against wives	83
3.4	Sex of children and violence against wives	84
3.5	Household composition and violence	85
3.6	Wife's education and physical violence	88
3.7	Wife's working status and physical violence	90
3.8	Occupational prestige and physical violence	91

3.9 Social class and physical violence 93
3.10 Wife's caste and physical violence 95
3.11 Wife's religion and physical violence 96
3.12 Traditionality and physical violence 99
3.13 Values in favour of violence and abuse 101
3.14 Objective dependency and physical violence 103
3.15 Subjective dependency and physical violence 105
3.16 Total dependency and physical violence 107
4.1 Violence in the presence of others 112
4.2 The reactions of the victims to violence 116
4.3 Victims who shared their bad experience 119
4.4 Types of advise extended by informal sources 120
4.5 Who reconciles first after the quarrel 122

APPENDICES : I—VI

I.1 Husband's education and occupation 200
I.2 Husband's education and income 200
I.3 Husband's occupation and income 201
I.4 Scores taken together on all the variables 202
I.5 Comprehensive social class 202
II.1 Scores regarding traditional sex based roles 206
II.2 Traditional sex based roles 207
III.1 Scores on value orientation 210
III.2 Value orientation and violence 211
IV.1 Scores on objective dependency 213
IV.2 Objective dependency of the respondents 214
V.1 Scores on subjective dependency 216
V.2 Subjective dependency of the respondents 216
VI.1 Score on total dependency 217
VI.2 Total dependency of the respondents 218

Preface

Different familial networks are governed by different quality of interpersonal relations between them. During the last few decades a number of instances regarding the quality of intra-familial relationships have come to the notice of general public which have forced the sociologists to accept the dictum "family is the centre of warmth" with cynicism. A number of researches have been conducted during the last two decades and it has now been established that family has a darker side also.

Violence by men against women and specifically against their wives is not a new problem, what is new, however, is public admission that wife abuse occurs in Indian families. Asymmetrical relations are the part of Indian social system. Husbands continue to dominate and use violence to maintain their supremacy. When wives meekly accept such a position, there is no conflict in the conjugal unit and family presents a picture of consensus and integrity. It is only when such asymmetrical relations are challenged that conflict and subsequently violence emerge.

Violence in one form or the other was found quite widespread in the present study. Asymmetrical gender relations became very prominent even with regard to different forms of violence used by spouses against each other. When a wife perceives injustice or is abused she may become angry but keeping in view the social definitions and societal reactions she may think twice before initiating any step which would result in serious retaliation from her husband or permanently break off the relationship. Dependency acts as a condition forcing these women to continue living in the abusive marital relationship mainly because they lack alternative support system. They have been socialized not to break up the marital relationship even under adverse conditions. Those women who have ventured to get their abuse terminated could do so only by terminating the marriage. The present book poses a serious question regarding the pitiable conditions of women victims who continue to live in abusive marital relations with the hope that things may improve.

The book has been divided into six chapters. The first chapter provides an overview of the problem of wife abuse. To start with the definitions of wife abuse and how extensive the problem is in our society. Subsequently, the precipitating factors which led to violent relationships have been discussed. Thereafter, the major theoretical frameworks have been presented with relevant critique of each. Finally, I have presented my perspective to enable the reader to understand my approach to the problem.

In the second chapter, an attempt has been made to find the presence or absence of violence against wives as well as the nature and extent of such violence in day to day life of the respondents under study.

Third chapter deals with physical violence against wives and its correlates—Demographic Variables, Social Variables and Dependency. Fourth chapter on coping behaviour has been divided into two parts. The first part relates to reactions of the victims to different forms of violence and second part deals with coping behaviour pattern which the victims adopt to deal with the violence.

To get a greater insight into dynamic aspect of conjugal relationship eight case histories are reported in chapter five. In the sixth and last chapter an effort has been made to summarize the empirical findings and draw inferences related to the issue under study.

Madhurima

Acknowledgements

The present study is based on my doctoral work which I was able to accomplish with guidance and encouragement of my dear father late Prof. Amarjit Mahajan. His insight and dedication has inspired me at different stages of completion of this work.

I also wish to thank Prof. P.N. Pimpley, Dept. of Sociology, Panjab University, for critical evaluation of the work which helped me a lot to improve the quality of manuscript.

I owe a great debt to my dear mother, who motivated me to complete and publish the work. I am thankful to my husband Mr. Harish Verma for his co-operation and understanding. He was a constant source of moral support.

I am thankful to my friend Mrs. Peeyushi Jain for much needed help and guidance.

I would like to thank all my respondents who provided me valuable time, precious information and full cooperation. I would also like to thank members of Punjab Istri Sabha, Chandigarh and Mrs. Grewal, Secretary of Family Counselling Centre, Chandigarh for their valuable help.

Madhurima

1 Introduction

Based on consensus model, the family sociologists have treated family as contributing to stability and order which is achieved through the process of socialisation of younger generation (Gelles, 1979; Goode, 1971; Kulkarni, 1982; Straus, 1980a). It is through familial association that social definitions and values are transmitted from one generation to next. It is for this reason the family has been treated as a "transmission belt" between an individual and society. Keeping in view, functions that a family performs for an individual and society it is treated as a basic institution of society. Such overemphasis of its contribution for bringing about stability gives scant attention to the conflicting interests of its members which are part and parcel of the role relationships. As social system is the outcome of both associative and dissociative processes, family being a "mini society" has also both positive and negative aspects which are inbuilt in its network of relationships.

Cooperation and conflict are normal features of familial relationships. However, presence of these features in the intimate relationships create a paradox. On the one hand, there is what Steinmetz and Straus (1974) have called the "Myth of family non-violence" which depicts cultural harmony and on the other hand, there seems to be social norms which grant the right to a few members to abuse other family members. Family sociologists have unfortunately overemphasized the positive aspect of familial relations and have neglected the other set of normative pattern regulating relation between family members.

During the last few decades a number of instances regarding the quality of intra-familial relationships have come to the notice of general public which have forced the sociologists to accept the dictum "family is the centre of warmth" with cynicism. A number of researches have been conducted during the last two decades and it has now been established that family has a darker side also. Family has also been seen as the source of assaults, violence and homicide. Gelles (1979) opines that people are more likely to be hit, beaten up, physically injured or even killed in their own homes by other members of the family. Other scholars have drawn the same conclusion. They contend that in the United States of America, violent crime occurs more frequently in the home than outside. Violence perpetrated among the members of the family is more common than violence among strangers (Dobash and Dobash, 1979; Freeman, 1979; Martin, 1976; Walker, 1979). Similarly Levinson (1989) on the basis of a cross cultural study of 90 societies came to the conclusion that family violence exists in one form or the other in 75 societies. He further argues that most people in the world have been at some time either the perpetrator, or the victim of or a witness to violence between members of their family.

Family violence range from any use of force in the family setting, including sibling fights, child and elderly abuse, and spousal conflicts. Similarly, violence conveys different meanings to different persons. From the legal perspective it refers to assaultive acts that lead to visible injuries both physical and mental. Mental health professionals include both assaultive and non-assaultive acts which are injurious to mental health of the victim. Sociologists tend to measure violence by the degree of its acceptance by society and from perspective of the victim, violence indicates transgression of the level of tolerance. The feminists include all patterns of discrimination under the category of violence. From power dynamic perspective, violence refers to abuse of power. Additionally, the terms 'violence' and 'abuse' have been distinguished. Violence refers to all forms of physical aggression while abuse refers to all physical and non-physical acts that cause physical and emotional injury to the victim. Taking into account different operational definitions adopted by researchers, they can be ranged from physical assaults to denial of freedom.

Gelles (1972) has defined family violence as day to day patterned and recurrent use of physical violence like pushing, slapping, punching, knifing, shooting and throwing objects by one member of the family at another'.

Gelles and Straus (1979a) added 'intention or perceived intention' but family violence for them remained physical in nature. Most of the studies on family violence have limited their scope to 'physical violence' involving members of the family. These studies (Downes, 1982; Gelles and Straus, 1979a; Levinson, 1989; Miller; 1976) have overlooked verbal and psychological violence like humiliation, insult and public embarrassment.

Garbarino and Gilliam (1980) highlight four basic features of the concept of abuse in intrafamilial relations. They are : the intentionality of the act, the effect of the act on the victim, the value judgement made about the act and the standard on which the judgement is based. Such definitions emphasise that violence, abuse, maltreatment have to be examined in a cultural context. Further, to enlarge the area of research neglect, abandonment, emotional exploitation have also been included under the label of abuse (Leonard and Jacob, 1988).

Pagelow (1984) adopted a broad concept of family violence by taking into account physical, verbal and psychological aspects of violence. He defined family violence as, "any act of commission or omission by family members and any condition resulting from such acts and inaction which deprive other family members of equal rights and liberties and/or interfere with their optimal development and freedom of choice".

These definitions have accordingly effected the nature and quality of research. The concept of family violence not only ranges from physical assault through psychological abuse to denial of freedom but also involves different network of relationships. Further, one cannot overlook the fact that different familial networks are governed by different normative patterns resulting into differential quality of interpersonal relations between them. Hence it would be problematic to club them together for explicating the nature and quality of interactions between them as well as for analytical purposes. Different familial network of relations are not only conceptually distinct but the causative factors of violence between them are also likely to be different. It is, therefore, most appropriate to limit one's field of research to one network at one time. It is for these reasons that subsequent discussion revolves around marital relationship only.

Out of different intra-familial network of relations, husband-wife relationship is basic on which family revolves. The quality of interaction between them would have repercussions on the whole family. Marital happiness will not only facilitate the adult members to perform their roles effectively and efficiently but will also facilitate for the creation of the congenial atmosphere and proper socialization of the progeny. On the other hand, marital conflict will not only lead to rupture in the family but would have adverse effect on the children.

Keeping in view the importance of husband-wife relationship in the family as well as the distinctive nature of quality of interaction between them, it would be most appropriate to investigate the nature, extent and precipitating factors which lead to conflict and violence in the conjugal relationship. There are additional reasons for restricting the present study to conjugal violence. One, a large number of studies report that wife beating occurs in more societies around the world than any other type of family violence. Second, most social and behavioural scientists working in the field of family violence have conceptualized it as a unidimensional phenomenon. Third, and the most important of all is the women's lower status. Husbands use violence against wives to reinforce their dominant position because use of coercive methods by the husbands has tacit societal approval. The studies further indicate that husbands resort to this behaviour pattern because they are physically more strong and do not visualize that their wives will hit back. Further, such victims are likely to continue living in the violent marital relationship because of their economic and social dependency.

It would be most appropriate to explicate the process by which wife abuse became a social problem in the Indian context. In the patriarchal Indian society the relationship between a man and a woman as husband and wife was of asymmetrical type. Sexual division of labour provides the husband's role as a provider and the wife is made responsible for upkeep of household. Such a division of labour gives rise to asymmetrical relations. As and when such asymmetrical relations are challenged, marital discord occurs because men would not give up their dominant position. Even when wife does not question her husband's absolute authority she is still abused. Mane (1991) on the basis of her analysis of ancient Indian literature reports that wives were meant to be beaten occasionally and it was a normal behaviour pattern. It was seen by husband, often as a manifestation of his power over his wife, a right which most husbands did not omit to exercise. Prominent Hindi poet Tulsidas wrote in his famous epic, *Ramacharitamanas*, "An animal, a rustic, a drum and a woman all require beating." In most cases of wife beating the reasons were extremely petty but related to breach of code of feminine conduct or poor performance of domestic activities.

Although husband and wife are treated as "two wheels of a cart", sexual intimacy fosters emotional interdependence. In the ancient literature wife is treated as a husband's other half (*ardhangini*). They are to perform all religious ceremonies together. They are supposed to enjoy the fruits of their action together. Wife is also considered to be the glory of home, the symbol of prosperity to family, the better half of husband, his friend, philosopher and guide. As a mother she is superior to ten fathers, superior to anything else on the earth (Majumdar, 1980). Manu declares that gods are pleased with those households where women are held in honour (Majumdar, 1980).

Due to asymmetrical roles, conflict is also inherent in conjugal network of relationship. Women assumed subordinate position and were denied equal status with men. They meekly suffered discrimination, disgrace and dehumanizing practices. Further, their economic dependence exposed them to various kinds of oppressions and exploitations. They accepted their sufferings because of the lack of alternative support system. During the 19th and 20th centuries a number of legislative steps were taken, first, to put an end to the exploitative practices against women and secondly to raise their position vis-a-vis men. These were the Social Reform Movement of the 19th century and the Nationalist Movement of the 20th century. Both these movements raised the question of equal status of women. The issues which attracted the attention of the social reformers of the 19th century were Sati, the ill-treatment of widows, the ban on widow marriage, polygamy, child marriage, denial of property rights and education to women. The following social reformers felt that these social evils should be eradicated by raising consciousness and making people sensitive to the injustice perpetrated on women. Raja Rammohun Roy, Ishwarchandra Vidya Sagar, M.G. Ranade, Mahatma Phuley, Swami Dayanand Saraswati, Swami Vivekananda were the main social reformers who raised their voices against some of the unjust practices.

Another very powerful force which helped to change the position and attitude towards women was the Nationalist

Movement particularly during the Gandhian phase. Women left the seclusion of purdah in large numbers not to join women's movement per sė but to participate in the struggle for independence from colonial rule. Gandhi listed equality of women in his Nine-Point Programme, but women's rights were not the primary goal of national movement. However, women gained political experience and confidence which extended their sphere of action beyond the home.

Serious attempts were made to elevate the status of women after the independence of India. An awareness of the need to remove social disabilities of women was created. Educational facilities were made available to them and a few urban based fortunate women could take advantage of these facilities. Techno-social changes provided opportunity for women not only to get modern education but also opened up new avenues for gainful employment outside their homes. In the recent years an increasing number of educated women have started accepting occupational roles of various types. These women are now competing for various positions along with men. They work not because they have to but because they like to. More women are seen working in non-traditional jobs and are also holding decision making posts. Political participation of women has also increased. Further, the constitutional recognition of equal status for women and progressive legal enactments have undoubtedly empowered Indian women with juridical equality. This change in their orientation has brought about a new awareness about their position as well as their resistance to exploitative social order. Equipped with modern education and economic independence they no longer accept asymmetrical marital relationship and are now claiming egalitarian way of living which implies change in the traditional role relationships between husband and wife. Men are not likely to accept the new position of the wife and may use greater force and violence to retain their traditional position. To highlight the plight of women victims, women organizations which are urban based have also started taking up such issues like dowry, domestic violence and rape cases to create public awareness.

In spite of the best efforts, women continue to suffer. Various protections failed to make any visible dent in their status. Patriarchal values and normative structure established some two thousand years ago still persist though in a different garb. The problems of women have become more serious since the discrimination and disabilities operate in more subtle and covert ways. The reality of the subordinate position of women is indicated through adverse sex ratio of girls, the growing domestic violence, increasing number of dowry deaths and rape cases. According to a recent survey conducted by UNICEF in India, every sixth female child's death is due to gender discrimination. Gender based inequities permeate almost every aspect of growing girls' social and cultural environment. For an average girl in India, the privations of poverty are significantly aggravated by value systems, norms and mores, which define and not infrequently, disparage the role of women (*Times of India,* 1995).

As the present study is confined to dynamics of conjugal relations, it will be suffice here to state that problem of wife abuse in our country play an important role in highlighting lower status of women.

REVIEW OF LITERATURE

It was during the second half of 1970's that social scientists in the West started conducting studies to find out the nature and the extent of violence against wives in the intra-family network. Subsequently, they also tried to identify the precipitating factors which led to violent relationship between the marital partners. Based on the results of the researches for almost two decades, the social scientists were able to work out not only the coping mechanism adopted by the victims but also different treatment programmes for the batterer and the battered. Further, a few sociologists have attempted to develop conflict tactic scale with the help of which the researcher would be able to identify the violence prone couples. Unfortunately, in India very few studies have been conducted in this area, except dowry related problems. However, from the late 1980's a few isolated attempts have been made to find out the nature of the problem as well as the precipitating factors which led to violence against wives. In review of literature, different researches under the broad headings of incidence of violence against wives, precipitating factors and coping mechanisms shall be discussed. The studies conducted in India and other countries have been grouped together.

Incidence of violence :

David Levinson (1989) an anthropologist after going through the records of human relations area Files at Yale University comes to the conclusion that wife beating is the most common form of family violence around the world. In a study of 90 societies, he finds that wife beating occurs occasionally in 74.5 per cent of the societies and it never occurs or very rarely occurs in 15.5 per cent.

A number of studies have been conducted in the United States to find out the incidence of assaults against wives, the estimates of these studies vary from one study to another. The most conservative estimate suggests that 12 per cent of all wives in the United States are physically abused by their mates each year (Straus, Gelles and Steinmetz, 1980). Other studies in the United States have suggested that incidence is as high as 50 per cent (Straus, 1978) to 60 per cent (Gelles, 1974; Walker, 1979). In a representative United States Survey which was specifically conducted to measure the violent acts among the intimates with the sample of 3300 families, Straus et. al. (1980) estimated that there were 3.9 million instances of spouse abuse annually. Two other surveys conducted in the United States also report alarming results. An estimated 20 per cent of the adult residents of Suffolk County, Long Island, have hit or been hit by their spouse (Nisonoff and Bitman, 1979). Szinovacz (1983) found that 26 per cent of the women had been abused in the sample of 103 couples from Pennsylvania towns.

Three state surveys conducted in the United States have focused exclusively on violence against wives. A Harris Poll of Kentucky housewives (Schulman, 1979) found that 10 per cent had been abused during the year and 21 per cent had ever been abused. A North Carolina sample revealed that 21 per cent had ever been beaten as adults by their husbands (Genteman, 1980). Finally, a probability sample of 1210 female residents of Texas, aged 18 or older found that 8.5 per cent had been abused during the year and 29.7 per cent had been abused 'ever' (Teske and Parker, 1983).

Data from the Second National Family Violence Survey conducted in the United States (Straus and Gelles, 1986), it was noted that in 16 per cent of the homes, some kind of the violence between the spouses had occurred in the year prior to the survey in 1986.

Some scholars are of the opinion that wife battering is quite widespread in all the cultures, though the problem is hidden away in some cultures as a "private matter" (Seager and Olson, 1986).

Different studies have been conducted around the world as reported by Levinson (1989) which show the presence of wife beating in different societies, Bororo of Brazil (Baldus, 1937); Kpelle of Liberia (Erchak, 1984); Serbs of Yugoslavia (Erlich, 1966); Azande of Central Africa (Evans-Pritchard, 1937); Moosi of Mali (Hammond, 1964); Ojibwa of Wisconscin (Landes, 1937); Somali of Somalia, (Lewis, 1962); Ganda of Uganda, (Mair, 1940); Quechua of Evader, (Muratoria, 1981); Greece (rural), (Sanders, 1962); Hare of Canada (Savishinsky, 1976).

A number of studies have been conducted in the United Kingdom (England, Wales, Scotland and Northern Ireland) which firmly establish that the wife abuse is a social problem (Hanmer, 1989; Johnson, 1985; Maidment, 1985). Small scale neighbourhood research projects aimed specifically at women, have had greater success in providing information on crimes against wives (Hanmer and Saunders, 1984; Radford, 1987), than the government sponsored national incidence surveys (Chambers and Tombs, 1984; Hough and Mathew, 1983; 1985). These government surveys have been remarkably poor at gaining information from woman, while non-random surveys give a tantalizing taste of the magnitude of sexual and other violent crimes against wives (Bains, 1987; Hall, 1986). Hanmer (1989) on the basis of a study of West Yorkshire in England reported 67 per cent of violence incidence against wives by their husbands within a period of one year as reported by police officers.

Hatty (1989) reported that in Australia, violence against wives has been most prolific in New South Wales. In another study it was found that out of 500 randomly selected sample, 106 cases reported wife abuse in New South Wales (Hatty and Sutton, 1986).

A study on 1000 families in New Zealand indicated that over a span of six years of family life the wife assault rates ranged between 8.5 per cent and 33 per cent. However, at the yearly basis the wife assault was limited to 3 per cent of cases under study (Fergusson et al., 1986).

Another study conducted in Netherland, indicates that violence against wives has become a common feature. The study does not, however, indicate the extent and frequency with which such violence takes place (Zoomer, 1983). In a longitudinal study conducted on 100 Catholic Mestizo households in Caipi, an Ecuadorian farming community in 1976 and 1983, it was noted that wife abuse was a common feature of the community (Stolen, 1990).

No official figures for domestic violence exist in Russia because it is not defined as a crime in Russia's criminal code. Khotkina (1995) reported on the basis of research by Sociologists and Human Rights Groups that about 14500 women died as a result of domestic violence in 1994 in Russia alone.

Unfortunately in India, no nationally representative sample survey has been conducted to find out the extent of the problem of wife abuse. However, a few sample surveys have been conducted in metropolitan cities to highlight rising crime against women. (Ahuja, 1987; *Indian Express*, 1994; Misra, 1994; Munshi, 1994; *Times of India*, 1994; *Tribune*, 1995). The data used in these sample surveys have been restricted to cases of physical aggression only. Even the figures on physical violence hardly reflect the enormity of the scale of aggression as they are based on police data which depend on complaints registered and not on the number of actual incidents.

In marriage, too, innumerable women have been at receiving end. In a bid to control the sexuality of women, many an insensitive husband has been known to indulge in the most barbaric forms of wife abuse, both of the body and mind. A very few studies have been conducted to find out the frequency of wife abuse. Grewal (1982) in a sample of 117 cases of the lower class at Chandigarh found that approximately 66 per cent of the husbands use verbal violence and approximately 33 per cent use physical violence against their wives. Singh (1985) in a study conducted in a village of Punjab found that violence in different forms existed in 50 per cent of the cases out of the sample of 114 cases belonging to different caste groups. Mahajan and Madhurima (1995) conducted a study in a village of the Union Territory of Chandigarh. They found that out of total number of 115 households belonging to the lower class 75 per cent of the households experienced one or the other form of violence in the conjugal unit.

A study conducted by the women's cell of the Majitha police district has revealed that wife beating by inebriated husbands is on the rise where alcohol is back in the open after militancy in Punjab petered out. Each day a number of battered wives, thrown out of their homes by drunken husbands, throng to the women's cell at the district headquarters along with their parents and members of the Panchayat to seek justice (*Tribune*, 1994).

A number of studies highlighting the dowry related

problems in Indian marriages have identified a number of atrocities committed against women by their husbands and in-laws (Agnes, 1993; Ganker, 1993; Gautam and Trivedi, 1987; Muzumdar, 1992; Paul, 1992; Prasad, 1989; Shah, 1989; Singh and Renuka, 1989; Sugumar, 1989; *Tribune*, 1995; Verghese, 1980).

Wife abuse is considered a private affair in the Indian society and it is difficult for the researchers to find out the extent of the problem in the general population. Hence depending upon snow balling technique a few studies have been conducted on the known cases of the battered women to find out the severity of the violence (Ahuja, 1987; Jain, 1992; Kaushik, 1989; Misra, 1994; Rai, 1994; Sharma, 1992).

Taking into account the reasons for seeking divorce, Chaudhary (1989) in his study found that 17.5 per cent of the cases had filed application for divorce because of physical assaults on them by their husbands.

Bhatti (1989) while taking into account different forms of violence concluded that 88 per cent of women in lower class were the victims of physical and verbal violence in contrast to 43 per cent from the middle class and 35 per cent from the high income class were the victims of physical violence. With regard to emotional and intellectual violence he found that the representation of the upper and middle classes was more as compared to the lower class.

With the exception of the United States, in no other country a national sample survey on wife abuse has been conducted. Keeping in view the paucity of reliable information on wife abuse in different countries in the general population, it is difficult to give any estimate regarding the extent of the problem. Nevertheless, different studies establish that wife abuse or wife battering is quite widespread around the world. So far as the studies conducted in India are concerned, most of them are limited to self-identified abused women and the concept of abuse has also been reduced to physical violence only.

Precipitating factors :

A number of studies have been conducted to identify the precipitating factors which lead to wife abuse. Some of the scholars have attributed abuse to the personality factors either of the batterer or the battered or to both. Most of the sociologists have tried to identify the social variables which are responsible for differential behaviour pattern attributing it to socialization, normative pattern, value system, traditional sex role orientation, social class background, etc. For the purpose of convenience, instead of taking into account individual studies, different studies have been grouped together on the basis of commonality of their themes.

Personality disorders :

Many researchers assume that identifiable psychopathology exists among the battering husbands (Ptacek, 1988) and they may often suffer from various personality disorders. They have been described as passive aggressive, obsessive compulsive, paranoid, sadistic and addiction prone (Faulk, 1977; Gleason, 1993; Shainess, 1977; Snell et al., 1964) or suffering from neurological or biochemical disorders (Elliot, 1977; Schauss, 1982). These researchers are of the opinion that these personality disorders directly involve abusive behaviour. Andersen et al. (1991) reported that these personality disorders are severe and carry a negative prognosis. They imply a lack of emotional empathy for the feelings of others.

Similarly, abused women are described as aggressive, masculine, frigid and masochistic (Ball, 1977; Snell et al., 1964). Others find battered women as unassertive, shy and reserved (Weitzman and Dreen, 1982).

Straus (1980a), on the other hand, claims that it is a myth that violence is used only by mentally disturbed people. He argues that fewer than 10 per cent of all instances of family violence are caused by mental illness or psychiatric disorders. Similar views have been expressed by other researchers (Browning, 1983; Dvoskin, 1981; Stark and Flitcraft, 1988).

Gelles and Cornell (1990) argue that it is difficult to interpret behaviour of the battered women in terms of personality disorders because one never really knows whether the personality factors found in the battered wives were present before they were battered or are the result of their victimization. They further argue that personality studies of the battered women frequently use small samples or clinical samples and often fail to have comparison groups. Thus generalization from these studies is difficult and demonstrating that battered women are actually different from non-battered women is nearly impossible using these data (Gelles and Harrop, 1989).

Low self-esteem :

Many researchers suggest that batterers have low self-esteem and they use violence to compensate the feelings of inadequacy and to prove masculinity (Boyd, 1978; Coleman, 1980; Gayford, 1975; Gelles, 1980; Kalmuss and Straus, 1982; Kaplan, 1972; Labell, 1979; Martin, 1976; Rosenbaum and O' Leary, 1981a; Straus et al., 1980; Walker, 1979, 1981). Man uses violence to compensate for his feelings of inadequacy because violence can be a vehicle for achieving a more positive attitude toward the self if the individual has experienced its being subtly condoned (Johnston, 1988; Kaplan, 1972; Stith and Failey, 1993).

The battered women have also been described as having low esteem and feelings of inadequacy and helplessness (Ball, 1977; Hilberman and Munson, 1977-81; Shainess, 1977; Star et al., 1979; Walker, 1979).

Lack of assertiveness :

Wife batterers have been described as having difficulty in expressing verbally what they think, feel and want (Ganley and Harris, 1978) and as being non-assertive both in their families and in the outside world (Browning, 1983; Ganley and Harris, 1978; Rosenbaum and O' Leary, 1981a; Saunders, 1982; Sonkin et al., 1985). Ganley and Harris (1978) note that assaultive men appear to be poor listeners, are unable to communicate directly and confuse assertiveness with aggression. Although many batterers may have good verbal skills in some areas, such as manipulation they tend not to use these skills in expressing their feelings assertively.

Stress :

The presence of stress, both internal and external has been found to be strongly related to the risk of wife abuse (Ganley and Harris, 1978; Gelles and Cornell, 1990; Mahajan and Madhurima, 1995; Neidig and Friedman, 1984; O'Leary et al., 1988; Straus, 1980c). These men have learned to respond to stress with attempts to control others with violence. Straus (1980c) concludes that it is not stress per se that is the cause of marital violence, violence is but one of many responses to stress. He further argues that stress is a mediating variable that may occur in combination with other variables to make violence more likely.

Self-blame :

A number of studies have established that aggressors do not own the responsibility of their violent behaviour towards their wives. Abusive men rarely define their violence as deviant behaviour and attempt to rationalize their behaviour through minimization, confusion, denial of attention, intoxication, loss of control and projection of blame on to women (Adams and McCormick, 1982; Bhatti, 1985, 1989; Dobash and Dobash, 1979; Lata, 1989; Mahajan, 1989a; Ptacek, 1988; Shah, 1989; Saunders, 1982; Straus et al., 1980).

The battering males may induce guilt in their victims by blaming them for the abuse until they come to blame themselves. Blaming the victim is frequently used to justify the use of coercive power (Cantos et. al, 1993; Kipnis, 1976).

The victims also endorse the contention of their aggressors. They assume the responsibility and suffer from the guilt that they provoked their husbands to be violent. (Ferraro and

Johnson, 1983; Flemons, 1989; Hilberman, 1980; Hilberman and Minson, 1977-1981; Miller and Carol, 1983; Pagelow, 1981a). Anderson et al. (1991) argue that self-blame is common in the battered women who invest more and more efforts in the relationship to make it work and blame themselves for the failure.

Pregnancy :

Several researchers have suggested that women experience violence at unusually high rates during pregnancy. Two types of explanations are given for it : (1) children are considered intruders by fathers and (2) pregnant wives are perceived as unwilling or unable to retaliate to violence (Dobash and Dobash, 1979; Gelles, 1972; 1988; Helton, 1985; Kaplan, 1972; Pagelow, 1981a; Stark et al., 1981; Teske and Parker, 1983; Walker, 1979).

Jealousy :

Different studies have enumerated a number of additional factors responsible for wife beating. Sexual jealousy, a form of insecurity is a common theme in the literature on violent marriages (Bhatti, 1989; Dobash and Dobash, 1979; Hilberman and Munson, 1978-81; Mahajan, 1989a; Mohan, 1989; Pagelow, 1981a; Parihar, 1989; Stacey and Shupe, 1983; Walker, 1979). The battered women have also endorsed that jealousy in one form or another was the main source of their husband's violent behaviour (Daly et al., 1982; Rounsaville, 1978; Roy, 1977; Whitehurst, 1971).

Marital satisfaction :

Some studies indicate that violence is negatively correlated with marital satisfaction (Hoffman et al. 1994; Kratcoski, 1984; Lystad, 1982; Martin et al., 1987). On the other hand, there are some studies which indicate existence of violence in satisfied couples. There is a belief that love and violence go together (Brinkerhoff and Lupri, 1988; Byles, 1982; Dutton, 1988).

Alcohol :

Many researches have held use of alcohol on the part of husband to be an important factor for wife abuse (Ahuja, 1987; Bhatti, 1989; Bordin, 1981; Brekke and Saunders, 1982; Coleman et al., 1980; Grewal, 1982; Hastings and Hamberger, 1988; Mahajan, 1989a; Mohan, 1989; Parihar, 1989; Shah, 1989; Singh, 1985; Snell et al., 1964, *Tribune,* 1994).

Some research studies, however, find that although there is a strong relationship between alcohol and violence, physical violence in families actually declined when drunkenness occurred "almost always" (Coleman and Straus, 1983). Alcohol as such is not an immediate antecedent of violence in a majority of families in which violence occurs (Kantor and Straus, 1987).

Cross-cultural studies of alcohol use and studies of marital violence suggest that alcohol itself does not lead to violence rather, men drink to have a socially acceptable excuse for violent behaviour (Gelles, 1974).

Sex differences :

There are many studies which suggest that females are less aggressive than males. Hence females are always victims of male aggression. Physiologists have attributed violence to genetics and hormones (Eme, 1979; Kaplan, 1972; McFarlane et al., 1954; Sears, 1961; Shaffer et al., 1980).

Race :

Some studies have tried to find out association between race and wife abuse. It is argued that Blacks use more violence against their wives as compared to Whites (McAdoo, 1981; Straus et al., 1980; Willie, 1981). These researchers are of the opinion that there is more marital violence in Blacks because they are also subject to different types of stress, discrimination and frustration. There are, however, a few studies in which it was reported that Whites were more violent both inside and outside their homes (Fagen et al., 1983).

Another group of researchers argue that there is no significant difference between the proportion of Black and White women who were the victims of marital violence (Casanave and Straus, 1979; Lockhart, 1987). It is further argued that race has no effect on marital violence, however, when social class positions are controlled, Black women experience more violence. Thus the issue of race remains enigmatic and warrants further investigation.

Social class :

A number of studies highlight that wife beating is more common in the lower classes (Ahuja, 1987; Bhatti, 1985; Gaguin, 1978; Gelles and Cornell, 1983, 1990; Grewal, 1982; Mahajan and Madhurima, 1995; Prescott and Letko, 1977; Saunders, 1982; Young, 1963).

The use and approval of physical violence in the lower class can be explained in terms of "Culture of Poverty" (Lewis, 1959). It has been argued that for the lower class people physical violence is normal and socially transmitted behaviour pattern (Davis, 1963; Whitehurst, 1974). Lower class husbands use physical force against their wives in order to give vent to their frustrations. According to frustration aggression explanation developed by Dollard and his associates (1939), aggression should be directed against the source of frustration. However, members of the lower class cannot show their aggression against those who are highly placed, hence their aggression is displaced.

On the other hand, several studies show that wife battering cuts across the class boundaries (Berk et al., 1983; Dobash and Dobash, 1979; Giles-Sims, 1983; Hilberman, 1980; Mahajan, 1989a; Martin, 1976; Star et al., 1979; Steinmetz, 1977; Straus et al., 1980; Walker, 1979; 1984).

Further, dowry related violence against women in the Indian society is a phenomenon of the middle class families. The low incidence of violence in the upper and middle classes can be attributed to their resources with the help of which they are able to keep their violence as 'private' but it does not mean that women in the middle and upper classes are free from such abuse (Gelles and Cornell, 1990; Margolin et al., 1988).

Employment status :

Wife abuse has been found to be associated with employment status of the husband. Wife battering is more in families where the husband is unemployed (Fitch and Papantonio, 1983; Gaguin, 1978; Gayford, 1975; Lewis, 1987; Prescott and Letko, 1977; Rounsaville, 1978; Straus et al., 1980). This may be due to number of factors, loss of income may increase the batterer's stress, lack of employment may be seen as a failure to live up to his status expectation that man should be the family provider (Hornung et al., 1981; Gelles and Cornell, 1990; O'Brien, 1971) or lack of a job may increase the time spent at home, increasing the opportunity for violence. It is further argued that men who are employed part-time have even higher rates probably because they do not have full time jobs and ineligible for unemployment or other benefits (Straus et al., 1980).

Steinmetz (1977) on the other hand argues that occupational environment (rather than employment status per se) was an important stimulus to violence and survey data points that clerical, service workers or managers and professionals are at a highest risk (Gaguin, 1977; Schulman, 1979; Stark and Flitcraft, 1988). Iwarimie-Jaja (1989) however, indicates that husbands working in unskilled occupations are more likely to be abusive than those working in skilled occupations and men in professional occupations were the least abusive.

Wife abuse has also been associated with employment status of wives. It is argued that women who stay at home and do not work outside the home as paid worker are at greater risk of being abused. When women have few personal resources severity of violence against them also increases (Iwarimie-Jaja, 1989; Levinson, 1989; Mitchell and Hodson, 1983; Schwartz, 1990). Hornung et al. (1981) on the other hand reported that housewives had a lower risk of violence than employed women.

Power imbalance :

Power imbalanced relationships are associated with spousal abuse, especially when the imbalance threatens the males power (Harris and Associates, 1979). Wife beating occurs far more often in families where all the decisions are made either by the wife or the husband (Adler, 1981; Bowker, 1983; Coleman and Straus, 1986). It is believed that wife beating tends to decrease in frequency when decision making becomes more egalitarian (Bowker, 1983; Coleman and Straus, 1986; Straus et al., 1980). Hauser (1982) however, argues that equal power is seen as a lower position for the husband and as a higher position for the wife, as a consequence, husbands refuse to accept egalitarian way of living and violence continues.

Values :

It is argued that violent wives as well as violent husbands express values in favour of violence than do non-violent husbands and wives (Briere, 1987; Levinson, 1989; Margolin et al., 1988; Straus, 1980b). Saunders (1982) suggests that if a man believes that use of violence is acceptable he may be less likely to internalize controls that would inhibit violence.

Traditional sex-role orientation :

The male batterer is characterized as holding traditional sex stereotyped values (Coleman, 1980; Gelles, 1980; Rosenbaum and O'Leary, 1981; Smith, 1990; Walker, 1981; 1988). Researchers argue that violence tends to erupt when there is a clash of ideologies between traditional, conservative, patriarchal husbands and non-traditional liberated wives (Walker, 1984; Whitehurst, 1974). Traditional male sex-role socialization places strong emphasis on men being in control in all aspects of their lives and batterers tend to overidentify with these dysfunctional and stereotypic masculine values and expectations (Gondolf, 1985; Straus, 1976). They hold high expectations of their own abilities to regulate their feelings and behaviours and are often described as rigid. Their patriarchal belief system grants them privilege and power to enforce their expectations on their partners using violence, if necessary (Carmen, 1981; Gondolf, 1985; Pagelow, 1981a; Smith, 1990; Yllo, 1983).

Social learning :

A large number of studies show that violence is a learned behaviour. Batterers have been abused as children or they have witnessed their fathers beating their mothers and as adults they also use violence against their wives as a means to an end (Ceaser, 1988; Erlanger, 1979; Freeman, 1979; Gelles, 1972; Hotaling and Sugarman, 1986; Kalmuss, 1984; Malone et al., 1989; O'Leary, 1988; Pagelow, 1981b; Rosenbaum and O'Leary, 1981b; Shupe et al., 1987; Straus et al., 1980; Ulbrich and Huber, 1981).

There are other researchers who do not find significant relationship between social learning and wife abuse (Emery, 1989; Gelles and Cornell, 1990; Rosenbaum and O'Leary, 1981b; Telch and Lindquist, 1984). They argue that violent background does not always predetermine a violent adulthood. Although the chances of being an offender and victim are increased if one grows up in a violent home, there are many violent people who had limited exposure to violence as children and some people who experienced extremely violent childhoods grow up to be non-violent persons (Gelles and Cornell, 1990).

The social learning model assumes that the battering male is violent with his wife in order to control her behaviour (to get rid of what he sees as aversive in her behaviour and to get her to behave as he wishes). Despite the power of the theory in accounting for wife battering, the applications of the model have also been limited by failing to deal directly with "internal" maintaining conditions for violent marital behaviours (Emery, 1989). Instead the literature has focused rather exclusively on "external" contingencies (Emery, 1989) which is problematic because the goal of aggressive behaviour is often to inflict pain rather than to attain some external instrumental end (Berkowitz, 1983; Emery, 1989).

Status inconsistency :

Status inconsistency between the spouses is also considered to be risk factor in wife abuse. Wives having higher occupational status than husbands have high risks of being abused particularly life threatening violence because such a situation disturbs the traditional position of the husbands (Demaris, 1987; Hauser, 1982; Hornung et al., 1981; Hotaling and Sugarman, 1986; Mohan, 1989; Yllo, 1983). Male dominance and female subordination is viewed as normal conditions but when some inconsistency develops in the status of either husband or wife, wife abuse results (Bhatti, 1989; Brienes and Gordon, 1983; Carmen, 1981; Dobash and Dobash, 1979; Hoffman et al. 1994; Martin, 1979; Mohan, 1989; Moore, 1979; Norman, 1985; Parihar, 1989; Stith and Failey, 1993).

Dependency :

Dependency is considered to be positively related with wife abuse. Those wives who do not have independent source of income and are psychologically more committed to their marital partners are at greater risk of being abused. Lack of any alternative support forces them to continue in the abusive relationship (Dobash and Dobash, 1979; Kertzman, 1980; Levinson, 1989; Mahajan, 1989a; Marsden, 1978; Mitchell and Hodson, 1983; Roy, 1977; 1982; Strube and Barbour, 1983; Truninger, 1971; Walker, 1978).

Wife assaulters have also been characterized as being extremely dependent on their partners (Bernard and Bernard, 1984; Browning, 1983; Coleman, 1980; Elbow, 1977;

Fault, 1977; Ganley and Harris, 1978; Hilberman and Munson, 1977-81; Saunders, 1982; Sonkin et al., 1985; Walker, 1979). Stordeur and Stille (1989) argue that dependency creates emotional conflicts for the batterers as they are likely to be afraid of loosing real intimacy. They fear that they will be abandoned, as a consequence when such a situation comes they become violent, homicidal or even suicidal in an attempt to prevent their abandonment.

The above noted studies on the precipitating factors leading to wife battering highlight one or the other factor. There is hardly any study which takes into account holistic approach and accounts for different precipitating factors. Further, taking into account the social definitions, one set of precipitating factors is likely to play pivotal role in one culture and another set of precipitating factors may be important in another culture. In short, the precipitating factors have to be seen in a cultural context.

Coping mechanisms :

Equipped with rich data on the incidence and nature of wife battering the sociologists in America have started working out the coping mechanisms to deal with problem of wife abuse. They not only look at the reactions of the victims but also the strategies adopted by the victims. Recently they have also started working out the programmes for the perpetrators of violence as well as for the victims for reducing conjugal violence.

Victims' reactions :

Different researchers report that victims experience a variety of reactions as a consequence of abusive behaviour of their husbands such as terror, shame, degradation, guilt, humiliation, constant anxiety, apprehension and depression (Gelles and Harrop, 1989; Hilberman and Munson, 1977-81; Hilberman, 1980; Marsden and Owens, 1975; Schechter, 1982; Star et al., 1979; Walker, 1978; 1988).

Violence against wives has negative consequences not only for the victims but also for the whole family. In battering relationships the women are always isolated from outside sources of social support (Boulette and Andersen, 1985; Ponzetti et al., 1982; Straus et al., 1980). Further, it leads to low self-esteem of mother in the eyes of her children. Moreover such families become the training grounds for young to be violent (Browne, 1988; Giles-Sims, 1983; Martin, 1976; Nicarty, 1982; Straus et al. 1980; Walker, 1979; 1981; 1984).

There is also a growing body of research that suggests that wife beating may lead directly to suicide or suicidal attempts (Back et al., 1982; Counts, 1988; Pagelow, 1984; Stark and Flitcraft, 1985). It may not be beatings per se that lead wives to kill themselves but beatings that are abusive and that bring shame to women. Mitchell (1990) explains the case of Wape women, a pacific cultural ethos where wife beating is rare experience, when it occurs, it is a humiliating experience. So suicide is a culturally accepted response and is seen as a self-empowering act.

Coping with abusive behaviour :

Researchers have tried to study different coping mechanisms used by the abused women to deal with abusive behaviour. Many researchers report that battered women specifically resist the notion that they should leave their battering husbands. First, because the battered women feel that they have invested too much (time, effort, money and emotions) (Brockner and Rubin, 1985; Brockner et al., 1981; Foss, 1980; Strube, 1988). Secondly, due to 'psychological entrapment' where women give exclusive value to their marriages over and above other aspects of their lives may be at risk of being battered (Dutton, 1983; Dutton and Browning, 1988; Dutton and Painter, 1981; Strube, 1988) and thirdly, battered women may suffer from "learned helplessness" in that they come to expect that no relationship exists between their actions and the outcomes. After trying and failing to prevent the abuse they may give up and become unable to learn that there is a way out of the situation (Boulette and Andersen, 1985; Munshi, 1994; Rai, 1994; Walker, 1979, 1983). Abramson et al. (1978) argue that learned helplessness is more likely when the victim of abuse attributes the abuse to internal, stable and global causes.

In addition to above mentioned reasons, other researchers have also mentioned different factors such as lack of alternative support system, self-image, social stigma, dependency, presence of small children and fear of living alone and embarrassment to admit that she has stayed in such a bad situation for so long, etc., which force women to remain in the violent relationship (Bhatti, 1989; Bergman et al., 1988; Chapman and Gates, 1978; Edgell, 1980; Mahajan, 1989a; Mahajan and Madhurima, 1995; Martin, 1979; Parihar, 1989; Roy, 1977; Russell and Ven, 1976; Shah, 1989; Strube and Barbour, 1983; Walker, 1979).

Some researchers argue that many abused women cope with violence by leaving the abusive relationship. It is argued that women who are employed, who get support from their family of orientation, friends and who do not have children are more likely to leave the abusive relationship (Gelles, 1976; Moore, 1979; Okun, 1988; Strube, 1988).

Treatment for the batterers :

As the problem of domestic violence has gained recognition, some researchers have suggested different treatment programmes for the batterers such as individual therapy, marital and family therapy, psychoeducational or psychotherapeutic group approach, community intervention and anger control techniques (Adams, 1988; Adams and McCormick, 1982; Gondolf, 1985; Roberts, 1984; Rosenbaum, 1986; Sonkin et al., 1985).

One study of abusive men who had been reformed in treatment indicated that they attributed their successful treatment to learning to accept responsibility for their problems, learning to become more empathetic and learning to redefine their conceptions of manhood (Gondolf and Hanneken, 1987).

It is believed that such programmes are not very successful in checking the abusive behaviour of the batterers (Gondolf and Fisher, 1991 ; Gondolf and Russell, 1986). Bowker (1983) argues that those who do stop physical violence heighten their psychological abuse. Those who do stop their abuse and violence are likely to do so as a result of constellation of interventions.

Treatment for the victims :

A variety of counselling approaches have been proposed for battered women (Gondolf and Fisher, 1988;1991; Rieker and Carmen, 1986; Turner and Shapiro, 1986). It is suggested that women should also think about resource allocation because it not only enables them to leave abusive relationship but also helps to 'equalize' the relationship (Gondolf and Fisher, 1991).

Andersen et. al. (1991) consider separation of the wife from the abusive husband as an important factor for the treatment of abuse. They also argue that the wife must not be encouraged to leave her husband until she has the resources to stay away either permanently or long enough to facilitate significant change in the husband's behaviour.

Other researchers have mentioned different counselling sessions for the battered women where the main aim is to reduce psychological dependence of victim, to reestablish her self-esteem, to combat traditional sex-role concepts, to dissuade her of beliefs that she can control the abuse and to decrease her acceptance or tolerance of the use of physical force in interpersonal disputes (Carlson, 1977; Gregory, 1976; Pagelow, 1978; Ridington, 1977-78; Straus et al, 1980; Vaugan, 1979; Walker, 1978, 1984).

Solution of the problem :

Ultimate aim of any scientific research is to suggest measures to control the problem after finding out the causative factors responsible for the existence of a social problem.

Keeping with this view, Straus (1979) with the help of 18 items of life stresses developed conflict tactics scale so that violence prone families could be identified. Efforts are being made to test the scale in different situations by various researchers.

Most of the researchers agree with the viewpoint that the root cause of wife abuse can be traced to societal values favouring use of violence and wives' objective and subjective dependency. Therefore, its solution lies in removing wives' dependency as well as bring about a change in the value system (Baum, 1987; Gil, 1979; Hotaling et al., 1988; Levinson, 1989; Linnel et al., 1984; Moore, 1979; Strube, 1988; Walker, 1979).

Absence of wife abuse :

Levinson (1989) on the basis of cross cultural study in 90 societies found that in approximately 16 societies there was absence of any kind of family violence. The absence is attributed to (i) equal share of husbands and wives in family decision making process (ii) wives being more powerful economically (iii) wives having informal support system, (iv) remarriage permissible to both husband and wife (v) and monogamous relationship and lack of premarital sex double standards. Kumagai (1979) and Mitchell (1990) also report the similar findings in other cultural groups.

The above mentioned researches on different coping mechanisms used for the purpose of reducing family violence have been evolved by psychologists which are individual based. As these techniques do not account for social definitions, normative pattern and socialization they fail to achieve the desired results. Even when psychological health of the batterer and the battered is restored, the "cure" would have no effect if the violent couples are sent back to the same social environment which had made them violent in the first place. In other words, unless social definitions are changed and women are allowed to have egalitarian way of life, wife abuse in one form or the other would persist.

Gaps in the available literature :

The review of the literature, no doubt helps in providing a guideline for future research on wife abuse, nevertheless, these researches cannot be used as a model for the present study for a number of reasons. First, there is no consensus among the researchers on the definition of wife abuse.

Secondly, most of the researchers have taken a very narrow aspect of violence, that is, physical violence and have overlooked verbal and psychological violence in the marital relationship which is sometimes more damaging than physical violence.

Thirdly, no study has taken holistic approach to explicate the precipitating factors of wife abuse.

Fourthly, the precipitating factors have to be seen in the cultural context, hence, the results of different studies conducted in the United States may not be applicable in Indian context.

Fifthly, most of the studies have not used qualitative research methodology to explain violent marital relationship. It is through qualitative research only that subterranean aspect of conjugal relationship can be understood. Additionally, in the Indian context no systematic scientific study has been conducted for understanding the nature of the phenomenon. No doubt, a few empirical studies have been conducted recently but even in these studies no theoretical framework has been used to explicate the problem of wife abuse in India.

Theoretical frameworks :

From the review of the literature it can be stated that scholars have used different theoretical frameworks to understand the nature and the extent of wife abuse, to identify the major social factors associated with the problem and to suggest ways to control violence against the wives. Instead of taking all the perspectives, I will restrict my analysis to sociological perspectives only, which have caught the attention of family violence scholars. Sociological perspective embraces the microscopic as well as macroscopic levels of analysis. It is for this reason that different theoretical frameworks used by family violence scholars will be discussed under the heading of micro level perspectives, which will include resource, exchange/control and symbolic interaction, and macrolevel perspectives which will include subculture of violence, conflict, patriarchal and general systems.

Resource theory :

Rests on the notion that decision making power in family relationships depends to a large extent on the value of resources each person brings to the relationship (Blood and Wolfe, 1960). Violence is used as a last resort to regain status quo ante (Goode, 1971). Resource theory has been revised and it has come to be called as status inconsistency theory. This perspective suggests that violence is more likely to occur when a man perceives his status inconsistent with his traditional power in the family which has been eroded because women's power has increased. He resorts to violence to compensate the loss of his power over his wife.

When this theoretical perspective was used in empirical research it produced inconsistent findings. For example, Allen and Straus (1980) provides some evidence that the more resources people have the less likely they are to commit family violence. However, Stark and McEvoy (1970) showed the opposite.

Exchange or social control theory :

Drawing from general exchange theory and social control theory, Gelles (1983) proposed an exchange or social control model of family violence. Gelles (1983) argues that unlike regular social interactions, intrafamilial relations cannot be broken off easily because members take into account the profit and loss they receive from such relationship. As a consequence when family members perceive injustice in a daily interaction, they become angry and resentful as a result violence erupts. He summarizes "People hit and abuse other family members because they can." The wife tolerates violence because of her greater investment in marriage and lack of alternative resources.

This theory does not account for the possibility of any change in the husband-wife relationship and also for the changing position of women who want to enter into marital relationship to have egalitarian way of life. Further it fails to take into account the chances of the victim hitting back and use of violence leading to a loss of status.

Symbolic interaction perspective :

Symbolic interactionism rests on three basic assumptions. First, social reality as it is sensed, known and understood. Interacting individuals produce and define their own definitions of the situation. Second, humans are capable of shaping and guiding their own behaviour and that of others. Third, in the course of taking their own standpoint and filling that standpoint with the behaviour of others, humans interact with one another. Interaction is seen as an emergent, negotiated and often unpredictable concern. Interaction is symbolic because it involves manipulation of symbols, words, meanings and language (Denzin, 1989). Stryker (1967) highlighted several indications of researchable questions that can be helpful in the study of family violence through the use of symbolic interactionism. The first question deals with differential commitments to family identities. The second question for a research deals with the consequences of differential commitments. The third question for research concerns an examination of the effects of identity. The fourth research question concerns about the relationship of crisis of identity. The fifth area of research deals with role taking and the final research question is concerned with the meaning held by individuals about things and words. Gelles and Straus (1979b) suggested that symbolic interaction view of family violence would explore the different meanings of violence people hold and the consequences of such meanings in situational setting.

Unfortunately symbolic interaction approach has not been used by the researcher to understand the phenomenon of wife abuse, hence, it is problematic to speculate about its applicability in the empirical situation. Further, symbolic interactions are inattentive to the importance of structural constraints and underestimate the extent to which choices are effectively foreclosed by given social circumstances.

Subculture of violence theory :

The theory suggests that some subcultural groups develop norms and values that emphasize the use of physical violence to a greater extent than is seemed appropriate by the dominant culture (Wolfgang and Ferracuti, 1982). Oscar Lewis (1959) has also explained family violence in terms of "Culture of Poverty". In certain groups, wife beating is more common because it is considered as a normal and appropriate way of behaviour. In these groups men have not been inculcated with sophisticated alternatives for resolving conflicts. For such men the most accessible targets in the intimate relationship are their children and wives. They use physical coercive methods to reduce their tension and stress.

Wolfgang and Ferracuti (1982) do not apply their thesis to violence within upper status groups. Further there are some studies which indicate that a large number of members of the lower segments of society are law abiding and on the other hand "white collar crimes" is the characteristic of the middle and the upper class.

Conflict perspective :

From the conflict perspective of conjugal violence, conflict could be viewed as one of the elements involved in social interactional processes within dyads and groups characterized by the positions of domination and submission (Steinmetz, 1978). However, the conflict perspective involves at least two distinct interpretations, drawn from two 19th century sources, Simmel and Marx. The Marxist version, modified by Dahrendorf, views intense conflict as the pervasive feature of the society itself and of social beings (Davis, 1980). Bipolar opposition of interest is the essence of the capitalist society therefore conflict is an inevitable feature of social process. The literature on conjugal violence generally ignores this version. Family violence theorizing reflects Simmel's version of conflict. This version views conflict as one of the universal forms of social interaction. Coser and other value conflict proponents reflect Simmel's notion of conflict as simply one of the processes of social interaction (Bersani and Chen, 1988). Conflict perspective helps in understanding the conflict in the intimate relationship. When wife who is supposed to assume submissive position questions the dominant position of the male partner, the husband uses violence as a powerful option for achieving his self-interests that is reinforcing his dominant position in the marital relationships (Sprey, 1974).

This perspective fails to account for those cases where husbands resort to violence even when the wives and husbands have common interest, that is harmony in the family relationships. Theoretically, what is needed is not only an enhanced understanding of intrafamily processes but also the placement of that family within the context of totality of values and beliefs with which they identify and that may set the conditions for violence. In societies in which violence is not an approved means of conflict resolution and husband is not empowered to use coercive methods violence against the spouses is absent (Levinson, 1989).

Patriarchal perspective :

Patriarchy, power dynamics and social inequality (Coleman and Straus, 1986; Dobash and Dobash, 1979; Finkelhor, 1981; Gelles, 1974; Meiselman, 1978; Star, 1980; Straus et al., 1980) can be explained together under one heading. Wife beating tends to occur more often in either wife dominant or husband dominant families but occurs most frequently when husband controls the family decision making. It is hypothesized that the greater the degree of inequality, the greater the violence to keep wife in a subordinate position. The same explanation has been utilized by the feminists who advocate that violence against wife is the outcome of male dominance in the patriarchal social structure. It is hypothesized that the greater the demand for equality by the wife the greater will be the violence against her in the patriarchal familial system to keep the wife in the subordinate position. Hence, violence against wife is seen as a means to an end.

This explanation, however, fails to explain why most powerful uses violence against the least powerful even if his power is not challenged by the subordinate. It has another drawback of being a theory that is essentially a single factor (patriarchy) explanation of violence toward women.

General systems theory :

Straus (1973; 1980a) tried to apply a general systems theory approach to explain family violence. According to him, family violence is a product of the system rather than of individual pathology. He argues that society expects a wife to be more committed to the marital relationship, this commitment represents a positive feedback loop that encourages violence in the future.

Further, relative power of husband and wife also becomes the source of conflict. If a husband feels that he should or must have power in the relationship, he may use violence to enforce that power. A husband may also use violence as a response to a wife's attempt to break off the relationship. He further believes that if once a wife accepts violent behaviour of the husband, it provides positive feedback and there are chances that incident will be repeated again. When wife gives into the violent behaviour of the husband, her response represents positive feedback to violence and it soon becomes an established pattern. When battered woman gets any support from her informal or formal group, it will lead to a change in the basic rules of the system. However, when she fails to get any support, pattern of violence is strengthened.

The general systems perspective fails to explain those situations in which wives fight back or they do not accept violent behaviour of their husbands in the first place. Given the size and complexity of the model it is not surprising that it has yet to be tested in its full form. Such a test would require research with individuals with families and across societies, a task beyond the resources of researchers today (Levinson, 1989).

Different theoretical perspectives discussed above indicate that sociologists are now seriously addressing themselves to the problem of family violence in general and conjugal violence in particular. They are developing micro and macro level perspectives which are expected to be comprehensive and useful for empirical verification both quantitatively and qualitatively. Unfortunately, no theoretical framework discussed above adopts a holistic perspective with the help of which the problem of wife abuse at the individual level and at the socio-cultural level could be explicated. The discrepancy may be attributed to theorists who are eager to argue for a specific theoretical perspective or theories instead of carefully developing them so that they can be subjected to research verification. To overcome this discrepancy, recently a new conceptual framework under the broad heading of dependency framework has been evolved and is being used to understand the phenomenon of wife abuse. As sociological perspective is expected to provide both microscopic as well as macroscopic levels of analysis, dependency framework fulfils this requirement. At the microlevel it can be easily operationalized to understand the dynamics of conjugal relations and at the macrolevel it can help in understanding victimization of women at the sociocultural level. It is for these reasons that for the present study, I propose to use dependency framework for understanding wife abuse in the Indian context.

Dependency framework :

Dependency has been defined differently. A few scholars take into account economic, social or physical dependency. For Blenkner (1969) dependency is "a state of being not a state of mind, a state of being in which to be old — as to be young —is to be dependent". This is similar to Clark's (1969) cultural perspective on dependency. Pillemer (1985) defined dependency as requiring assistance from another person or persons to continue living in the community. These explanations, however, give scant importance to psychological dependency.

Knopf (1975) has identified three degrees of dependency which are quite similar to those suggested by Otten and Shelley (1977) interdependency, survival dependency and excessive dependency. Foulke (1980) has drawn a scale where at one polar opposite of the continuum, there is independence and at the other polar opposite there is complete dependency. The first stage is of independency, second stage is of reciprocal dependency, third stage is of asymmetrical dependency and the final stage is of survival dependency.

Dependency designates certain conditions over which the victim has no control. These conditions may be her economic dependency or social definitions which force her to trace out her identity through her husband which make her more committed to marriage. Dependency framework has been used in three ways to explain wife abuse. In the first approach dependency is treated as a cause of wife abuse, whereas in the second it is treated as a condition forcing a woman to assume the role of the victim and thirdly the way in which partial non-dependency also results into wife abuse.

Women's social status as well as their access to various systems of resources are determined largely by their relationships to men through marriage. Women enter into marital relations as subordinate to men as their attributes height, age education, occupation, etc., are lower than men. Further, they are trained to be submissive and trace identity through their husbands. This dependency of the wife is fully exploited by the husband and he uses violence to reinforce his dominant position in the marital relationship. Hence, dependency is considered to be positively related with wife abuse (Dobash and Dobash, 1979; Mahajan and Madhurima, 1995; Marsden, 1978; Straus, 1976; Truninger, 1971; Walker, 1978). Further, dependency of husband over his wife is also treated as a cause of wife abuse (Bernard and Bernard, 1984; Coleman, 1980; Faulk, 1977; Ganley, 1981; Saunders, 1982; Sonkin et al., 1985). When husband is dependent upon his wife he resorts to physical violence because he is afraid of losing her. Thus dependency either of wife's or husband's is related to wife abuse.

There is another way in which dependency framework has been used to explain wife abuse. Marital dependency is not treated as a cause of wife abuse but as a condition which forces a battered woman to continue staying in the abusive relationship. Lack of alternative support system and wife's tolerance of violence force her to continue living with violent spouse (Bicchause and Hawker, 1995; Karp and Karp, 1994; Mahajan and Madhurima, 1995; Gelles, 1976; Martin, 1979; Roy, 1977; 1982; Strube and Barbour, 1983; Strube, 1988).

Family sociologists inspired by Marxian ideology have also used dependency framework to explain wife abuse. With partial release from dependency wife starts questioning asymmetrical power relations which results into her abuse because she continues to remain subjectively dependent upon her husband. This framework suggests that unless women are totally free from both 'objective' and 'subjective' dependency, they would continue to be abused. However, men would resist such changes and are likely to abuse their wives but it would be only a temporary phase. In the long run, freedom from dependency would result into freedom from abuse. A new type of role relationships will develop between husband and wife based on the ideology of egalitarianism (Kalmuss and Straus, 1982).

Dependency framework suggests that wife abuse is rooted in many factors. Hence, it provides a leeway to account for cultural context. Taking into account the research studies conducted in India on wife abuse, it is quite clear that they have very limited empirical base and much of the knowledge gained so far is anecdotal. It would be appropriate to start with broad based conceptual framework and dependency perspectives serves this purpose.

Objectives :

Keeping in view the gaps identified in the available literature on wife abuse and lack of systematic, scientific studies in India, the proposed study was undertaken with the following main objectives.

1. To find out the nature, extent and frequency of wife abuse. While exploring the nature of violence, an attempt will also be made to find out the frequency with which different types of violence namely withdrawal, verbal, psychological and physical are used. It will also be seen which partner uses which form of violence more against the other partner. Further, it will also be seen whether different types of violence are used in combination and to what an extent.

2. To identify the correlates of physical violence used against the wives by their husbands. Under correlates different demographic variables (age at marriage of the wife, present age, number of children, sex of the children and family composition); ascribed attributes (caste and religion); and achieved attributes (education, occupation and social class) will be associated with physical violence. An attempt will also be made to find out relationship between traditional sex based roles and wife battering. Further, it will also be seen whether the presence of values in favour of the use of violence instigates wife battering. Conversely, disapproval of such behaviour pattern protects her from being the victim of husband's physical violence. Additionally, an attempt will be made to find out whether dependency objective or subjec-

tive or both, is the cause or condition or instigating factor for wife abuse.

3. To explicate the coping mechanisms adopted by the victims to deal with the abusive relationship. While looking at the coping mechanisms, the reactions of the victims to different kinds of violence will be considered. Further, an attempt will be made to find out different strategies used by the victims to deal with abusive behaviour. Additionally efforts will be made to find out as to what an extent help is sought from informal or formal agencies to put an end to the abusive relationship and to what extent these agencies, are successful in solving the problems of the abused women. Lastly, an attempt will also be made to find out the reasons for which abused women continue to stay in the abusive relationships.

Methods of conducting study :

Sociologists in India for a number of reasons have remained indifferent to the phenomenon of intrafamily violence. Such indifference has resulted into very few empirical studies conducted on domestic violence in general and wife abuse in particular. A few isolated studies which have been conducted in India have very limited scope. Further in these studies no theoretical framework has been used for empirical verification. Under these circumstances, the present study is based on exploratory and descriptive designs of research to explore the nature of wife abuse.

For the present study violence refers to "an act carried out by a spouse with an intention to inflict harm or injury to the other spouse". The terms 'violence' and 'abuse' have been used synonymously. Violence has been further divided into four types : withdrawal, psychological, verbal and physical. 'Withdrawal' as a form of violence stands for "stoppage of normal communication, not eating, crying or going out of the house and drinking". 'Psychological' violence includes "humiliation, indifference, demeaning and degrading the spouse with an intention of doing psychological damage" to the victim. 'Verbal' violence stands for "use of abusive language, or calling names or even verbal threat of resorting to physical violence". 'Physical' violence implies the use of physical force with an intent to harm or inflict injury on the other spouse. It also stands for "assaulting, beating, battering, slapping, hitting, pushing and throwing objects with an intention to injure the victim".

Universe :

The study was conducted at Chandigarh which has a population of more than six lakhs. The city is one of the few planned cities of India and is divided into different sectors. The city at present serves as a capital for the states of Punjab and Haryana and is a Union Territory as well.

Sample :

Chandigarh, being a planned city has a housing pattern which is clearly demarcated. The living arrangement ranges from one room set to large bungalow type. For the purpose of giving equal representation to all the classes of people residing at Chandigarh, it was decided to have a purposive sample of 50 cases from each class as a preliminary step, the classes were identified according to their living arrangement. People living in one room sets or in huts were treated as belonging to the lower class. Those residing in houses consisting of two rooms were designated as belonging to working class. The middle class consisted of those persons who were living in houses consisting of 3 to 4 rooms and the upper class stood for those who were living in the houses having 5 or more rooms. For the purpose of comparison, a purposive sample of 200 households situated in different sectors were selected giving equal representation to all the four classes identified based on their living arrangements. However, for the purpose of analysis these cases were rearranged, taking into account the education, occupation and income of the head of the household. After dividing the three variables into four categories, gamma test was used to find the association between these three variables. After having established high association between these three variables, in order to avoid further discrepancy a comprehensive index was worked out for the purpose of identifying the social class. Weightages were assigned on these three variables, i.e., education, occupation and income. Individuals score could range from 3 to 12. Then the scores were arranged in ascending order to calculate quartiles in order to compute social class. The redistributed sample according to social class background came to be 54 cases from the lower class, 46 from the working class, 74 from the middle class and 26 from the upper class (See Appendix I).

Techniques (interview schedule) :

An interview schedule was constructed to collect the core data for the present study. Keeping in view the objectives of the study, different close ended questions were formulated. Interview schedule, thus prepared was pretested on two respondents of each class. The language of a few questions was redrafted in the light of the comments of the cases as well as to remove the possibility of ambiguities. The interview schedule had different sections to elicit information from the respondents. In addition to socio-economic and demographic background of the respondents and their husbands, information was also sought with regard to the constitution of their households, that is, in addition to their own children who were the other members residing with them. Further questions related to nature, extent and frequency of violence, precipitating factors of violence and coping mechanisms were also asked. There were three sections in the interview schedule which dealt with their level of traditionality, value orientation in favour or against violence and dependency.

Traditional sex based orientation :

The level of traditionality of the respondents was found out with the help of eight statements to find out association between wife abuse and level of traditionality. Each statement had three response categories. The reactions 'agree' designated endorsement of traditional sex based roles. Conversely, disagreement indicated non-endorsement of traditional sex based roles. To find out their level of traditionality scores were allocated to their reactions. Score '3' was given for agreement, score '2' for somewhat agree and for disagreement score of '1' was given. Depending upon the scores of the respondents, they were distributed into three categories, viz., high, medium, and low level of traditionality (See Appendix II).

Value orientation :

To explicate the role of value orientation favouring the use of violence for resolving conjugal conflict, the respondents were given a set of 12 statements. The response designating favourable attitude to the use of violence was given the score of '3' and disapproval was assigned the score of '1'. In this way, a respondent's score could range from 12 to 36. Depending upon the scores of the respondents they were accordingly divided into three categories—low, medium and high (See appendix III).

Dependency :

To understand the role of dependency in wife abuse it was divided into 'objective' and 'subjective' dependency. The level of objective dependency was found with the help of six statements, having two points scale. As objective dependency mainly dealt with factual information, dichotomous response categories in shape of 'yes' and 'no' were used. Any response which depicted the objective dependency of the respondent was assigned the score of '2' and any response indicating absence of dependency was allotted the score of '1'. In this way, each respondent's score could range from 6 to 12. Depending upon the scores, the respondents were divided into three categories of low, medium and high (See Appendix IV).

For the level of subjective dependency six statements

were used having three-point scale. The responses ranged from 'agreement' to 'somewhat agree' to 'disagreement'. Depending upon the statement, scoring was done. Any response depicting the subjective dependency was assigned the score of '3' whereas non-dependency was allocated with the score of '1' and partial subjective dependency was given the score of '2'. In this way scores ranged from 6 to 18 and accordingly the respondents were divided into three categories of low, medium and high level of subjective dependency (See Appendix V).

To see the effect of total dependency on wife abuse, subjective and objective dependency were grouped together under the label of 'total dependency'. Total dependency was calculated by taking the scores of both objective and subjective dependency. The respondents were divided again into three levels of high, medium and low dependency (See Appendix VI).

Case study method :

For greater understanding of the problem of wife abuse, eight case histories of victims were taken who had sought help from women organizations or with the police or in the judiciary. Two cases from each social class were taken. Their detailed case studies were recorded with the help of an interview guide. Each case study was recorded at several meetings with the victim. This technique was used to understand the developmental cycle of their married life. The temporal aspect of the cases revealed the onset of the violence, the period for which the abusive relationship continued as well as the strategies adopted by the victims to deal with the abusive situation. The case study method was used to find out the subterranean aspects of their married life. Further, the qualitative information gathered from the selected cases was also used to check the analysis based on the sample data.

Tabulation :

After collecting all the information it was transferred into a code design and were entered into computer. With the help of computer, simple frequency and cross tables were made. Percentages and measures of central tendency were calculated for analysing the data and making comparisons among the groups. Gamma statistic was used to find the relationship among education, occupation and income so that 'social class' could be operationally defined. Further, different quartiles were also calculated for dividing traditionality, value orientation and dependency into different levels.

The present study is of non-probability sampling and research design is of exploratory nature, therefore statistical tests are not used for the sample data.

2

Incidence of Violence

There are no official data on wife abuse available in different nations. There are, however, a few surveys conducted on family violence in different countries. These empirical studies indicate that violence against wives as well as children is quite widespread. The U.S. Bureau of Justice has published two reports on intimate violence based on the data collected by National Crime Survey. The major findings revealed that there were about 3.8 million incidences of violence among intimates (Gelles and Cornell, 1990). Similarly, in a nationally represented sample of 6002 individuals in 1986, Gelles and Straus (1987) concluded that in 16 per cent of the homes, some kind of violence between spouses had occurred in the year prior to the survey. More than one in four of the couples reported marital violence at some point in their marriages. David Levinson (1989) has examined records of the Human Relations Area Files at Yale University. These records contain descriptive and statistical information on a wide range of societies over time and around the world. Levinson reports that wife beating is most common and frequent form of family violence. Seager and Olson (1986) are also of the opinion that wife beating is quite widespread. They, further, contend that some cultures encourage wife beating as a man's right whereas in others the problem is hidden away as a 'private' matter.

A few isolated studies conducted in India have also endorsed the fact that wife abuse in one form or the other is quite common (Grewal, 1982; Mahajan, 1989a; Mahajan and Madhurima, 1995; Parihar, 1989; Saheli, 1986; Singh, 1985). These studies further contend that wife abuse is not only widespread but also transgresses the boundaries of caste, class, race and religion.

In the present chapter an attempt will be made to find out the presence or the absence of violence against wives as well as the nature and extent of such violence in day to day life of the respondents under study.

For the present study violence has been defined as "an act carried out by the spouse against another spouse with an intention of hurting the other". Further, for the purpose of analysis violence has been divided into four types, i.e., Withdrawal, Psychological, Verbal and Physical. While describing the incidence and frequency of different types of conjugal violence the incidents and frequency of violence by the husband towards his wife as well as wife's violence towards her husband are taken up.

'Withdrawal' as a type of violence designates withdrawal from normal interactions with the spouse. One resorts to such acts with an intention of harming or making the other spouse uneasy. In short, withdrawal stands for, stoppage of normal communication, not eating, crying or going out of the house and drinking. 'Psychological' violence means mental torture or agony which may be sometimes more damaging for the conjugal relations. This violence stands for, humiliation, etc., 'Verbal' violence stands for use of abusive language or calling names or even verbal threat of resorting to physical violence. 'Physical' violence stands for the use of physical force with an intent to harm or inflict injury on the other person.

To ward off any misunderstanding and confusion these four types of violence are not to be treated as occurring in a sequential order. It also does not imply that one type of violence is less damaging than the other types. At a given period of time a spouse may use one type of violence and another type at other moment or may be resorting to a combination of different types. It is only for the purpose of analysis that they have been divided into four types.

The nature of the present study is such that one cannot ask direct questions. Hence, to find out the presence or absence of violence in the conjugal relations, study was started with most trivial aspect of daily life. It was assumed that while living together there would be a number of occasions when a couple would have difference of opinion. In case these differences are not reconciled they may lead to arguments which may subsequently result into quarrels and fights.

The respondents were asked, "During your married life, was there any occasion when you and your spouse had difference of opinion?" There can be three possible answers to the question, "Yes, No, and Sometimes". Sometimes has also been included under the `Yes' category.

TABLE 2.1 **Difference of opinion between the spouses**

Response	*Frequency*	*Percentage*
Yes	198	99
No	2	1
Total	200	100

TABLE 2.2 **Difference of opinion leading to arguments**

Response	*Frequency*	*Percentage*
Yes	198	99
No	2	1
Total	200	100

The tabulation of responses indicates that in normal day to day life on a number of issues the partners have a difference of opinion. With the exception of two respondents, they admitted that they had difference of opinion and these differences also resulted into arguments between the spouses.

An attempt was also made to probe the issues on which the couple had arguments. It was noted that issues related to money matters resulted into arguments between the partners in 50 per cent of the cases under study. The other issues which led to arguments were matters related to child care, drinking behaviour pattern, suspicion regarding extra marital relations of the spouse, housekeeping and relations with parents-in-law. The tabulation of data helps to conclude that in addition to personal behaviour pattern like drinking, suspicion, etc., there were a number of issues related to family and kinsmen which led to arguments between the spouses. Hence, one factor cannot be held responsible for such arguments.

TABLE 2.3 **Issues on which spouses had arguments**

Issues	*Frequency**	*Percentage*
Money matters	100	50
Child care	96	48
Drinking behaviour	79	39.5
Suspicion of adultery	60	30
Housekeeping	47	23.5
Parents-in-law	44	22
Friendship circle	19	9.5
Miscellaneous	18	9
	N = 463	

Note *: The respondents were allowed multiple choices, hence total exceeds 200. However, percentages of each issue has been worked out based on 200 cases.

If arguing over certain issues does not stop or partners refuse to listen to each other it may lead to quarrels which may take different forms. Hence, the respondents were also asked, "Whether arguments between the partners led to quarrels?"

TABLE 2.4 **Incidence of quarrel**

Response	*Frequency*	*Percentage*
Yes	187	93.50
No	13	6.50
Total	200	100.00

With the exception of 13 cases all our respondents admitted that verbal arguments over different issues had resulted into some form of quarrel or fight with their spouses.

The above description simply identifies the issues on which husband and wife had quarrel with each other. But this description does not identify the spouse who initiated the quarrel as well as the precipitating factors. The spousal interpersonal relationship is based on mutual expectations from each other. If one partner does not behave in the expected manner or raises objection about a specific behaviour pattern of the other partner, such a situation may lead to quarrels and fights.

TABLE 2.5 **Which of the spouse initiated quarrel**

Spouse	*Yes*		*No*		*Total*
	Fre.	*Per.*	*Fre.*	*Per*	
Wife	125	(62.50)	75	(37.50)	200
Husband	144	(72)	56	(28)	200

Tabulation of data in Table 2.5 clearly indicates that conjugal discord and conflicts cannot be attributed to one partner alone. In 62.5 per cent cases the wives have assumed the responsibility of starting the quarrel, however, 72 per cent have also held their husbands responsible for initiating the quarrel. Though both the spouses play almost the equal role in starting the quarrel, the precipitating factors for each are likely to be different.

TABLE 2.6 **Instigators attributed to wife**

Factors	*Frequency**
Wife was rude to husband	60
Wife disobeyed the husband	40
Wife taunted the husband	35
Wife had some problem with her job	2

**Note* : Multiple choices were used by 125 respondents.

Wife's disrespectful behaviour pattern towards her husband, her disobedience and being nagging type are the main precipitating factors for spousal quarrel. Patriarchal norms give Indian husbands more power than wives. The effect of these norms result into asymmetrical and a hierarchical relationship, with the husband being in the dominant position. To assert his dominant position the husband is likely to impose his will on his wife. As and when the wife questions the dominant position of the husband or shows disrespect or does not obey her husband, such a situation precipitates the quarrels and fights. The husband is likely to reinforce his dominant position by intimidation or use of coercion against his wife. Further, as a consequence of such asymmetrical spousal relationship the wife assumes the responsibility for starting the quarrel rather than attributing to her husband. The 'self-blame' mechanism is adopted by wife to endorse her husband's dominant position in the family (Ferraro and

Johnson, 1983; Pagelow, 1981 a; Walker, 1979).

To exert his dominant position in the conjugal relationship the husband uses rude behaviour as a strategy to put his wife in a subordinate position. When this rude behaviour on the part of the husband is resented by the wife, the husband reacts back more vehemently. Hence, the rude behaviour pattern of the husband is the main precipitating factor of quarrel. Another main factor attributed to the husband relates to money matters or his job related problems. His failure to earn sufficient money and frustration at the job makes him very irritable and he gives vent to his

TABLE 2.7 **Instigators attributed to husband**

Response	*Frequency**
Rude behaviour	104
Drinking behaviour	35
Money matters and job related problems	38
Extra marital relations	9
	N = 144

**Note* : Multiple choices were used.

frustration by picking up a quarrel with his wife on flimsy grounds. Another reason for quarrel is husband's drinking behaviour pattern. Under the influence of the alcohol he may not only indulge in verbal violence or may even use physical force. Drinking behaviour of the husband leading to quarrel in the present study is limited to 39.5 per cent of cases. The results of the study do not support the findings of other researchers who have attributed family quarrels mainly to alcohol (Ahuja, 1987; Bhatti, 1989; Brekke and Saunders, 1982; Coleman and Straus, 1983; Mahajan, 1989a; Parihar, 1989). There were also a few cases where extra marital relations of the husband were the main factor of quarrel.

In addition to the above precipitating factors attributed to the spouses, other members of the family may also play an active role for initiating the quarrel between husband and wife. In the present sample, 29 cases reported that their parents-in-law were the main villain in the conjugal quarrels. Out of these 15 respondents attributed quarrels to dowry related problems. Their parents-in-law would always take up some issue related to insufficient dowry they brought. Researchers in India have treated dowry as a serious threat to conjugal relationship and it was considered as the main factor for family quarrels (Agnes, 1989; Gautam and Trivedi, 1987; Prasad and Vijaylakshmi, 1988; Singh and Renuka, 1989; Shah, 1989). In the present study dowry is one of the precipitating factors rather than the main factor for conjugal quarrels and was also confined to 15 cases only.

Quarrels and fights as a consequence of arguments may take different forms of violence. For analytical purposes violence has been divided into these categories withdrawal as a form of violence, psychological violence, verbal violence and physical violence. Further, to find out the frequency of such violence it would be interesting to know which of the partner uses which form of violence more against the other partner.

Withdrawal as a form of violence may not be physically harmful to the spouse though psychologically it may be. In human relationship especially in conjugal relations mutual understanding and interaction are of utmost importance to the spouses. If one spouse intentionally stops talking to other or starts avoiding his or her company it may be treated as a type of violence. However, the societal reactions to such type of interpersonal relations is not very negative and members of the group may not treat it as a form of violence. It is expected that wife would be resorting to withdrawal more frequently than husband because these methods are socially accessible to her. She may also resort to this form of violence as a consequence of other forms of violence used by her husband or she may use it as an insulation mechanism to avoid the possibility of serious retaliation from her husband.

TABLE 2.8 **Withdrawal used by the spouses**

Response	*Husband*		*Wife*	
	Fre.	*Per.*	*Fre.*	*Per.*
Yes	88	44	166	83
No	99	49.5	21	10.5
N.A.	13	6.5	13	6.5
Total	200	100.0	200	100.0

TABLE 2.9 **The Frequency* of withdrawal**

Response	*Husband*		*Wife*	
	Fre.	*Per.*	*Fre.*	*Per.*
Rarely	30	34.09	45	27.11
Occasionally	19	21.59	39	23.49
Very often	39	44.32	82	49.40
Total	88	100.00	166	100.0

**Note* : Restricted to 88 husbands and 166 wives.

In contrast to 44 per cent husbands 83 per cent of the wives resort to withdrawal. It may, however, be clarified that all these respondents do not use this mode regularly.

To find out the frequency with which withdrawal as a form of violence is used against the spouse tabulation of data has been restricted to these cases only (Table 2.9). In case of husbands who use withdrawal as a form of violence approximately 66 per cent of them use it very often or sometimes and only 34 per cent resort to it rarely. On the other hand, approximately 73 per cent of wives resorting to this form of violence use it occasionally and very often only 27.11 per cent use it rarely. Thus, it can be concluded that withdrawal as a form of violence is not only used more but also more frequently by wives than their husbands.

Psychological violence is still another form of violence used in the conjugal relationship. Humiliation of a spouse in the presence of others may lead to very damaging consequences for intimate relationship. Similarly demeaning and criticism of his or her abilities are not conducive to the development of close relationship between the spouses. Let me now explain to what an extent and with what frequency the cases under study use psychological violence against their spouses.

Tabulation of data (Table 2.10) with regard to psychological violence depicts a completely reverse position from that of withdrawal as a form of violence. In case of withdrawal more wives were resorting to it against their husbands whereas more husbands were found to be indulging in psychological violence against their wives. Table 2.10 reveals that in contrast to 35.5 per cent wives using psychological violence against their husbands 69 per cent husbands resorted to psychological violence against their wives.

With regard to the frequency with which such violence is used Table 2.11 reveals that out of 71 wives 30 (42.25 per cent) use it occasionally whereas out of 138 husbands 68 (49.63 per cent) use it very often. In short, not only more husbands resort to psychological violence but they also use it more often against their wives.

TABLE 2.10 **Psychological form of violence used by spouses**

Response	*Husband*		*Wife*	
	Fre.	*Per.*	*Fre.*	*Per.*
Yes	138	69.0	71	35.5
No	49	24.5	116	58
N.A.	13	6.5	13	6.5
Total	200	100.0	200	100.0

TABLE 2.11 **The frequency* of psychological violence.**

Response	*Husband*		*Wife*	
	Fre.	*Per.*	*Fre.*	*Per.*
Rarely	35	25.55	18	25.36
Occasionally	34	24.82	30	42.25
Very often	68	49.63	23	32.39
Total	138	100.00	71	100.00

**Note* : Restricted to 138 husbands and 71 wives who use psychological form of violence.

TABLE 2.12 **Verbal violence used by spouses**

Response	*Husband*		*Wife*	
	Fre.	*Per.*	*Fre.*	*Per.*
Yes	142	71	100	50
No	45	22.5	87	43.5
N.A.	13	6.5	13	6.5
Total	200	100.0	200	100.0

TABLE 2.13 **The frequency* of verbal violence**

Response	*Husband*		*Wife*	
	Fre.	*Per.*	*Fre.*	*Per.*
Rarely	41	28.88	35	35
Occasionally	44	30.98	29	29
Very often	57	40.14	36	36
Total	142	100.00	100.00	100.00

**Note* : Restricted to 142 husbands and 100 wives who use verbal violence.

Another form of violence identified for the present study is verbal violence. It includes shouting at each other and calling names. In case the arguments do not stop and quarrel persists, verbal violence is a natural consequence thereof. It is further assumed that husbands, to maintain their dominant position, would be resorting to this form of violence more as compared to their wives.

Table 2.12 indicates that more husbands (71 per cent) use verbal violence as compared to 50 per cent of wives using this form of violence. To understand the frequency with which verbal violence is used by the spouses tabulation was restricted to those cases only who resorted to verbal violence (Table 2.13). It was noted that in contrast to 65 per cent wives 71.12 per cent husbands were using it occasionally or very often. The tabulation helps us to conclude that though more husbands were using verbal violence against their wives but with regard to frequency with which it was used by the spouses against each other there was no marked difference.

Physical violence is not only a degraded human behaviour particularly if the parties involved are intimately related but is also deplored by the society at large. People may grudgingly tolerate other forms of violence but may react vehemently against physical violence. Hence, quarrels and fights between the spouses may not ultimately result into physical violence against each other. It is also likely that due to societal censor people may not accept that they are either perpetrators or victims of physical violence. It is, therefore, expected that only those spouses will admit the existence of such behaviour pattern who have either developed animosity in their conjugal relations or their abuse is in the 'visibility' of the public. Hence, it is assumed that only a few respondents would admit the presence of such type of behaviour pattern in their intimate relationship. Further, violence as a form of control is used by those members who have been accorded a dominant position in the family and they have more resources. Violence is used by parents against children and husbands against wives. This is not to say that wives do not strike back at husbands. However, in a family that is characterized by violence, it is the weaker and most vulnerable member who lives in fear and is likely to be the victim of dominant person. Moreover, women who act violently against their husbands are usually being treated violently by their husbands and these wives are only fighting back (Lips, 1991). Some of the researchers have labelled wives' violence as "passive" or "defensive" violence (Bowker, 1983; Gelles, 1974). It is implicit in these labels that it is the husband who takes the lead in physical violence and the wife only reacts back or uses defensive mechanisms to save herself from physical assaults. It should not, however, be overlooked that a culturally endorsed ideology of male dominance gives men a perceived right to extend power over women. It is therefore expected that more husbands would be acting violently against their wives rather than vice versa.

Table 2.14 indicates that a majority of wives do not indulge in this extreme form of violence against their husbands. It was, further, noted that in contrast to 33.5 per cent husbands only 8.5 per cent of wives resorted to physical violence against their spouses.

TABLE 2.14 **Physical violence used by spouses**

Response	*Husband*		*Wife*	
	Fre.	*Per.*	*Fre.*	*Per*
Yes	67	33.5	17	8.5
No	120	60	170	85.0
N.A.	13	6.5	13	6.5
Total	200	100.00	200	100.0

TABLE 2.15 **The frequency* of physical violence**

Response	*Husband*		*Wife*	
	Fre.	*Per.*	*Fre.*	*Per*
Rarely	25	37.31	6	35.29
Occasionally	23	34.33	6	35.29
Very often	19	28.36	5	29.42
Total	67	100.00	17	100.00

**Note*: Restricted to 67 husbands and 17 wives who use physical violence.

With regard to frequency there is not much difference between husband's violence against wives and vice versa. Out of 67 cases of husband's violence against wives, 37.31 per cent used it rarely and 28.36 per cent used it very often. In case of 17 wives resorting to physical violence 35.29 per cent used it rarely and 29.42 per cent resorted to it very often.

As stated earlier different types of violence do not constitute discrete categories but are likely to be used against the spouse in combination. Earlier different types of violence resorted to by husband and wife have been described separately. However, such a description did not help in understanding as to how the spouses react to a particular type of violence against each other. Now, an attempt will be made to know the proportion of wives being the victims of one or another or combination of different types of violence reacting with same type of violence or with other forms of violence against their husbands. To get a clear idea a comprehensive picture has been presented in Table 2.16.

Tabulation of data depicting husband's violence against his wife and wife's violence against husband clearly indicates that a large majority of the spouses resort to different types of violence simultaneously, i.e., one may use withdrawal and psychological forms of violence against the other spouse whereas the abused spouse in reaction may use either psychological or verbal violence or a combination thereof.

Taking into account withdrawal only as a form of violence, data reveals that 14 out of 200 husbands resorted to withdrawal only. On the other hand, 60 out of 200 wives used this form against their husbands. Out of these 60 wives 7 were the victims of their husbands' withdrawal, and rest of them were the victims of other types of violence or a combination thereof used by their husbands against them.

The above explanation which was restricted to withdrawal only does not depict the real picture. A closer look at the Table 2.16 indicates that there were 88 husbands who were using withdrawal along with other forms of violence against their wives. On the other hand, 166 wives were found to be using this form along with other forms of violence against their husbands. These 166 wives, who were the victims of all types of violence perpetuated by their husbands, e.g., psychological, verbal and physical, reacted against their husbands' violence by resorting to withdrawal in combination with verbal and psychological violence. It is for this reason that more wives than husbands were found to be resorting to withdrawal form of violence.

Use of psychological violence depicts a different picture. There were 16 husbands who were resorting to this mode of violence only against their wives. But, not a single wife of these cases were reacting back with the same form of violence. Twelve wives of these husbands were resorting to withdrawal only, one to verbal only, two to withdrawal in combination with psychological and one to withdrawal in combination with verbal and psychological. However, taking into account all those who were using psychological violence in combination with other forms of violence, there were 138 husbands who were resorting to psychological violence along with other forms of violence. In contrast 71 wives of these cases were reacting back with psychological violence in combination with other forms of violence and out of the rest a majority of them were taking shelter of withdrawal form of violence against their husbands.

Similarly, taking into account verbal violence it is noticed that 19 husbands were resorting to verbal violence only against their wives. However, none of the victims of these husbands reacted back with verbal violence only but resorted to other types of violence or combination thereof. There were 6 wives who were using verbal violence against their husbands but they were the victims of other types of violence and combination thereof.

In the total sample there were 142 husbands who were using verbal violence in combination with other types of violence against their wives but only 100 wives were using verbal violence in combination with other types of violence against their husbands who were the victims of verbal violence as well as other forms of violence.

With regard to physical violence no spouse was found to be resorting to it only, without resorting to other forms of violence. They were found to be using it in combination with other forms of violence, viz., withdrawal, verbal or psychological. It was found that 67 husbands used physical violence in combination with other types of violence against their wives and in response only 17 battered wives gave back in the same coin and a majority of these victims resorted to withdrawal, psychological or verbal or a combination thereof.

The above analysis needs further clarification. A spouse at a given period of time might have resorted to withdrawal or psychological or verbal form of violence and at another time might have used another form of violence. Hence, spouses reacting to violence might have used one form or one

TABLE 2.16 **The frequency with which the spouses use different forms of violence against each other.**

	W	*V*	*Psy*	*WV*	*WPsy*	*VPsy*	*VPh*	*Psy Ph*	*VPsy Ph*	*WV Psy*	*WV Ph*	*WPsy Ph*	*WVPsy Ph*	*Not appli-cable*	*Total*
Withdrawal	7	5	12	2	3	9	-	1	9	6	0	0	6	-	60
Verbal	1	-	1	-	1	1	1	-	-	1	-	-	-	-	6
Withdrawal Verbal	2	7	-	6	-	10	1	-	3	5	1	-	8	-	43
Withdrawal Psychological	1	3	2	-	1	3	-	2	7	2	-	2	1	-	24
Withdrawal Physical	-	-	-	-	-	-	1	-	-	-	-	-	-	-	1
Verbal Psychological	3	-	-	-	-	1	-	3	3	-	-	1	-	-	11
Verbal Physical	-	-	-	-	1	-	-	-	-	-	-	1	-	-	2
Verbal Physical Psychological	-	-	-	-	-	-	1	-	1	-	-	-	-	-	2

(Contd...)

	W	V	Psy	WV	WPsy	VPsy	VPh	Psy Ph	VPsy Ph	WV Psy	WV Ph	WPsy Ph	WVPsy Ph	Not appli-cable	Total
Withdrawal Verbal Psychological	-	4	1	1	-	7	1	-	1	6	1	1	3	-	26
Withdrawal Verbal Physical	-	-	-	1	-	-	-	-	-	-	-	-	3	-	4
Withdrawal Psy, Ph	-	-	-	-	-	-	-	-	-	-	-	-	2	-	2
W, V, Psy, Ph	-	-	-	-	1	-	-	-	1	-	-	-	4	-	6
No violence	-	-	-	-	-	-	-	-	-	-	-	-	-	13	13
Total	14	19	16	10	7	31	5	3	25	23	2	5	27	13	200

combination at one time and at another time might have resorted to another form or another combination. Therefore, there was always a possibility of overlapping which could be attributed to the fact that the respondents were asked to indicate the presence or absence of violence in conjugal relationship during the span of their married life rather than restricting to a single event or incidence or a specified time span. In short, it can be concluded that with the exception of physical violence other forms of violence are widespread in the conjugal relations. Further husbands had resorted to different forms of violence more with the exception of withdrawal against their wives and more wives, on the other hand, had resorted to withdrawal. Even if withdrawal as a form of violence is ignored, keeping in view its covert nature the other types of violence were found equally prominent. Thus violence in the conjugal unit is quite widespread.

After having observed that violence in conjugal relation is generic. The next chapter is restricted to physical violence against wives only. It does not, however, mean that other forms of violence in the spousal relations are not important. Bhatti (1985) is of the view that verbal violence, humiliation and public embarrassment are sometimes more damaging than physical violence. One reason for restricting the analysis to physical violence is that physical violence is theoretically and practically distinct from other harmful coercive acts (Etzioni, 1971). Physical violence, as a category of behaviour is conceptually distinct. From the practical point of view lumping all types of violence would create confusion, it would be impossible to determine what causes spousal violence. Unless physical violence is treated separately from other harm-doing acts it would be difficult to identify the factors which lead to wife abuse. Additionally, people generally exonerate withdrawal, psychological or verbal violence and do not treat them as 'violence'. It was perhaps for this reason that with the exception of thirteen cases all the respondents, without having any fear of being stigmatized, admitted the presence of different types of violence in their day to day life. Further, the very fact that they were continuing to live in such abusive relationships indicates their tolerance to these forms of violence. Physical violence is not only treated as violence but also attracts societal censure. It is this form which meets with condemnation by police, judicial system and society at large.

3

Correlates of Physical Violence

In the preceding chapter it has been observed that violence against wives is quite widespread in the conjugal relationship. The present chapter deals with physical violence against wives and its correlates. For the purpose of analysis, the correlates have been discussed under three sub-heads : Demographic variables, social variables and dependency. An attempt is made to explicate their role in making the wives victims of their husbands physical violence.

Demographic variables

To understand the nature of the social grouping as well as the quality of interrelationship that exists among the members, it is essential to understand their demographic background. Young children are expected to behave differently as compared with adult population. Similarly, age at marriage determines fertility span. Marital status is also linked with differential role performance and evaluation. Additionally, the presence or absence of children in the family gives rise to different types of role responsibilities to which the couples have to make adjustments.

To find out the correlates of wife abuse, the demographic variables which have been considered for the present study are : Age at marriage; present age; number of children; sex of the children and household composition.

Age at marriage:

Age at marriage does not differentiate battered from non-battered wives (Post et al. 1980; Stark et al., 1981) yet younger age at marriage puts a lot of stress for adjustment which may be exhibited in violent behaviour pattern on the part of young batterers. It can thus be assumed that women who are married at a younger age are at higher risk of physical violence.

TABLE 3.1 **Wife's age at marriage and physical violence**

(Age at marriage in years)

	Up to 18	*18-21*	*21+*	*Total*
Yes	27	19	21	67
	45.00	34.55	24.71	33.50
No	33	36	64	133
	55.00	65.45	75.29	66.50
Total	60	55	85	200
	100.00	100.00	100.00	100.00

Overall median age at marriage = 20.19 years
Median age at marriage of victims = 19.02 years
Median age at marriage of non-victims = 20.79 years

It is evident from Table 3.1 that women who got married at younger age were more victims of physical violence by their husbands in contrast to those who got married at later age. Further, it was noted that there was a progressive decrease in the percentages of victims of physical violence from lower age at marriage category to higher age group. Out of 60 respondents who got married below the age of 18 years, 45 per cent were the victims. In contrast to this who were married after the age of 21 years, only 24.71 per cent were the victims of physical violence. It is also interesting to note that median age at marriage of victims of physical violence was lower (19.02 years) than those of non-victims (20.79 years). It can, thus, be concluded that those women who married at lower age were at high risk of physical violence in comparison with those who got married at later age. In the Indian society although the age at marriage is increasing yet in the rural areas it still remains quite low that is, 17.81 years (Goel, 1988). Therefore, class and situational factors may play an important role in determining the age at marriage which in turn may be associated with violence because young couples are under lot of stress to adjust to new role responsibilities.

Present age :

A few studies indicate that wives of younger age group are at higher risk of abuse as compared with those of older age group because older women are not prone to file assault charges either because of traditional attitudes or because of the possibility of divorce (Shupe et al., 1987). The results of National Family Violence Survey conducted in America indicate that all forms of marital violence occur most frequently among those under 30 years of age (Straus et at., 1980). The rate of marital violence among those under 30 years of age was found to be more than double the rate for the age for 31 to 50 years (Ahuja, 1987; Dvoskin, 1981; Fagan et al., 1983; Gayford, 1975; Lupri, 1991; Straus et al., 1980; Shupe et al., 1987). To what an extent such a contention is applicable in the present study?

The data for the present study were tabulated to find out association between the age of the wife and her being victim of physical violence. The respondents were distributed into four age categories. There was a progressive decrease in the percentages of victims of physical violence from lower age category to higher age category. Among the victims of physical violence 45.45 per cent were below the age of 30

TABLE 3.2 **Wife's present age and physical violence**

(Present age of wife in years)

	Up to 30	*30-40*	*40-50*	*50+*	*Total*
Yes	20	27	16	4	67
	45.45	36.99	26.23	18.18	33.50
No	24	46	45	18	133
	54.55	63.01	73.77	81.82	66.50
Total	44	73	61	22	200
	100.00	100.00	100.00	100.00	100.00

Overall median age	=	39.04 years
Median age for victims	=	35.00 years
Median age for non-victims	=	39.24 years

years. In contrast to this those who were in the age group of 50 years above, only 18.18 per cent were the victims. Similarly, if the median age of the victims of physical violence is compared with non-victims, it was noticed that median age of victims was 35 years in contrast to 39.24 years median age of the non-victims. In short, an inverse relationship was found between the age of wives and their physical abuse. In other words, physical violence against wives of younger age group was more frequent as against those of higher age groups. The data of the present study support the findings of studies cited above. Wife abuse can occur at any age but the data on age indicate that wives of younger age are at higher risk of being abused. It may be due to the fact that younger couples are still learning to make adjustment with each other and addition of children in the family puts enormous demands and stresses on the younger people.

Number of children :

Presence or absence of children in the family is likely to affect the quality of relationship between husband and wife. Further, presence of more children in the family would create problem of management and proper training of the younger ones. Researches on the impact of children on marriages consistently show that the level of marital satisfaction and marital adjustment goes down after the birth of the first child (Rollins and Foldman, 1970). An additional child would imply a decrease in time for parents to pursue their own interests. Further, each additional child increases the work load and conflicts (Knox and Wilson, 1978). In the traditional societies like India, child care still remains under the domain of mothers and for any deviance on the part of child it is the mother who is blamed. Further, more children put a lot of stress on the limited resources of the family.

TABLE 3.3 **Children and violence against wives**

(Number of children)

	No child	*1-2*	*3-4*	*5+*	*Total*
Yes	4	31	26	6	67
	57.14	25.83	41.94	54.55	33.50
No	3	89	36	5	133
	42.86	74.17	58.06	45.45	66.50
Total	7	120	62	11	200
	100.00	100.00	100.00	100.00	100.00

Among the victims of physical violence it was found that the rate of violence against mothers who had five or more children or no child was more than double the rate for those who had one or two children. Keeping in view the number of children it was noted that there was a progressive increase in the percentages of victims of physical violence from one to two children category to women having five or more children or with no child. In short, it can be concluded that a large number of children in the family become a source of conflict resulting into violence against wife or mother. The highest percentages of physical violence was found in those households which had no child. It may be attributed to their younger age as well as wives' inability to have children because children are valued in the Indian society and those women who are unable to bear a child are ridiculed.

Sex of the children:

In the patriarchal society like India, greater importance is given to the male child. The female child is not only considered a liability because of associated dowry problems but mothers who give birth to female children only do not get much respect in the family as compared with those who give birth to male children. Lately with the help of amniocentesis the couples would like to know the sex of the child. In case the foetus is of the female sex, they go for abortion. A study of 8000 cases of abortion showed that 7999 of them involved a female foetus (Chowdhary, 1984). The high female foeticide reinforces the sex preferences prevalent in our society.

TABLE 3.4 **Sex of children and violence against wives**

	Males		*Females*		*Both*		*Total**	
Yes	20	33.33	11	33.33	34	34.00	63	32.64
No	40	66.67	22	66.67	66	66.00	130	67.36
Total	60	100.00	33	100.00	100	100.00	193	100.00

**Note* : Seven cases have been excluded who do not have any child.

The Table 3.4 does not indicate any association between the sex of the children and violence against mothers. The victims of physical violence were almost equally divided in the categories of those who had only male or female children of both the sexes. In the present study sex of the children in the family was not found to be associated with wife abuse.

Household composition:

Wives living in extended and joint households are required to make adjustments with a large number of kin in contrast to those who are living in nuclear households. Further, patrilocal residence and patriarchal structure of the family places women into subservient position. The men are more likely to act as sons rather than husbands. The parents-in-law and other kinsmen continue to have greater affiliation with the sons as compared with daughters-in-law. A number of cases have been reported where because of backbiting, the husbands have maltreated their wives. Hence presence of a large number of members in the family not only creates the problem of adjustment but they also act as instigators for wife abuse (Mahajan, 1989a; Prasad, 1989; Shah, 1989; Singh, 1985).

TABLE 3.5 **Household composition and violence**

(Household composition)

	Nuclear		*Joint*		*Total*	
Yes	56	32.94	11	36.67	67	33.50
No	114	67.06	19	63.33	133	66.50
Total	170	100.00	30	100.00	200	100.00

Although there was no marked difference in the percentage of victims living in nuclear and extended households, yet among the victims a relatively higher percentage (36.67) were found to be living in joint and extended households in contrast to those living in nuclear households (32.94). Similarly, among the non-victims no marked difference was found with regard to their pattern of living arrangement. Hence, the composition of household was not found to be associated with wife abuse.

From the foregoing discussion on the demographic correlates of wife abuse, it was found that the younger age at marriage, young wives (below the age of 30 years) and those having no child or a large number of children were at higher risk of being victims of physical violence. However, no association was found between the sex of the children as well as living arrangement and wife abuse. Based on the results of this exploratory research the following hypotheses can be formulated for verification in future researches.

1. The younger the age at marriage of the women, the greater is the possibility of their being battered.
2. The younger the age of wife, the greater are the chances of her being victim of physical violence.
3. The greater the number of children, a woman has the greater is the possibility of her being victim of physical violence of her husband.
4. The absence of child is likely to result in wife battering.

Social variables :

An individual's social milieu not only influences his social position, network of relationships and contents of learning but also his social behaviour pattern. Social behaviour is a function of the life situations which may be physical, economic, social or cultural or an interplay of these elements (Hill and Hausen, 1960). It is assumed that persons having differential life situations would react differently to the same stimuli. It is, therefore, essential to explicate the role of these social variables for understanding the quality of conjugal relationship. The social variables considered for the present study are educational and occupational status of the respondents, their social class background, their caste and religious background, their attitudes regarding traditional gender roles in the family and their value orientation in favour of use of violence for the resolution of conflict.

Education :

Formal education helps an individual to know what is happening outside one's immediate surroundings. It also facilitates him to develop rational outlook towards life. Education widens the horizon and makes the individual more knowledgeable. Education also helps an individual to get jobs of high prestige and with high economic returns. Further, higher education enhances one's social prestige. Efforts have been made to find out association between the level of education one has and the quality of interpersonal relations.

A few studies indicate that the less education a person has, the more likely he or she is to approve of and support violence (Straus et al., 1980). Some other studies, however, contradict their findings and on the other hand, they are of opinion that couples with the lowest educational levels are less prone to violence than those who had attained higher education (Stark and Flitcraft, 1988). It is argued that low education level does not cause violence but it aggravates the frustration. The reason for more violence among those who have higher education, may be that women with high education may not endorse the traditional role relationship and this may be considered as threat to the dominant position by their husbands. However, education can provide people with alternatives for resolving family disagreements. It is, therefore, expected that with the help of education individual learns different mechanisms to resolve the conflict in the conjugal relationships.

TABLE 3.6 **Wife's education and physical violence**

(Wife's education)

	Illiterate and Illiterate	*Upto middle*	*Matric and Diploma holder*	*Graduate*	*Post Gradiate Professionals*	*Total*
Yes	25	10	10	11	11	67
	44.64	32.26	28.57	25.58	31.43	33.50
No	31	21	25	32	24	133
	55.36	67.64	71.43	74.42	68.57	67.50
Total	56	31	35	43	35	200
	100.00	100.00	100.00	100.00	100.00	100.00

The educational background of the victim wives indicates that those who have low educational attainment (Upto middle standard) or higher educational attainment (Professional and Post-graduation and above) had over representation as compared with those who had moderate level of education. There is a progressive decrease in the percentage of the victims from illiterate educational category upto graduation with the exception of those who had higher education. This curvilinear distribution of victims of violence indicates that women who have no education or have higher educational attainment are more prone to physical violence by their husbands. The women with low education designate their complete dependency because with low educational background they will not be able to have economic independence or would be engaged in occupations with low economic returns and low prestige. In the case of those who have higher education they may be in better position to gain economic independence and with the higher education they may start questioning the dominant position of their husbands. Such a threat is not tolerated by the husbands and they use physical violence as their ultimate resource to maintain their dominant position in the family.

Occupation :

Occupation is an important indicator of a person's position in society. It is believed that the higher the education one has, the higher the occupation one holds and the higher the prestige he gets in society. Conversely, the lower the occupation, the lower will be the economic returns and as a consequence thereof, there are likely to be higher frustrations and greater marital conflicts. Many studies indicate that persons engaged in occupations of lower prestige are more likely to resort to physical violence against their wives to give vent to their economic stresses (Gelles and Cornell, 1990; Shupe et al., 1987; Straus et al., 1980). It is also argued that women who stay at home and are not engaged in paid work outside their homes are at somewhat greater risk of being physically abused than those engaged in paid work (Levinson, 1989). This is probably because housewives are perceived to contribute less to family subsistence and are consequently valued less than women who are engaged in paid work outside the home. Wife beating is far less common in societies in which women have independent economic and social resources, perhaps because these resources are valuable enough to make a husband think twice before acting in ways that might force his wife to terminate the marriage (Kalmuss and Straus, 1982; Levinson, 1989).

In the sample (Table 3.7) there are only 65 women respondents who were found to be engaged in paid work. Out of these 47.69 per cent were victims of physical violence of their husbands. On the other hand, out of those not engaged in paid work outside their homes, only 26.67 per cent were physically abused by their husbands. The results of the present study support the findings of Hornung et al. (1981)

who, in one representative sample, found housewives had a lower risk of violence than working wives. The reason housewives are abused less than working wives is because keeping in view their economic dependency they may have "Learned helplessness" with the result they have developed tolerance of such violence and do not share with outsiders that they are being abused or they would endorse the traditional gender roles and would not question the authority of their husbands. Hence, they do not provoke their husbands to use physical violence to maintain their dominant position in the conjugal relationship. On the other hand, the working wives may not accept the dominant position of the husband in family decision making and raise questions about asymmetrical conjugal relations. Such a situation may prompt the husband to use physical force to retain his dominant position.

TABLE 3.7 **Wife's woking status and physical violence**

(Working status)

	Not engaged in paid work outside the home		*Engaged in paid work outside the home*		*Total*	
Yes	36	26.67	31	47.69	67	33.50
No	99	73.33	34	52.31	133	66.50
Total	135	100.00	65	100.00	200	100.00

TABLE 3.8. **Occupational prestige and physical violence**
(Occupational prestige of the working wives)

	Low		*Medium*		*High*		*Total*	
Yes	16	61.54	10	47.62	5	27.78	31	47.69
No	10	38.46	11	52.38	13	72.22	34	52.31
Total	26	100.00	21	100.00	18	100.00	65	100.00

The general contention that working gives economic independence to women, hence, they would be relatively free from abuse is also not found to be correct in the present study. On the other hand, it is the working women who are abused more than the non-working women. The association between wives' working status and her physical abuse will become more clear if the type of occupation in which these women are engaged in, is taken into consideration.

As the number of respondents under the working category were limited to 65 cases only, their occupations were grouped under three categories, i.e., occupations with low prestige, medium prestige and high prestige. The data reveal that the percentage of the victims goes on decreasing from low occupational prestige category to higher prestige category. In short, there was inverse relationship between occupational prestige and physical violence, i.e., the lower the prestige of paid work, the greater was the violence against wives. The results indicate that it is not the working status per se which provides women freedom from physical violence of their husbands but it is the nature of the occupation and associated prestige and economic returns which facilitate women to be free from physical abuse.

Social class

The concept of social class has been defined by several sociologists. The most prominent among them are Marx, Weber, Warner, Dahrendorf. They have, however, given emphasis to different attributes. One salient feature of different definitions is that members of a class group have common style of living and value orientation. Wolfgang and Ferracuti (1982) in their study of subculture of violence have even divided a class into subclasses depending upon value orientation of the members. Similarly, a number of scholars have tried to find out association between class background and family violence. One set of studies maintains a positive association between lower class and wife battering (Gaguin, 1978; Gelles and Cornell, 1983; Saunders, 1982; Straus et al., 1980). Whereas some researchers do not endorse their findings and they have contended that wife battering transgresses the boundaries of class (Berk et al., 1983; Dobash and Dobash, 1979; Hilberman, 1980; Steinmetz, 1977; Walker, 1979, 1984).

In the present study an attempt has been made to find out association between class background and wife beating. The class background of the respondents has been worked out based on education, occupation and income of the husbands of the respondents because a majority of the women respondents were not found to be working and hence, had no independent income of their own. While selecting the sample their living arrangement was taken into consideration and 50 cases from each house type were included in the sample, which were redistributed into different social classes. The class background of the respondent was also divided into lower, working, middle and high for the purpose of finding out differential behaviour pattern, i.e., wife abuse in different classes. (The methodology adopted for working out social class has been discussed in Appendix I.)

TABLE 3.9. **Social class and physical violence**

(Social Class)

	Lower		*Working*		*Middle*		*Upper*		*Total*	
Yes	28		14		20		5		67	
		51.85		30.43		27.03		19.23		33.5
No	26		32		54		21		133	
		48.15		69.57		72.97		80.77		66.5
Total	54		46		74		26		200	
		100.00		100.00		100.00		100.00		100.00

The data indicate that in contrast to 19.23 per cent victims of physical violence in the upper class, there were 51.85 per cent victims in the lower class. There is a progressive decrease in the percentages of victims of physical violence from the lower through the middle to the upper class. Similarly, among the non-victims the higher per cent (80.77) belong to the upper class. In short, women belonging to the lower class were at a higher risk of being physically abused by their husbands. The results of the study indicate inverse relationship between class background and wife battering. These findings support the contention of those researchers who found that women belonging to the lower class were at a higher risk of physical violence which was attributed to their way of life. The use and approval of physical violence in the lower class has been attributed to what Lewis (1959) calls, the culture of poverty. The concept implies that the poor people have a distinct subculture. Due to common experiences they have developed certain attitudes and behaviour pattern which have been transmitted from parents to children. These include the casual resort to physical violence, an inability to plan for the future, seeking of immediate gratification, weak impulse control and fatalistic attitude towards the future. Davis (1963) while describing the 'class-linked' violence contends that physical violence in the lower class families is normal, socially approved and socially inculcated type of behaviour. Similarly, Whitehurst (1974) while making a distinction between the middle and the lower class families with regard to control over violence, maintained that violence-responses were much more built into lower class subculture as a means to achieve some goals to assert independence and masculinity. The members of the lower class are subject to a lot of economic pressures and strains and they cannot show their resentment and frustration against those who are highly placed and hence they give vent to their frustrations at the slightest provocation by beating their wives on whom they can exert their power. Indirect support to this explanation is found in the work of Allen and Straus (1980). Their study of relationship between distribution of power and resources between spouses and wife abuse indicated that in blue collar families, husbands who did not possess clear resource superiority over their wives tended to use violence to maintain their power in the family more than husbands who possessed such resource superiority. On the other hand, members of the middle and upper classes have more resources and can keep their violence private and additionally, because of the sensitivity of the issue and embarrassment, the victims are not likely to admit its existence in their conjugal relationship.

Caste :

Individual's social status is determined by his ascriptive and acquired attributes. In the Indian society ascriptive attributes, like caste, determine not only his social milieu as castes are hierarchically placed but also his opportunities to acquire new attributes. Although an individual is now theoretically permitted to achieve any position and support any ideology yet caste plays an important role in influencing his behaviour pattern. Keeping in view the importance of caste in the Indian society, it will be worthwhile to find out an association between caste and wife battering.

TABLE 3.10 **Wife's caste and physical violence**

(Caste)

Response	*Brahmin*	*Khatri/ Arora*	*Jat/ Rajput*	*Trading Caste*	*Backward Caste/ Schedule caste*	*Others*	*Total*
Yes	9 26.47	10 23.26	12 31.58	4 36.36	28 43.08	4 44.44	67 33.5
No	25 73.53	33 76.74	26 68.42	7 63.64	37 63.64	5 55.56	133 66.5
Total	34 100.00	43 100.00	38 100.00	11 100.00	65 100.00	9 100.00	200 100.00

The distribution of the victims of physical violence according to their caste background indicates that respondents belonging to the lower castes group and those who have not specified their caste were more victims in contrast to the respondents belonging to the higher castes. Among the twice-born, the respondents belonging to trading castes were at a higher risk in contrast to Khatris and Aroras. Similarly, among the non-victims the higher percentages of respondents were found among the twice-born. The higher frequency of physical violence present among the members of the lower castes may be attributed to their lower class background. Similarly, among those cases who have not specified their caste, most of them belonged to Muslim and Christian religion and these respondents were having lower socio-economic status. The association between caste background and physical violence would remain incomplete unless their economic status is also considered. Preceding analysis has indicated that members belonging to the lower class were more likely to resort to physical violence for the resolution of conjugal conflicts.

Religion :

Religion is an important institution which instills a particular philosophy of life in an individual. His outlook towards himself and others as well as his behaviour pattern are likely to be influenced by his religious belief system. Is wife abuse a characteristic of a particular religious group? To find out an answer to the question religious background of the respondents was considered.

TABLE 3.11 **Wife's religion and physical violence**

(Religion)

Response	*Hindu*	*Sikh*	*Muslim*	*Christian*	*Total*
Yes	46 32.86	16 32.00	2 50	3 50	67 33.5
No	94 67.14	34 68.00	2 50	3 50	133 67.5
Total	140 100.00	50 100.00	4 100	6 100	200 100.00

No clear-cut association was found between religious background and physical violence against wives. Among the two main religious groups present in Chandigarh, there was no marked difference in the percentage of victims. In case of Muslims and Christians 50 per cent of the respondents belonging to these religious groups were the victims of husband's violence. This again may be attributed to the low economic status of the respondents. The results of the present study do not establish any association between religion and wife battering.

Traditional gender roles :

The family as a social institution lays down norms and values to regulate the behaviour of the members of the social group. Family as a social group is structured in such a manner that one member, usually the husband, assumes the dominant position and the other members take up subordinate positions. The family provides a social setting where husband and wife play complementary roles (Parsons and Bales, 1955). One of the conditions which maximises the cooperative elements in the family is the similarity of social values and ideologies which promotes not only cohesiveness and harmony but also helps in the proper functioning of the group (Nye, 1982).

In the patriarchal traditional societies, like India, sex role expectations favour male dominance in the family. Traditional ideology promotes and serves to justify male dominance as well as helps in cultivating a belief system among the husbands and wives as to how they should behave in the marital relationship.

Motivated by traditional ideology, division of labour in the family was worked out into a male provider and a female to focus more narrowly on the domestic realm. Such a task specialization and differential evaluation helped men not only to have greater control over economic resources but also a greater access to power in the family. The power structure in the family is maintained through the actions of the members involved in the relationships. Those at the top of the power structure behave in dominant ways and they do not hesitate to use coercive methods to retain their dominant position (Dobash and Dobash, 1979; Finkelhor, 1983; Lips, 1991).

Attempts have been made to find out association between traditionality and wife abuse. A number of studies have concluded that men who were more traditional in their attitudes towards women were more likely to become wife abusers (Rosenbaum and O'Leary, 1981a; Kalmuss and Straus, 1982; Straus et al., 1980; Walker, 1981). Some importance is also given to sex role orientation of the victims. Walker (1984) is of opinion that non-traditional wives if paired with traditional husbands are at higher risk of being abused. An attempt has been made in the present study to find out correlation between wives' traditional orientation and their being victims of abuse.

Traditional sex role orientation of the respondents was worked out based on the responses to eight statements (Appendix II). The level of traditionality was further divided into three: High, Medium and Low, to find out association between level of traditionality and wife battering. It is assumed that respondents who have low level of traditional role orientation are at higher risk of physical violence than those at high level of traditionality because wives with low level of traditional orientation are more likely to question asymmetrical power relations in the family.

Data on traditionality and wife abuse reveal that there is a progressive decrease in the percentage of victims from low level of traditionality to high level of traditionality. In contrast to 22.86 per cent of the wives showing high level of traditional sex role orientation, 40.32 per cent wives indicating low level of traditionality were the victims of physical violence by their husbands. Similarly, among the non-victims, their percentages go on increasing from low level of traditionality to high level of traditionality. In short, it can be con-

TABLE 3.12 **Traditionality and physical violence**

(Traditionality)

Response	*Low*		*Medium*		*High*		*Total*	
Yes	25	40.32	34	33.01	8	20.86	67	33.5
No	37	59.68	69	66.99	27	77.14	133	66.5
Total	62	100.00	103	100.00	35	100.00	200	100.00

cluded that wives with non-traditional sex role orientation are at higher risk of being physically abused. The results of the study partially support the findings of Walker (1984) and Whitehurst (1974). The reason for wives showing less traditional sex role orientation being victims of physical violence may be attributed to their attempt in questioning the traditional power structure in the family. The husbands in such situation are likely to use physical force as the last resort to maintain their dominant position.

Value orientation :

The norms and values relating to intra-family violence indicate cultural contradiction. On the one hand, there is a myth of family non-violence (Steinmetz and Straus, 1974) which reflects cultural norms for the family as a group characterised by love and harmony. On the other hand, there seems to be social norms which imply right of the family members to strike each other (Straus, 1976). The legitimation of violence in the family is explicit and mandatory — as in the case of rights and obligations of the parent to use a necessary and appropriate level of physical force to adequately train and control a child.

Data reported by Straus (1980c) showed that violent wives as well as violent husbands express more approval of violence than do non-violent husbands and wives. Levinson (1989) in his cross cultural study on family violence came to the conclusion that wife beating was more common and frequent in societies in which adults solved conflicts by resorting to physical violence, indicating attitude in favour of violence.

The cultural norms and values permitting and sometimes encouraging husband to beat wife actually reflect hierarchical and male dominant type of society like India. The right to use force exists, as Goode (1971) concludes, to provide the ultimate support for the existing power structure of the family in which the wife assumes a subordinate position. Based on these studies it can be concluded that physical violence against wives would be more common in those families which possess proviolence values to resolve spousal conflicts.

Respondents' values in favour or against use of violence in the family were obtained from their reactions to 12 statements. Their scores were divided into three categories depicting low, medium and high scores (See Appendix III). This exercise was done with an assumption that the respondents with high score on values in favour of violence in the family would be at a higher risk of being victims than those with low score.

The data did not depict any clear-cut association. On the other hand, it was noted that those respondents who had medium score on values favouring use of violence to resolve family conflict were more victims in contrast to those who had high or low score. The reason for lack of association may be attributed to the fact that there is a lot of gap between values and actual behaviour pattern. Secondly, the values were taken of the wives rather than the husbands who were the perpetrators of physical violence against their wives. The respondents might be holding values against the use of

TABLE 3.13 **Values in favour of violence and abuse**

(Values)

Response	*Low*		*Medium*		*High*		*Total*	
Yes	23		37		7		67	
		31.94		35.58		29.17		33.50
No	49		67		17		133	
		68.06		64.42		70.83		66.50
Total	72		104		24		200	
		100.00		100.00		100.00		100.00

violence but had no control over the values and behaviour pattern of their husbands.

The above discussion on social variables highlights certain salient features which contribute to husbands' physical violence against wives. Lower caste background, low and high educational attainment, lower working status, lower social class background and low level of traditionality were found to be contributing factors for husbands' physical violence against wives. However, no association was found between religious background and value system of the respondents and their being victims and non-victims of physical violence.

Dependency :

Dependency is a state, both physical and mental, depicting assistance from a person or persons for continuing living in the community. The human child has to depend upon his parents for his growth, development and social recognition. The Indian society has placed women in a state of dependency as a daughter on her father, as a sister on her brother, as a wife on her husband and lastly as a mother on her son. Further, sexual division of labour and gender roles accentuate these differences. Additionally, patriarchal social norms not only grant control of family resources and property to men but also provide dominant position to them. To maintain their dominant position, the husbands are likely to use coercive methods including physical violence against their wives. Sometimes physical violence is used as a means to an end and at other times as an end in itself.

Dependency is also treated as a cause of physical violence in the conjugal relationships. Researches have utilized this explanation in two ways. In case, a wife is completely dependent, both physically and socially, her husband exploits her dependency and uses violence at whim to reinforce his dominant position in the conjugal relationship (Dobash and Dobash, 1979; Mahajan, 1986; Marsden, 1978; Straus, 1976; Truninger, 1971; Walker, 1978). A few scholars are also of opinion that when a husband is dependent upon his wife he resorts to physical violence as a last resort against his wife as he is afraid of losing his spouse or a person on whom he can exert his dominant position. Hence, dependency of husband over his wife is also treated as a cause of wife abuse (Bernard and Bernard, 1984; Browning, 1983; Coleman, 1980; Elbow, 1977; Faulk, 1977; Ganley, 1981; Ganley and Harris, 1978; Hilberman and Munson, 1977-81; Saunders, 1982; Sonkin et al., 1985; Walker, 1979).

As the present study is limited to wife abuse, the analysis is limited to wife's (victim's) perception regarding the conditions which make her dependent upon her husband and how this state of dependency results into her being abused. To find out association between wife's dependency and her abuse, dependency has been divided into objective and subjective. It does not, however, mean that we can draw watertight compartments between the two. In certain cases objective dependency may lead to subjective dependency, whereas in other cases even though there is no objective dependency yet the individual remains subjectively dependent upon her spouse.

It can, however, be assumed that a wife who experiences

both objective and subjective dependency is at higher risk of being abused in contrast to those who have only objective or only subjective dependency.

Objective dependency

For the purpose of analysis wife's objective dependency stands for conditions like not working, i.e., being economically dependent upon husband; not having any property in her name; not receiving any financial assistance from her family of orientation; inability to live alone; inability to do shopping alone, and inability to go outside the city alone. Further, level of objective dependency may vary from case to case hence, objective dependency was further divided into three levels: low, medium and high. (The procedure adopted for assigning scores as well as for dividing into three levels have been discussed in Appendix IV.) The wives who are objectively dependent upon their husbands are at higher risk of being abused because it would be difficult for these women to come out of the abusive relationship as they do not have the resources to live alone. Their objective dependency is also known to their spouses who may fully exploit the situation knowing fully well that their wives would not be able to leave them. It is further envisaged that wives who have high level of objective dependency are at greater risk of being abused.

TABLE 3.14 **Objective dependency and physical violence**

Response	*Low*		*Medium*		*High*		*Total*	
Yes	29		25		13		67	
		31.87		32.89		39.39		33.50
No	62		51		20		133	
		68.13		67.11		60.61		66.50
Total	91		76		33		200	
		100.00		100.00		100.00		100.00

Table 3.14 indicates that wives with high level of objective dependency are physically abused more in contrast to those who have low level of objective dependency. This is evident in the percentages of the victims at different levels of dependency. Similarly, the percentage of non-victims goes on decreasing to high level. There were 33 respondents who had high level of objective dependency, out of which 60.61 per cent were not the victims of physical violence. The results of the study support the contention of a few scholars who are of opinion that high level of women's marital dependency is not associated with wife abuse because husbands of dependent wives can maintain their dominant positions without resorting to violence as their wives are in no position to question their dominance (Allen and Straus, 1980; Brown, 1980; Goode, 1971; Mahajan and Madhurima, 1995; Whitehurst, 1974). Although no cause and effect relationship can be established between dependency and wife abuse yet the data show an indicative trend that wives who have high level of objective dependency are abused more as compared to those who have low level of objective dependency.

Subjective dependency :

A few scholars contend that objective dependency of the wife per se does not result into her abuse but is mediated by her tolerance (Saheli, 1986; Walker, 1979). One may, however, raise the question why she develops this tolerance to abuse? One reason may be that she remains subjectively dependent upon her husband because her social reality has not been constructed outside the marital relationship. In Indian society marriage is a must for every woman, unless she adopts a life of celibacy. Remaining unmarried or living a life of a divorcee is looked down upon. Hence, whether a wife is objectively dependent upon her husband or not she remains subjectively dependent. It is not, however, true in the case of husbands. Remarriage after divorce or separation is easily available to a man than a woman. Such a discriminatory practice perpetuate subjective dependency in the wives.

Subjective dependency in the present study stands for, not leaving the husband even under adverse circumstances; divorce not considered good; perception that married women even if abused enjoy higher status than divorced; lack of support from kin; greater commitment and more devotion to marital relationship. It is also expected that wives are likely to have different levels of subjective dependency. Depending upon their scores they are divided into three categories : low, medium and high (See Appendix V). It is expected that wives having higher level of subjective dependency will be at higher risk of being physically abused in contrast to those having lower level of subjective dependency.

TABLE 3.15 **Subjective dependency and physical violence**

(Subjective dependency of the wife)

Response	*Low*		*Medium*		*High*		*Total*	
Yes	17		34		16		67	
		23.94		37.36		42.11		33.50
No	54		57		22		133	
		76.06		62.64		57.89		66.50
Total	71		91		38		200	
		100.00		100.00		100.00		100.00

The results of the study indicate that in contrast to 23.94 per cent wives having low subjective dependency more than 42 per cent of the wives with high level of dependency are the victims of physical violence of their husbands. There was a steady increase in the percentage of abused wives from low level of subjective dependency through medium level to high level of subjective dependency. Taking into account 38 cases having high level of subjective dependency it was noted that more than 42 per cent were the victims of husbands' physical violence and approximately 58 per cent were free from being physically abused. Although, no positive correlation could be established between subjective dependency of wife and her being victim of physical abuse yet the high percentage of victims having high level of subjective dependency designate a partial association between subjective dependency and her being battered. The reason for high percentage of such victims can be attributed to wife's commitment to marriage and her inability to use alternative mechanisms to get out of the abusive relationships. Such a situation forces her to cultivate tolerance and continue living in the abusive relationship. Similarly, the husband uses coercive methods to assert his dominant position in the familial network of relationship because he is confident that his violent behaviour would not be challenged and he can attain the desired goal, that is, subduing his wife. The results of the present study on subjective dependency and wife abuse partially support the findings of other researchers (Kalmuss and Straus, 1982).

Total dependency :

Subjective dependency in certain cases may be treated as a consequence of objective dependency. In other cases subjective dependency may not be the outcome of objective dependency. It was for this reason that these two facets of dependency were treated separately, however, to find out the impact of dependency on wife abuse both objective and subjective dependencies have to be combined. In other words, to find out the validity of dependency framework to explicate wife abuse, both the facets of dependency are combined to find out their combined effect on physical violence.

The total dependency scores of the respondents have been arranged into three categories—low, medium and high (See Appendix VI). The data indicate that wives with higher level of dependency are at higher risk of being abused in contrast to those with lower level of dependency. In contrast to 27.42 per cent of wives with low level of dependency more than 35 per cent of the wives with higher level of dependency

TABLE 3.16 **Total dependency and physical violence**

Response	Low (Total dependency)		Medium		High		Total	
Yes	17		35		15		67	
		27.42		35.71		37.5		33.50
No	45		63		25		133	
		72.58		64.29		62.5		66.50
Total	62		98		40		200	
		100.00		100.00		100.00		100.00

were the victims of husbands' physical violence. The percentage of non-victims goes on decreasing from lower level of dependency to higher level. Under these circumstances, though no clear cut correlations could be found between dependency and wife abuse yet it was found that with the increase in the level of dependency there was an increase in the percentage of victims.

The above discussion on the correlates of physical violence against wives indicates that younger age at marriage, lower class background and dependency force them to assume a victim's role. In short, no single factor can be held responsible for wife abuse. Hence, for the purpose of understanding correlation of physical violence against wives multiple factors should be taken into account.

4

Coping Behaviour

Violence against wife in one form or the other was found to be quite widespread in the cases under study. To find out the correlates of violence, the analysis is restricted to physical violence in the preceding chapter because it is felt that physical violence as a form of behaviour is different from other types of violence. Moreover, physical violence against wife was not found to be present in some families, a situation providing an opportunity to identify the factors present in the families of battered women and likely to be absent in the families of non-battered women. Physical violence against wives was found to be more common in lower class as compared with that of upper classes. However, violence of different forms was found to be quite generic, cutting across class boundaries and was also found to be present in all age groups having different attributes. Additionally, domestic violence in one form or the other is not considered seriously unless it involves homicide or physical injury against an intimate. It is commonly recognized that much of what would be called aggravated assaults, become domestic disturbances or comparably minor offences if they occur in domestic situations.

From the stand point of the victim, violence is violence whether it is verbal, psychological or physical. Therefore in this chapter on coping behaviour, all the victims will be considered in order to find out their reactions to violence as well as steps they take to deal with the abusive situation.

Researchers in the area of family violence in the United States have spent about 20 years in understanding the nature and the extent of the problem. After identifying major social factors associated with the problem of wife abuse they have advocated different coping mechanisms for the solution of the problem.

Different researchers have given attention to develop programmes for the wife batterers, such as individual therapy (Adams, 1988; Adams and McCarmick, 1982; Rosenbaum, 1986); marital and family therapy (Adams, 1988; Heppner, 1981; Weitzman and Dreen, 1982); psychoeducational or psychotherapeutic group approach (Roberts, 1984); Anger control techniques (Edleson, 1984; Ganley and Harris, 1978; Purdy and Nickle, 1981; Saunders, 1984; Sonkin et al., 1985; Star, 1983); cognitive behaviour strategies (Emery, 1989) and coordinated programmes involving group treatment and community intervention (Gondolf, 1987; Gondolf and Hennekin, 1987).

In addition to research on batterers' treatment programmes, researches have also suggested treatment techniques for the victims (Andersen et al., 1991; Bowker, 1988; Gondolf and Fisher, 1991; Gelles and Cornell, 1990; Sedlak, 1988; Turner and Shapiro, 1986). Andersen et al. (1991) argue that separation of the abused wife from her husband is an important factor for the treatment of abuse and ultimately for her survival and yet when she leaves her husband, she exposes herself to an ever increasing risk of violence. Thus a wife must not leave her husband until she has the resources to stay away either permanently or long enough to facilitate significant change in the husbands' behaviour. Gondolf and Fisher (1991) argue that it is the woman's separation that is the prime motivator for a man's attending counselling in the first place, once batterer "gets her back" he is much more likely to drop out of counselling and batter again.

Although different researchers in the United States have started working on the solution of wife abuse, yet they are unable to reach at a consensus because most of them are naive. Gondolf and Fisher (1991) argue that there is high drop out rates in such programmes. After such programmes their battering ceases but psychological abuse heightens. Stordeur and Stille (1989) argue that patriarchal society will not change overnight and that men in society who are reaping the rewards of violence will resist relinquishing their domination, men who attempt to give up their violence will be faced with covert and overt pressures from other men to come back in line with the attitude of masculine superiority.

The procedures advocated by these researchers may not be applicable to the Indian cultural situation. First, because the available knowledge regarding violence against wife is only anecdotal but there is also no consensus on the definitions of wife abuse. Additionally, no national sample survey has been conducted in India to find out the extent and the severity of the problem. Under these circumstances efforts should be made to assess the nature and the extent and the severity the problem as well as to identify the factors associated with wife abuse. Further, coping involves three sets of behaviour pattern. First, reactions to violent relationship; secondly, procedures adopted to deal with abusive relationship and thirdly, to develop mechanisms for countering violent behaviour pattern or getting freedom from abusive relationship. Because of above noted reasons this chapter is restricted to only the reactions of the victims to different forms of violence as well as the steps they take to deal with the situation.

I

Husband's violence against wife is not a continuous process but revolves around relative peace and violence. There would be certain periods when the partners exhibit complete sympathy, understanding and love for each other. On other occasions the relationship would be marred with violence. Most of the women who are victims of their husbands' violence are of the view that conflicting situation in their intimate relationship is transitory. It is perhaps with this false hope that they continue living in the abusive relationship.

The perceptions of abuse by victims are likely to be different depending upon their training, life situation and availability or non-availability of alternatives. They, in turn, are likely to have ramifications on their reactions to their abusive situation. Further, their reactions are likely to be coloured by the presence or absence of other members in the household. In case, the conjugal violence takes place in the absence of other members of the family or outsiders, the victims are likely to react differently as compared with those victims who are abused in the presence of others. Victims who are abused in the presence of others are more likely to feel humiliated as they may develop a feeling of having been let down in the eyes of others. The victims are likely to react sharply even to the mildest form of abuse in case such abuse takes place in the presence of children and in-laws. In case of children, the victims may feel that their limited area of authority over children has been eroded. On the other hand, if the abuse takes place before the in-laws and outsiders, the battered women are likely to feel that they have been let down in the estimation of their in-laws and outsiders. Such victims are more likely to develop a feeling of helplessness. Before taking into account the victims' reactions to their abuse it is therefore essential to know, in whose presence their abuse had taken place.

TABLE 4.1 **Violence in the presence of others**

In the presence of	*Frequency**
Children	159
In-laws	49
Outsiders	25
No one	24

**Note*: Multiple choices were used by the respondents, hence total exceeds 187.

Out of 187 cases of victims of violence, only 24 victims informed that their abuse took place in the absence of other members of the family or outsiders. It is only in these cases where violence can be labelled as a "private matter" between husband and wife. In a majority of cases (159 out of 187) their abuse took place in the presence of their children. Such a situation is likely to create a sense of powerlessness among the victims. Further it would have negative effect on the children. A number of researchers are of an opinion that children who are brought up in violent families are more likely to become violent parents (Gelles, 1974; Pagelow, 1981b; Straus et al., 1980). It was only in 25 cases where women were abused by their husbands in the presence of outsiders. Such a situation is likely to create greater humiliation and shame for the victims. Approximately one-fourth of the victims were abused in the presence of their in-laws. Their abuse may be attributed not only to interference in the conjugal relationship by the in-laws but also depicts stronger ties with family of orientation of the husband than his family of procreation. As the respondents were allowed multiple choices it was noticed that a number of victims told that they were abused in the presence of other members of the family as well as outsiders. These are the victims who are more likely to be depressed as the charm of their married life starts fading away.

Studies conducted on wife abuse and victims reactions report a high incidence of depression among the victims. Wife abuse has been claimed to produce reactions among the victims such as "paralyzing terror" (Hilberman and Munson, 1977-81), "terrifying intimidation" (Schechter, 1983), "shame and degradation" (Marsden and Owens, 1975) and "humiliation and isolation" (Walker, 1978). A number of clinical studies report a high incidence of depression and anxiety (Hiberman, 1980; Star et al., 1979; Rounsaville and Weissman, 1978; Walker, 1978). The literature on psychological problems of battered women consistently report depression, anxiety and somatic problems. The samples of the battered women in these studies are exclusively the samples of women who come forward and seek help, hence are not the representative samples of the abused wives. It is quite probable that there may be psychologically troubled and more anxious abused wives who have not sought such help. Keeping in view the methodological shortcomings and the small size of the sample and lack of comparison group, it becomes difficult to draw any generalization with regard to reactions of the abused women. Further, it is not known whether they have been abused on single occasion or repeatedly. Additionally, psychological distress experienced by battered women was initially thought to be responsible for their battering (Shainess, 1979; Straus et al., 1980). Recently researchers have proposed that depression, anxiety and somatic disorders reported by battered women are the consequences of their being abused rather than a cause (Gelles and Straus, 1988). Based on Second National Family Violence Survey in the United States, Gelles and Harrop (1989) examined the effects of violence against women as per the information provided by 3002 female respondents. Women who reported experiencing violence also reported higher level of depression, anxiety and somatic disorders. Such a situation has prompted these battered women to contemplate suicide and a higher percentage of them had reportedly made suicidal attempts in comparison to non-battered women.

The battered women may also develop a feeling of helplessness as they may find themselves unable to check the violent behaviour of their husbands as well as they find that social definitions are unsupportive in helping them to come out of the abusive relationship. The abused women often suffer from, what Walker calls "Learned helplessness" (Walker, 1979; 1983), in that the victims come to the conclusion that no relationship exists between their actions and the outcomes (violence). After trying and failing to prevent the abuse of their husbands they give up. In addition, learned helplessness is more likely when the victims of abuse attribute the abuse to internal, stable and global causes (Abramson et al.,

1978). There is, however, another side to this learned helplessness. The helplessness on the part of the victims is created by their perpetrators of violence. It is in this context that Kipnis (1976) opines that battering males may induce guilt in their victims by blaming them for the abuse, until they come to blame themselves. Blaming the victims is frequently used to justify use of coercive power (Adams and McCormick, 1982; Bhatti, 1985; 1989; Star, 1980; Walker, 1979). Further, the battering men arouse fear in the victims by frightening them with threat of abandonment and of physical violence and by actual physical violence of varying severity (Andersen et al., 1991). Additionally, the victims are forced to develop a feeling of powerlessness and helplessness because they find that social support system would not come to their rescue, hence they continue to suffer humiliations in silence with the hope that things may improve.

There would be a few cases who may not accept a victim's role and as a consequence of being abused by their spouses, they may develop a feeling of hatred and may also become vengeful. Keeping in view the cultural ethos and status of women in India, where a wife is expected to treat her husband as God (*Pati Parmeshwar*) few victims of such abuse may develop a feeling of hatred against their husbands.

In the present study an attempt was made to find out the reactions of the victims to their abuse. It was expected that most of the victims would give their reactions which would be self-directed rather than directed against the perpetrators of violence, i.e., their husbands.

Keeping in view the reactions of the victims of different types of violence in the conjugal relationship it was noted that a majority of the cases (146 out of 187) had developed a feeling of depression. The results of the present study support the findings of Gelles and Straus (1988) and Gelles and Harrop (1989) that high level of depression was a consequence of their being abused by their husbands.

Further, a number of respondents assumed the responsibility of provoking their husbands to be violent and hence,

TABLE 4.2 **The reactions of the victims to violence**

Reactions	*Frequency**
Depressed	146
Humiliated	52
Shameful	14
Lonely	3
Powerlessness	28
Trapped	11
Guilty	23
Fearful	4
Hatred against husband	11
Vengeful	3

**Note* : Multiple choices were used by the victims, hence total exceeds 187 cases.

started blaming themselves for their abuse. These cases developed a feeling of guilt (23 cases) in them and indirectly endorsed the contention of their abusers that they had "asked for it". A number of researchers have also come to this conclusion in their studies in which the victims assumed the responsibility of provoking their husbands to be violent and suffered from the feeling of guilt (Ferraro and Johnson, 1983; Hilberman, 1980; Miller, 1983; Pagelow, 1981b). Additionally, a few respondents became afraid after having been abused by their husbands. These were the cases who have been threatened of dire consequences by their husbands if they did not act according to their dictates. As a consequence of their abuse they became very fearful and hence, their conjugal relationship was marked with fear rather than mutual love and understanding.

As expected, a few victims blamed their husbands for their violent acts. There were only 11 cases who developed hatred against their husbands because of their violent behaviour pattern against them and three cases as an outcome of their being abused developed animosity and hostility to such an extent that they became vengeful and would like to take up some action against their perpetrators of violence. It can, thus be assumed that these cases who have developed hatred and enmity against their abusive spouses are likely to seek intervention from the formal agencies so that they could teach a lesson to their abusers.

The above description regarding the reactions of the victims helps in concluding that in spite of being abused by the husbands, the women in India suffer in silence and do not develop a feeling of hatred against their spouses. It does not, however, mean that they have not reacted to their abuse but their reactions were self-directed rather than directed against the abusers.

II

The second part of this chapter deals with coping behaviour pattern which the victims adopt to deal with the violence. The strategy an individual adopts depends upon ones perception of the abusive situation. The analysis of the reactions of the victims to their violence indicated two types of reactions. One, self-directed and the second as 'other directed'. However, keeping in view one's training, socialization, life situations and the possibility of getting help from kin and others, one would act accordingly. It is further, envisaged that marital relationship is marked both by mutual sympathy and conflict. When two persons interact there may be a number of issues on which they think alike as well as have difference of opinion. Keeping in view the quality as well as the permanency of relationship, some incidents of dispute between the partners or sporadic incidents of conflict or violence may be accepted by the partners as part and parcel of their intimate relationship. As stated earlier conjugal relationship is not marked with continuous conflicts and fights but there are occasions when such conflicts stop and partners have cordial relationships. Hence, the conjugal relationship revolves around love and conflict and there is a tendency on their part to overlook certain sporadic incidents of disputes. The basic assumption of exchange theory that human interaction is guided by the pursuit of reward and avoidance of punishment is not applicable to the husband-wife relationship particularly in the Indian society. The following writers Homans (1961) and Blau (1964), Gelles (1983) believe that an individual who provides a reward to another thereby places him or her in debt, so that the second individual must furnish benefits to the first in return. The interaction will continue if rewards come equally to both the parties, if not, it will be broken off. However, intrafamilial relations, particularly, husband-wife relationship, cannot be broken off easily. As a consequence, when a partner perceives injustice or is abused, the individual may become angry but keeping in view the social definitions and societal reactions a person may think twice before initiating any step which would permanently break off the relationship.

Each victim of abuse is likely to work out her own strategies to deal with abusive situation in the conjugal relationship. It is only when violence becomes recurrent and individual strategies fail to bring about change in the violent behaviour pattern of the spouse, the victim may feel quite helpless. It is this helplessness on the part of the victim which would force her to seek some assistance from other persons. Frieze et al. (1980) found that members of the wife's family are more likely to be sought out help to end battering than any other informal help source. Among the formal agencies police were likely to be approached than other formal sources. Almost similar conclusions were drawn by Pagelow (1981a, 1981b) with regard to use of formal sources. Based on in-depth interviews of the victims Bowker (1983) came to know about different techniques used by the women to get their husbands to stop battering. These techniques were clustered into three types: (a) personal strategies, including talking, promising, threatening, hiding, passive defense, aggressive defense and avoidance; (b) use of informal help sources, including family members, in-laws, neighbours, friends and shelters; and (c) formal help sources, including the police, social service agencies, lawyers and district attorneys.

It is expected that the victims would first use informal help sources before seeking formal help in case she is not able to check the violent behaviour of their husbands. Further, the help from the informal sources would not imply asking them to intervene but by sharing one's experiences with them and seeking their advice for dealing with the abusive relationship. It was in this context that the victims were asked, whether they shared their abusive experiences with their relatives and close friends?

TABLE 4.3 **Victims who shared their bad experience**

Response	*Frequency*
Yes	50
No	137
Total	187

It is interesting to note that a majority of the victims (137 out of 187) did not share their abusive marital relationship experiences even with their relatives and close friends but preferred to rely upon their own strategies to deal with the abusive situation. It needs an independent study to find out the reasons as to why these cases have not shared their experiences with their informal sources for seeking their advice to tackle the abusive situation as well as the reasons why they are continuing to stay in the abusive relationship. As the scope of the present study was limited to finding out the coping behaviour pattern of the victims, the description would be limited to only those cases who have sought informal and formal help to deal with the situation.

Out of 187 victims of violence, only 50 cases shared their

experiences with their informal help sources, i.e., kin and close friends. Out of these 50 cases, 36 cases were the victims of physical violence of their husbands and 6 victims were adopting "passive" and "aggressive-defence" mechanisms. In the remaining 14 cases, they were free from physical violence but were the victims of verbal and psychological violence of their husbands.

As stated earlier, when the victims' own strategies to deal with violent situation fail, they are likely to approach their informal group to seek advice to face the situation. As the victims themselves have failed, they seek their advice with the hope that by acting on their advice, they will be better equipped to change the behaviour pattern of their husbands so that they could have cordial relations with their spouses. Whenever there is a conflict between husband and wife and this conflict is brought to the notice of informal group of the conjugal unit, there would be certain persons who would show sympathy to the victims and others may take the side of the husbands. Depending upon the nature of the abuse, the reactions of the informal group are likely to vary. Further, some members of the informal group may advise the victims to patch up for the purpose of saving their marriage whereas others may simply lend lip-service but would not give any concrete advice. Still others, are likely to advise the victims either to seek help from formal agencies or to break off the abusive relationship.

TABLE 4.4 **Types of advise extended by informal sources**

Advise given	*Frequency**
Advised to patch up	29
Advised to seek formal help	10
Advised to break off	8
Showed no interest	15

**Note* : Restricted to only 50 cases, and the respondents were allowed multiple choices.

Data reveal that in a majority of the cases, the members of the informal group advised the victims to patch up with their spouses. Indirectly these members valued their continuation in the conjugal relations and advised them to reconcile to the situation for the purpose saving their marriage. As in the case of the victims, their informal group also endorsed the traditional values, wherein it is the wife who is expected to yield irrespective of the fact whether she is at fault or not. Just in opposition to this, 10 victims were advised to seek help from formal agencies and in 8 cases the members of informal groups even advised for breaking off marital relationships. In addition to these, there were 15 cases where the victims found the attitudes of the members of their informal group not of much help because they showed indifference to their problem.

After seeking the advise of the members of the informal group the victims are not likely to translate the advise into practice irrationally and immediately. They would reevaluate their situation and would work out their own strategies to deal with the situation. To the marital partners the richest payoff of well managed conflict comes with yielding after a fight (Bach and Wyden, 1974). Any intimate relationship implies some readiness to yield one's own self-interest when it clashes with that of a partner. Give and take relationship between husband and wife also implies bending one's own will to the wishes of the other. Yielding, no doubt, involves loss of self-respect but those who value the relationship yielding is a small price so long as it leads to cessation of the conflict and an improvement in the quality of the relationship. Given the lower status of women in our society, as well as the stigmatized position of the single woman, the victims are likely to take the initiative of patching up the differences because they do not like to break off the relationship permanently (Dutton and Painter, 1981; Saheli, 1981; Strube, 1988; Truninger, 1971). It does not, however, mean that it is only the women who move first in the direction of reconciliation. In the conjugal relationship both the partners are likely to patch up if they value the relationship. The husband, the perpetrator may also realize his mistake and may become very apologetic over his behaviour pattern (Straus, 1980a). It is, therefore, expected that both the partners would take the initiative for reconciliation, however, more wives than the husbands are likely to take the first step.

TABLE 4.5 **Who reconciles first after the quarrel**

Spouse	*Frequency*	*Percentages*
Wife	44	23.53
Husband	33	17.65
Either husband or wife	110	58.82
Total*	187	100.00

*Not applicable 13 cases have been excluded.

The data indicate that in a majority of the cases (58.82 per cent) both the partners take the initiative to patch up, i.e., sometimes the husband reconciles first and at other times, it is the wife who takes the initiative for reconciliation. Either husband or wife here means that whosoever realizes his or her mistakes first, takes the initiative for reconciliation. Secondly, more wives than the husbands take the first step for reconciliation. Further, out of 33 husbands who tried to reconcile first after the quarrel, 78.79 per cent were also the initiators of the quarrel whereas in cases of 44 wives who tried to reconcile first, only 59 per cent had started the quarrel, but less percentage of husbands had tried to reconcile. On the other hand, less number of wives had started the quarrel but a higher percentages of them had taken the steps for reconciliation. The results reinforce the dominant position of husbands in the conjugal relationship.

In spite of reconciliatory approach of the wives to put an end to the conjugal quarrel, it might erupt again and again and might force them to seek help from some formal agencies. Their decision to involve formal agencies in the intimate relationships is not an abrupt or a spontaneous response to one isolated violent act on the part of their spouses. Their decision is an outcome of recurrent violent behaviour of the spouses as well as based on negative experiences over a period of time. It has been argued that the battered women are in a kind of "social trap" in which an immediate pay off obscures the violent events that precede it. In this process the relationship alternates unpredictably from periods of violence to periods of relative peace, thereby creating hope that things could be made to be alright if the women can just keep things running smoothly (Dutton and Browning, 1988; Dutton and Painter, 1981). However, when the situation escalates and goes beyond their control only then, they would venture to seek the help from the outside sources. It, however, does not mean that all the victims of their husbands' violence would seek intervention from formal sources after having failed to control the abusive behaviour pattern of their husbands. A number of victims may be ignorant about the type of the formal help available or they have developed "learned helplessness" and reconciled to their fate or they may be afraid that such intervention instead of helping them may enhance the severity of abuse against them. This is an area which needs an independent study, particularly in Indian setting where research on conjugal violence is very much limited. After having failed in their personal strategies to deal with violent situation they seek help from the informal groups. In case such help also does not yield any result and violent situation persists as a natural consequence thereof, they may seek help from the formal agencies. It is, however, expected that few victims of husbands' violence will seek intervention from formal agencies. It is in this context the victims were asked, "Had they sought help from the formal agencies for resolving the violent situation?"

It is surprising to note that out of 187 cases of husbands'

violence only 16 victims had sought help from outside formal agencies. Nine victims sought the intervention of influential persons who could have some control over their husbands and seven victims sought the help of women organizations like Panjab Istri Sabha. However, when such intervention failed to yield the desired results two victims had sought help from the legal counsellors and one case sought help from Crime Against Women Cell of the Police Department.

It would be in the fitness of the thing to explain the background of such victims who have sought help from the formal agencies. Out of 16 such cases, 14 were the victims of their husbands' physical violence and among these 14 cases there were 5 victims who had also used 'defensive violence' against their violent husbands. The remaining two cases were the victims of other form of violence. It is surprising to note that out of 67 victims of battering, only 14 battered women have sought help from the formal agencies. The results of this study do not support the contention of Gelles (1976) that the greater the severity of battering, the more likely the victim would seek intervention from formal agencies. As to why the remaining cases have not sought such help can be the subject matter for another independent study. As the present study has been restricted to only those cases who sought help from the formal agencies, the subsequent analysis will be restricted to only those 16 cases.

With regard to the educational background of the victims who sought help from formal agencies, it was found that either those respondents who were less educated or had high educational qualifications sought such help. Out of 16 cases, 9 had graduated and above. On the other hand, 6 cases who were either illiterate or had education up to middle level sought such assistance. Although it is difficult to draw any generalization based on 16 cases yet it is safe to conclude that women who are highly educate or had lower level of education seek assistance from the formal agencies and women, who belonged to middle category.

With regard to the working status of the victims who had sought intervention from the formal agencies, no clear cut trend was noticeable. Out of 16 cases, 5 were those who were not engaged in any paid work outside the household. In addition there were 3 cases who had lower occupational status. In contrast to these, 8 victims were engaged in occupations of medium prestige. In other words, the victims having higher educational attainment but engaged in medium prestige occupations are more likely to seek help from formal agencies.

The class background of their spouses was also checked and no distinction was found with regard to their class affiliation. These 16 cases were equally distributed in all the four social classes, however, with the exception of the victims of upper class, the cases belonging to other three classes were the victims of physical violence of their husband and in the upper class out of four cases, only two were the victims of physical violence and remaining two cases were the victims of other forms of violence. In short, no clear cut association was found between the class background and seeking help from formal agencies.

With regard to the type of help advanced by these formal agencies, it was noted that in 6 cases the women organizations provided them social or moral support implying thereby, listening to their problems sympathetically and assuring them that their injustices would be vacated. In five other cases, help in the shape of counselling was extended. The women organization as well as the influential persons had a meeting with their husbands, and family of orientation of both the spouses. In these cases attempts were made to seek the assistance of the kin of both the partners for settling the dispute between the conjugal unit. One victim was helped in filing a divorce case against her husband. There were four victims who informed that these formal sources neither came to their rescue nor gave them any constructive advice.

To what an extent the intervention of the formal sources was helpful to the victims? In other words, were the victims able to have congenial relationship subsequent to intervention from the formal sources? Out of 16 cases, 5 victims gave the reply in affirmative. These victims contended that after the intervention from the formal agencies, their abuse at the hands of the husbands had stopped. However, out of these 5 cases one had already sought divorce and 4 have been provided legal separation. As all these five cases were not staying with their abusive partners, they got freedom from daily quarrels and abuse. In the remaining 11 cases even after the intervention of the formal agencies their abuse has not stopped. Despite their efforts at the personal level, informal level and intervention from the formal sources their abuse continues and in the absence of other alternatives they are continuing to stay in the abusive relationship. In short, it can be concluded that intervention even by the formal agencies has not helped the victims to get freedom from violence of their spouses. They can be relieved of the abusive situation only when they leave their perpetrators. In case they become aware that leaving the abusive spouse is the best mechanism to get rid of violence but when they continue to stay with the abusive partner and suffer, one may raise the question, why do they stay with them? A number of studies have been conducted to find out answer to this question. Legal writer Elizabeth Truninger (1971) lists seven factors that help to explain why women do not break off relationships with abusive husbands. These are : (a) the women have negative self-concepts, (b) they believe their husbands will reform, (c) there is economic hardship, (d) they have children who need a father's economic support, (e) they doubt they can get along alone, (f) they believe divorcees are stigmatized, and (g) it is difficult for women with children to get work. Strube and Barbour (1983) argued that the more committed a woman is to the relationship the harder it is to justify psychologically that leaving is the best decision. Similar ideas have been reported by other research who argue that economic and psychological dependency, social stigma, presence of small children, lack of alternative support system and embarrassment to admit that she has stayed in such a bad situation for so long, force her to remain in violent relationship (Bergman et al., 1988; Bhatti, 1989; Kalmuss and Straus, 1982; Kertzman, 1980; Mahajan, 1989a; Parihar, 1989; Pleck, 1987; Walker, 1979). However, another group of researchers explains their stay in terms of cost and benefit. They feel that women have invested too much in the shape of time, effort and emotional involvement that they can't think of leaving the relationship (Brockner et al., 1981; 1982; Foss, 1980; Tiger, 1980).

Marriage in India is not a social contract. It is not contracted to seek personal happiness from the marital relationships. Marriage is considered as a social and religious obligation. This is more true in case of Indian women whose destiny in life has been marriage and motherhood. The Indian women right from their childhood are trained to be submissive, expected to develop patience and courage to face different odds in life but not to seek separation from their spouses. Although legally she is allowed to seek divorce because of the atrocities of her husband, yet social definitions, values and norms have not undergone appropriate changes to create congenial situation for her to go for divorce if circumstances so demand. Consequently, divorce for women is still stigmatized. Under these circumstances, it is not easy for her to terminate the marital relationship even though it is abusive. Additionally, she may be economically, psychologically and socially dependent upon her husband or she had made so much emotional investment in her marital relationship and children that she would continue to suffer rather than go for the last resort, i.e., separation or divorce.

To get a clearer picture the remaining 11 cases were asked the obvious question, why do they continue to stay in the abusive relationship? These respondents indicated different compulsions and gave a number of reasons which force them to continue staying in the abusive relationship, e.g., for the sake of children, for the sake of family reputation, with the hope that things will improve one day and that they could not think of alternative way of living. The data of the present study support the contention of some researchers (Gelles, 1976; Martin, 1979; Roy, 1977; 1982; Strube and Barbour, 1983; Strube, 1988). They have also concluded that a number of conditions influence their decision to tolerate violence of their spouses and they are forced to continue living with their abusive partners.

The foregoing analysis on the reactions to husbands' violence and coping behaviour of the victims highlights subjective dependency of the Indian women to their marital relationship. This subjective dependency is the outcome of their socialization, life situations, social definitions, values and norms and lack of alternative support systems. Hence, the objective conditions not only influence the victims' reaction to husbands' violence but also their coping behaviour pattern. Additionally, their perception that other alternative ways of living, e.g., single, divorcee or separated are no substitute for married life forces them to develop tolerance to violence and they continue living with their abusive spouses with a hope that things may improve.

5

Case Studies

Research on the problem of wife abuse is an area where one technique of data collection would not be sufficient to explicate the intricacies of the marital relationship. In spite of well thought of interview questions and good rapport with respondents, there would be a number of events and circumstances which will remain buried in the formal interview situation.

After marriage the husband and wife have to make a number of adjustments to come up to the expectations of each other as well as for the purpose of having congeniality, understanding and peaceful atmosphere. This is more true in the Indian society where the marriages are arranged by the parents and the married partners start knowing each other only after the marriage. Due to structural gender inequality women are not treated as equal partners in marital relationship. Even during their childhood they are not only discriminated but are required to develop a submissive personality configuration. In the Indian society, marriage and motherhood are treated as the destiny of women. Under these structural constraints, it is the women who are required to make greater efforts and sacrifices in making adjustment in the marital relationship than men. Undoubtedly, for the sake of having congenial marital relations, both the partners are expected to make some sacrifices but this is more true for the women.

Violence in the conjugal relationship does not erupt suddenly but is a result of continuous interactions between the partners. There would be a number of occasions where they agree on certain issues but on others they may have a difference of opinion. When these difference of opinions persist and both husband and wife decline to give due weightage to the viewpoint of the other partner, it may lead to quarrels and fights. Further, some new developments may take place in the marital relationship which may become a sore point. Still in other cases a change in the behaviour pattern of a spouse may be resented by the other partner. In households, where in addition to husband and wife, other kinsmen reside, they may also contribute in creating difference of opinion between them. Under these circumstances, it becomes essential to explicate the developmental cycle of the marital relationship. It is for this reason that case study method has been used in the present work to supplement the core data collected with the help of an interview schedule.

Intensive study of an individual's behaviour over a period of time and in various situations is called a case history or case study method (Ryckman, 1978). This method is particularly useful because it attempts to find the meaning of the recorded data within the life of the individual and only later on in terms of classes of individuals.

In the present work, case study method is used to highlight the dynamic aspect of conjugal relationship. As stated earlier, violence in the conjugal relationship is not a continuous process. Though there are certain periods in the marital relationship, which are relatively peaceful and harmonious yet there are certain time where there is conflict resulting into violence against a spouse. This aspect can be best highlighted with the help of case study method.

For the present study, case histories of eight victims of violence have been taken. These eight cases belong to different classes. Two cases from each of the four classes, viz., upper, middle, working and lower have been recorded. The cases selected were interviewed on several occasions, so that detailed information could be procured. Keeping in view the objective of the study indepth interviews, probings and observations were relied upon to bring out subterranean aspects of their conjugal relationship. The cases have been presented in a systematic manner, viz., their background, incidents giving rise to violence, the resultant outcome of violence, their personal strategies, circumstances forcing them to seek help from the formal institutions, their decision to continue in the abusive relationship, etc. For highlighting developmental aspect, time element has been used. To maintain the secrecy and confidence of the respondents their names have been substituted by fictitious names. Each case has been described separately followed by case discussion. After the detailed description of the cases an attempt is made to highlight certain commonalities and variations in the circumstances of these cases which have precipitated the discord. How the victims dealt with adverse life situations, is discussed.

CASE STUDY I : MRS. KANWAL

Kanwal (40) comes from a Jat Sikh family. Her father was working as a doctor in defence services. She has one elder sister who is married to a doctor. After graduation, at 21, Kanwal's marriage was arranged with a Major in the Army, who subsequently became a Colonel. Her father-in-law is a well-known industrialist of Punjab. Her husband is the only son of his parents. Three daughters were born out of the wedlock.

Coming from a family of defence personnel, she was well acquainted with the social practices prevalent in the defence services. It was a common practice that the couples participated in different social and official parties where drinks were normally served. In the beginning she tolerated the drinking behaviour of her husband. She tried her best to persuade her husband not to indulge in heavy drinking and misconduct towards other women under the influence of liquor. In spite of her best efforts, her husband did not change his habits and this became a sore point in their marital relationship.

During her first pregnancy and subsequent to the child birth she used to avoid attending social gatherings. Her absence from such parties was treated by her husband as a blessing in disguise. He drank heavily and flirted with other women. However, his misconduct used to be conveyed to her by her friends. She felt very bad about such happenings. As and when she would enquire from her husband about his misconduct he would shout at her and would humiliate her by praising other women. He would even try to find fault with her, pertaining to her dress, make up and outer personality configuration which she resented a lot and even used to loose her temper. One year after their marriage and birth of the first child their verbal fights became very common.

During six years of their married life she gave birth to three daughters. In early 1980's her husband was transferred to a non-family station and she came to Chandigarh along with her daughters to stay with her in-laws. It was during this period that she brought to the notice of her mother-in-law the behaviour pattern of her husband. Instead of appreciating her agony her mother-in-law blamed her for not being able to win over her husband as well as for giving birth to three daughters. Being fed up with the taunts of her mother-in-law, she went to her father's place at Delhi along with her daughters to stay there till her husband was posted to a family station. She narrated to her parents the humiliations hurled upon her by her mother-in-law as well as flirtatious behaviour of her husband. She was consoled by her parents and was advised to remain submissive.

During her stay at her parents' house she received very loving letters from her husband. He would even come to meet her and the daughters for a week or so during holidays. On his visits he would behave normally and act as a loving husband and father. He would take them for shopping and on outings. In this way he left the impression with her parents that he was a normal loving husband who cared for his family's well being. After about a year when he was posted at Chandigarh, Kanwal and her daughters came to join him.

At Chandigarh, Kanwal found that her husband had not changed a bit and indulged in his routine behaviour pattern of heavy drinking and flirting with other women. She got very annoyed. Every attempt of correcting him resulted into quarrels, shoutings, calling names and even physical fights. During these fights they even started throwing objects at each other.

To have a peaceful and happy married life she sought the counselling of common family friends, who instead of counselling her husband suggested that she should be tolerant and submissive for the sake of her daughters. She got frustrated, became lonely and broke all contacts with these common friends. She remained completely aloof and spent most of her time in her household activities and with her daughters.

The continued humiliating behaviour of her husband forced her to seek help from some outside agency. With the assistance of her friends she contacted a women's organization and sought its intervention. On her request the members of the organization went to their house and tried to plead her case with her husband. In their presence Kanwal's husband did not utter a single word but as soon as they left he became furious and even threatened to kill her. Her parents-in-law also accused her of lowering their prestige in the eyes of the neighbours. Kanwal's father was also asked to rush to Chandigarh and in his presence everybody accused her of involving outsiders in family affairs. Her father also sided with her in-laws. He even pleaded with her to remain calm and be tolerant because her husband being the only son would get all the property of the family and she would ultimately get all the assets which she would need for the marriage of her daughters and her own maintenance. She felt very bad at the behaviour of her father who instead of taking her cause asked her to continue suffering.

Keeping in view her humiliating situation, many a times she thought of seeking divorce from her husband so that she could live a peaceful life with her daughters. She is economically dependent upon her husband as she is not doing any job. Her parents are also not likely to extend her any support. Moreover, her daughters who are in the age group of 15-18 years, are also not in favour of her seeking a divorce. Under these circumstances she is forced to continue living in an abusive relationship. However, being brought up in the family of defence officials she is not able to reconcile to her present fate. As and when some quarrel takes place or hot words are exchanged she does not take them meekly but gives back in the same coin. The quarrels, exchange of hot words and fights are regular features in her family, yet she is continuing to live with her husband in the hope that her husband would mend his ways and she would have a happy future life.

Discussion :

(1) The case belongs to an upper class, where wife is educated but economically dependent on her husband.

(2) The precipitating factor for giving rise to conjugal violence is alleged infidelity of the husband, who also indulges in heavy drinking which is very much resented by the wife.

(3) The abuse against the wife started after one year of the marriage. The severity of violence increased after six years of marriage and the wife is victim of abuse for the last 18 years.

(4) The wife does not play a submissive role while reacting to aggressive behaviour of the husband, resulting into increase in the frequency and intensity of conjugal violence. Further, she was failed to gain sympathies of her informal group.

(5) Formal sources have also failed to put an end to conju-

gal violence. On the other hand, involvement of outside agencies in the family matters has been widely criticized by her informal group. As a result violence escalated against her.

(6) In the absence of alternative support system, her economic dependency and for the sake of female children, she is continuing to live in the abusive relationship.

CASE STUDY II : MS. SHANTI DEVI

Shanti Devi is 42 years old, a graduate, belonging to the state of Haryana. Her father was a businessman. She has three brothers and one sister. She is the youngest of them all. At a very young age, she lost both of her parents. Her brothers looked after her. She was married at the age of 27 to a man of her own caste. Her husband is an engineer and was working as a manager in a private concern at the time of her marriage. Her husband is three years older to her. Shanti Devi's husband has one brother.

After marriage she went to stay with her in-laws in the village as immediately after marriage her husband went to Iraq on a short official trip. After returning from Iraq, he got transferred to Visakhapatnam. He went there alone and she was again left with her in-laws as he had to look for a suitable accommodation there. Though Shanti Devi was well looked after by her in-laws, she insisted on joining her husband. When he did not call her to join him for the whole year, she reached Visakhapatnam and started staying with him. It was at Visakhapatnam that she came to know about her husband's extra marital affair and the reason of his reluctance in not bringing her to this city. She overlooked infidelity of her husband and continued with her married life. Her husband took good care of her and provided her all the basic necessities.

After a gap of one year Shanti gave birth to a daughter. Her husband took good care of her during her pregnancy. She was also maintaining contacts with her brothers and sister. She gave birth to another daughter after one year.

During this period her husband treated her and the children well. She had no complaint against him except occasionally she got upset over her husband's extra marital relationship. She had reconciled to her fate and her routine family life went on normal. After one year her father-in-law and subsequently her mother-in-law expired. She and her husband came to their native place to pay homage to the parents. After their death, her brother-in-law along with his family continued to stay in their ancestral home.

After four years of her marriage her husband was transferred to Haridwar, Shanti along with her daughters accompanied him. At Haridwar her husband met his old friends and he started spending more time with them which created suspicion in the mind of Shanti because she was quite aware of her husband's waywardness. After a few months, she came to know about her husband's infidelity from his friend's wife. She enquired from her husband about the allegations but he vehemently refuted but she had an inkling that her husband was not telling her the truth. Whenever he would come home late she would ask probing questions about his whereabouts which were resented very much by him and he started abusing and humiliating her. After some time he also got involved with his officer's minor daughter. Not only did he loose his job but with a shaved head and blackened face he was made to sit on a donkey. This sort of insult was too much for them. With all sorts of assurances and promises to mend his waywardness he brought her back to his ancestral home. She did not inform her brothers about his extra marital relationships because she thought that they would not be able to help her. She tried to adjust with a hope that he would mend his ways after the humiliating experience at Haridwar.

At first Shanti did not have any problems with her husband's sister-in-law who was also staying there but after some time family tussles started as her husband was unemployed. Later on, when her husband got a job as a Project Assistant, they established an independent kitchen but continued to stay in the same house.

Within six months of their arrival, Shanti's husband again started with his immoral behaviour. He developed an affair with his brother's married sister-in-law. He started visiting her regularly and gave her expensive gifts. Shanti came to know about the affair from her neighbours. She felt very bad about it. She tried her best to persuade her husband in checking his waywardness. After having failed she asked her brother-in-law to intervene and help but he refused bluntly. Left with no alternative she thought of meeting that lady's husband. She asked him to check his wife's behaviour. To her surprise he also expressed his helplessness. Her husband came to know about her prying endeavour and became very furious over her intervention in checking his relations with the other woman. He bluntly told her that he would continue to have relations with the other woman. Such a situation became unbearable for Shanti Devi. She stopped having sexual relations with her husband. This made him even more furious. He started abusing and beating her. He even stopped providing her for the basic needs.

In order to end her mental agony Shanti decided to leave her husband. Before doing so she thought of teaching a lesson to that lady who disturbed her family life. She went to her place and abused her. On the way to bus stand she met her brother-in-law who suggested her not to take this hasty and drastic step of leaving her husband. She was amenable to the suggestion provided he helped her in checking her husband's waywardness. He, however, showed his helplessness. In the meantime her brother-in-law's son informed her husband that she was leaving the house with the daughters. Her husband came to the bus stand and forcibly took her back and locked her in a room. At night when he came back home he was fully drunk and he started beating her with anything he could lay his hands on. Her daughters tried to save her but they too were beaten. Subsequently her brother-in-law came and saved her. As a consequence of severe beating she had a black eye and a broken tooth. She was even denied any medical aid in spite of such injuries.

After this incident her husband stopped coming to the house for two to three days at a stretch. Whenever she tried to enquire from him anything about his absence she was given harsh treatment. Many a time on the slightest protest he would beat her badly. Her life became miserable. She even tried to commit suicide by consuming poison but was, however, hospitalized and saved. Her husband told her that he was not going to allow her a simple death, she would be tortured physically and mentally before her death.

The continuous threat of getting killed and loss of mental peace forced her to leave her husband's house. After remaining in abusive relationship for seven years she ran away alongwith the daughters taking a small amount of cash. This time, she took a train and reached a small town near Ambala. She got refuge in an Ashram. After a gap of ten days she left for Chandigarh where her sister lived.

Shanti's sister had full sympathies for her but she could not provide her shelter because of her poor economic condition. She, however, got her daughters who were 8 and 9 years old admitted in a school, where their fees were remitted. Her sister also made living arrangement for her in Dev Samaj Mandir.

Shanti's husband tried to trace her. He came to her brothers' house and informed them about her desertion. He also came to Chandigarh and after meeting her sister came to know about her whereabouts. Her husband asked her to go back with him. She refused to do so because she had already made up her mind not to live in the abusive relationship. Further she felt that her husband's extra-marital relations would be bad influence on the daughters. On her refusal her husband sought the help of her brothers. Her brothers warned her that if she did not go back to her husband, they would not help her as she had brought disgrace to their family by leaving her husband. In spite of these threats she did not go back with her husband.

Instead Shanti sought help from a woman's organization at Chandigarh. She asked for shelter and job. She was made warden of the destitute home for women and since then she is staying there. The Women's Organization at Chandigarh tried to resolve her marital conflict. Her husband was invited to Chandigarh but they failed to reach to any agreement. Her husband wanted her either to return back or to seek divorce. She did not accept either of these proposals. She, however, allowed her daughters who were in their early teens to visit their father who was at Ranchi at that time. On returning back her daughters informed her that one lady was staying in the house of their father and he was interested in marrying her once he secured divorce from Shanti. Her husband has since filed a divorce petition against her on the ground of desertion. She has received the legal notice and sought legal advice from her advocate. She is not interested to divorce her husband unless she gets sufficient maintenance from him because she needs the money for the welfare of her daughters as she herself is not in a position to provide adequately for them.

Though Shanti Devi's husband is not concerned about her and wants to divorce her, yet she loves him and does not want to loose him. For the last four years, she is staying away from her husband.

Discussion:

(1) The case belongs to upper class, where wife is educated but economically dependent on her husband as she was not engaged in paid work outside the home.

(2) The main factor of physical violence against wife is infidelity on the part of her husband.

(3) The wife continues to accept the extra-marital relations of her husband till his deviant behaviour was not known to her informal group and her husband acted as a good provider. It was only when she started questioning her husband's waywardness that she became a victim of physical violence.

(4) Wife's abuse started after four years of marriage.

She continued to suffer the violent behaviour of her husband for seven years.

(5) Her attempt to seek intervention of informal group for checking immoral behaviour of her husband enhanced her physical abuse.

(6) Physical violence became recurrent and the purpose of which was to create fear in the victim.

(7) In spite of her economic dependency, presence of female children and no support from informal group she got separated from her husband when severity of violence became unbearable.

(8) Although she has been separated from her husband for four years and is now economically independent yet she does not want termination of relationship because of her subjective dependency.

CASE STUDY III : MS. MANJIT KAUR

Manjit Kaur is 24 years old Jat Sikh lady. She is B.A., B.Ed. Her father is a superintendent and her mother is a housewife. She has one younger brother who is a student. She got married at the age of 23 to a science graduate of her own caste. Her husband is four years elder to her. He is working as a manager in a private firm at Chandigarh. He has two elder married sisters and his father is a big landlord.

Immediately after her engagement her fiance started visiting her regularly. He insisted on taking her for outing. Her parents did not favour it but subsequently they granted permission to go out. Everytime Manjit and her fiance were alone and her fiance would talk about money. He would tell her that all his friends' wives have brought lots of dowry. He would even tell her about his sisters' marriages, how much money was spent on their marriages, etc. She realized that he was hinting her to bring a large dowry. She knew that her parents would do their best yet she started feeling scared and doubting the intentions of her fiance. Manjit did not talk to her mother on this because she was a heart patient but she gave some hints to her father who did not take it seriously.

Her father, however, assured her that everything would be alright. He told her that her parents-in-law were very nice people and it might be her fiance who due to immaturity said such foolish things. She was asked not to take the matter seriously and concentrate on her B.Ed. examinations.

Manjit was still to sit for her examinations when her-in-laws started insisting on an early marriage. Though she wanted to go for marriage only after taking her examinations but her in-laws did not agree to it. Later on, after many requests, her marriage was fixed on the next day of her last paper. She could not study properly for her examinations as she had also to devote time on wedding preparations. She told her fiance that she was not likely to get good marks and to her surprise he was happy to hear this. He told her that it was blessing in disguise for him otherwise she would have insisted on doing job and he hated working wives because they tend to become very proud of their earnings. She was very depressed and disturbed to hear his morbid ideas. In spite of the fact that her views clashed with that of her fiance, she did not say anything and agreed to marry him taking into consideration the feelings of her parents.

Immediately after her marriage, Manjit had to face hostile attitude of her husband and parents-in-law. They started showing resentment towards her parents. Her father-in-law started complaining about the food served to the guests at the wedding. He told Manjit that her father should have informed them well before the marriage that he was financially in a bad shape so that they would not have brought so many guests. Her sisters-in-law also made sarcastic remarks about her jewellery and quality of the clothes. Her mother-in-law started feeling sorry for having married her only son in such a poor family, which could not even give a vehicle to him. Her husband also joined them in humiliating her and her family. Her husband did not talk to her properly. She felt isolated and depressed. During her first visit to her parents after the marriage, her husband misbehaved with them. He refused to eat or drink anything and insisted on leaving immediately. She hardly got time to talk to her parents, but her parents could judge from her expressions and her husband's misbehaviour that something was wrong. They also accompanied them to her in-laws' place and enquired from them the reason of their displeasure. Her parents-in-law started complaining about the insufficient dowry they had received. They humiliated her parents, who did not say anything and heard everything silently. When her parents left she was humiliated and accepted their taunts helplessly.

In this way a month passed, but every day she was harassed and humiliated. She was not allowed to visit her parents. After a month, she went to Kanpur with her husband to his sister's house. Her husband continued to make insulting remarks about her father. She tried to dissuade him but he would not listen to her. Instead he would talk about poor reception given to the marriage party and poor quality of gifts to all the relatives.

Even after coming back from Kanpur her husband refused to take her to her parents. Manjit was confined to the house. Left with no alternative she wrote a letter to her parents informing them about her plight. She knew that her husband and his parents were after seeking more dowry and once their demands were met they would behave better towards her. She even asked her parents to make arrangements of some hard cash.

One day, her mother-in-law's friends came to visit them. Her dowry items were shown to them. Her mother-in-law abused her parents and called them names in front of the guests. Manjit, did not like her rude behaviour and asked her mother-in-law not to use bad language for her parents. Her mother-in-law became very angry. She called her names and threatened to teach her a lesson. Manjit's mother-in-law was very much agitated. She felt quite humiliated in front of her guests because Manjit, being a daughter-in-law, who was not supposed to utter a single word in her defence, had demanded from her mother-in-law not to abuse her parents. Such a behaviour of Manjit was considered an insult by her mother-in-law. In the evening, when her husband came from the office, her mother-in-law started crying and twisted the whole incident. Her husband became very angry at her after listening to his mother. He started shouting at her and even called her names. Her mother-in-law caught hold of her hands and her husband started beating her. She was slapped, pushed, kicked and her head was struck against the wall.

Her mother-in-law felt very happy at her victimization. Her husband threatened to kill her if in future she ever tried to misbehave with his mother. Manjit could do nothing but cry helplessly. She developed a feeling of being trapped.

Next day, when Manjit's husband left for the office, she told her mother-in-law that she was going to her parents' house. Her mother-in-law asked her to stay back. She, however, did not listen to her and left the house with some of her belongings. In this way within six months of her married life, she left the house of her in-laws and went to stay with her parents. On reaching there she narrated her miseries to her parents. She also informed her parents that her in-laws were very greedy and they could even kill her for dowry. Her parents became very scared after hearing her tale of woes.

In the evening her husband came to take her back home. Manjit refused to go with him. Her father asked for an explanation from her husband for his misconduct and violent behaviour. Instead of feeling ashamed at his behaviour he started shouting at them. He started threatening her father and brother that if they did not send Manjit with him they would not live to see their daughter. Her husband created a public scene at her parents place. Her brother asked him to leave because he was not in his senses and further, they did not want to keep contacts with such greedy and ill-mannered people.

Manjit continued to live with her parents. Her parents never asked her to go back to her in-laws. They also realized that she would not be treated well there again. Her husband also did not come to meet her again. In the meantime, her B.Ed result was out and she managed to secure a job in a private school.

Her parents contacted her maternal aunt who was a social worker and was in contact with different women's organizations. She agreed to help her. Manjit went with her to a women's organization. She lodged a complaint against her husband in their office. In the subsequent meeting her husband was summoned, who no doubt attended the meeting, but did not agree to any of the charges levelled against him. On the other hand, he started criticizing her and her parents for being arrogant and rude. Instead of arriving at any compromise, the matter worsened because of the adamant attitude of her husband. He agreed to take her back provided she leaves the job and breaks contact with her family of orientation. Manjit refused to accept her husband's conditions and on the other hand, told him that she was willing to live with him provided he leaves his parents' house to which he did not agree. As a result, Manjit was left with no alternative but to go in for divorce. Her parents also endorsed her decision.

At the time of recording of the case, Manjit Kaur's petition for divorce was pending in High Court. She was happy that she was able to get relief from violent and humiliating married life. She was trying to forget her previous experience as a nightmare and was optimistic about her peaceful future life.

Discussion :

(1) The case belongs to the middle class where wife is young and educated but was not engaged in paid work.
(2) The precipitating factor responsible for abuse is dowry.
(3) Parents-in-law were instrumental in instigating the husband to use physical violence against the wife.
(4) Wife became victim of violence immediately after her marriage. Within six months of her marriage she left

the abusive relationship.

(5) She continued to suffer psychological abuse for six months but when such abuse was followed by physical violence she decided to seek outside intervention.

(6) Wife sought help from parents who readily accepted her and even helped her to become economically independent.

(7) In order to bring an end to conflicting situation, formal agencies were also involved but instead of solving the problem, the situation worsened.

(8) Absence of any child, economic independence, support from family of orientation and younger age of the wife facilitated her to come out of the abusive marital relationship which she is contemplating to terminate legally.

CASE STUDY IV : Ms. SAVITA

Savita is 28 years old, a graduate, belonging to a Hindu Khatri family. Her father is a superintendent in Government office at Chandigarh and her mother is housewife. She has one brother who is working as a clerk in one of the Punjab Government offices. She got married at the age of 26 years. Her husband is the only son of his parents. He has one sister who is married. Her father-in-law was working as a clerk before starting the business of spare parts of scooters. Her husband works with his father and his mother is a school teacher.

Savita's marriage was settled through matrimonial advertisement in a local newspaper. Before marriage her in-laws informed them that the entire business was being managed by their son and as a retired person her father-in-law was only helping his son in the business. They also told her parents that they were in favour of simple marriage and they were against dowry. Her parents readily agreed to their proposal and accordingly performed a simple marriage. They did not give her anything in dowry.

Immediately after the marriage, Savita was treated nicely by her husband. After a few weeks her mother-in-law started grumbling for dowry and started accusing her parents for not giving anything. She felt very bad and talked to her husband who paid no attention to her complaints, instead he told her that she should accept meekly whatever her parents-in-law would say failing which her life would be miserable. Being fed up with the taunts of her mother-in-law Savita requested her mother to give some items of furniture and household articles to please her mother-in-law so that her humiliation could be stopped. Her parents provided her furniture and some household articles, which her in-laws accepted happily. On receipt of these gifts situation remained normal but after a month her mother-in-law again started harassing her. She asked Savita to bring a scooter from her parents. Savita knew that her parents would not be able to fulfil their growing demands. Therefore she did not tell anything to her parents and continued to tolerate her mother-in-law's taunts. She requested her husband to intervene and stop the humiliation which he refused. Being of a carefree nature, he would not take any complaint against his parents seriously. He would prefer to roam about with vagabond boys instead of going to the shop regularly. He would bring different kinds of modern dresses and would insist her to wear them. As Savita was not accustomed to wear the modern dresses she was very reluctant to put them on but on persistent insistance of her husband, she would wear them. Her husband would then take her to his friends who were not only illiterate but also indulged in vulgarity. They would share dirty jokes in her presence. She used to object to their misconduct but her husband would take everything very lightly. He would drink and smoke in their company till late at night and she was forced to sit with them even if she felt uncomfortable in their company. As she did not want to displease her husband she did not protest but failed to reconcile to the embarrassing situation.

After a few months of her marriage, Savita noticed a

change in the behaviour of her father-in-law. He would ask her husband about their sex life in her presence. She used to feel highly embarrassed but would not say anything. Her father-in-law even tried to make sexual advances towards her. When one day she was alone, her father-in-law tried to molest her. She reprimanded him and spoke harshly. Savita even threatened him that she would report everything to her mother-in-law. In the evening when her husband came home, she told him about his father's misconduct but he refused to believe such allegations.

After this incident her father-in-law stopped making advances towards her but started instigating her husband against her. Her father-in-law told her husband that he would like to open a new shop but was short of Rs. 50,000 therefore, he should arrange the amount from Savita's parents. Her husband asked her to bring money from her father. It was at this stage that Savita came to know that her husband was economically dependent on his father and he had no shop in his name or had any independent source of income. Further, she knew that her father would not be able to arrange for money. She pleaded with her husband that he should not insist on that issue but he refused to yield to her requests. Her in-laws also used to join her husband in harassing her and their behaviour became very rude. They would even call her names. Savita was not able to comprehend the changed attitude of her in-laws. Whenever she complained to her husband about the changed attitude of his parents regarding dowry he would get angry. He warned her that she could stay with them only when she had arranged money from her parents.

Savita was sent to her parents' place to bring the demanded money. She narrated everything to her parents. Her mother consoled her and told her father to make arrangement for some money. Her mother sold some of her jewellery and her father also took loan but they were able to arrange only Rs. 10,000. Her father took her back to her in-laws. He gave Rs. 10,000 to her father-in-law because Savita was pregnant and her parents wanted her to continue the marital relationship. Her father-in-law kept the money but abused her father for bringing a small amount.

After this incident Savita's parents stopped coming to her place. Her husband started drinking heavily. Whenever she objected to it she was beaten. One day, she found some drugs in her husband's pocket and on enquiry he readily accepted that he was taking drugs. She was shocked and disturbed over his drug addiction. She informed her mother-in-law about her husband's addiction but they did not show any interest in solving her problems. His drug dependency made Savita miserable. He stopped taking any interest in his work. He would come home late at night and sleep during day time. Savita pleaded with him for giving up the bad habit but he could not change. He started stealing from the shop whenever he needed money for buying drugs. He had become completely dependent on drugs.

One day, his father came to know about his stealing habit and reprimanded him in front of the servants. Her husband became very angry with his father but vented it on her. He asked her to bring money from her parents. On her refusal she was beaten badly. Next day he took her to her parents' place and asked for some money from them. When they refused to give him money he started shouting outside their house. She tried to stop him but he continued shouting till he got some money after which he brought her back.

After a gap of every three or four days Savita's husband would go to her parents and would collect some money for drugs. Her parents were in an awkward position but could do nothing. She had full sympathies for her parents but was not in a position to check her husband's behaviour pattern. Again after a few days he asked her to bring more money from her parents. She bluntly refused to oblige him. On her refusal he gave her a severe beating, as a result she became unconscious. Her in-laws did not intervene. Her husband threw her out of the house. Somebody from the neighbourhood informed her father who came immediately and she was taken to a nursing home. Her father and brother wanted to inform the police but her mother stopped them. Savita remained in the nursing home for a month and later gave birth to a son. During this period, neither her husband nor her in-laws came to visit her.

In spite of indifferent attitude of her husband and her in-laws Savita's parents went to inform her in-laws about the birth of their grandson. They also took some sweets and fruits with them, thinking that her in-laws would feel happy at the birth of their grandson and things might improve for their daughter. Her parents' hopes were shattered when her in-laws neither accepted the sweets and fruits nor talked to them properly. On the other hand, her parents-in-law abused Savita of having immoral character and even alleged that the new born was not their grand child. Her parents could not tolerate such misconduct on their part and came back in disgust. They informed her about the treatment they received at her in-laws house. She also felt bad but could do nothing.

After a month, her husband came to her parents' place. He felt sorry for his rude and violent behaviour towards Savita. He asked for their forgiveness. He even accused his parents for instigating him against Savita. He told her parents that he had stopped taking drugs and would like to start a new and an independent life. He asked Savita's parents to send her with him and he would live separately from his parents. They were surprised to see a change in his behaviour. Savita thought that her prayers for having peaceful married life were answered. Her parents were a bit reluctant to send her back but he pleaded for forgiveness and asked for one more chance and assured them that he would not repeat his mistakes. He also told them that he had even rented one room set so that he could live with Savita away from his parents. When Savita's parents agreed to send her with him, he asked Savita to leave the child with her parents and she could visit him everyday. She agreed and left the child with her mother. Savita's parents gave them a few utensils, beddings and other things so that they could start their new household.

Savita and her husband stayed together in the new house. During this period Savita's husband treated her well. Everyday she visited her child. Her parents were happy that at last her husband has improved his ways and their daughter was having peaceful life. He, however, did not start any new business and continued to visit his father's shop. After one and a half month, her husband told her that his parents were alone and he wanted to stay with them. She told him that if his parents would treat her well she would also accompany him. He, however, refused to take her with him and asked her to go back to her parents. She went back to her parents and told them about her husband's new decision. Her father immediately went to her in-law's house. Her father-in-law did not allow him to get inside. Her husband came out and joined his father in insulting him. He told her father that he had stayed with Savita for one and a half month just for fun. He had no intention to keep a 'whore' as his wife. It was a great shock to her father. Her father accused him for ruining his daughter's life. Savita's father warned them of dire consequences for their mistakes. Her father-in-law and husband reacted and called him names. Her husband started behaving like a mad person. He took off his clothes and started running on streets abusing her father. In this way, he created a public scene to embarrass her father. Her father came home and told her the whole episode. That day she felt so miserable that she wanted to commit suicide. Her parents and brother consoled her and told her to be bold and face the reality.

Next day, her father lodged a criminal case of dowry harassment against her husband and in-laws with the police. They also approached different women's organizations, and a 'dharna' was staged outside her father-in-law's shop. She developed animosity against her husband and in-laws. Police helped them to recover all the dowry items as well as cash.

With the help of her father she was able to get the job of

a clerk six months after she gave birth to her son.

At the time of recording of this case study, she was working as a clerk in a Government office. She has been staying with her parents for the last one year and they are also looking after her child. Her divorce case is pending in High Court and she is likely to get the custody of her child. After having gone through traumatic experiences of her married life, she is not thinking of remarriage after divorce. She is very proud of her parents who have not only provided her shelter but have also helped her to be economically independent. It was with their sympathy and understanding of her anguish that she was able to come out of the abusive marital relationship.

Discussion :

(1) The case belongs to a middle class family where the wife is more educated than husband but was not engaged in any kind of paid work. Her husband, was economically dependent on his parents.

(2) The main precipitating factor of her abuse was dowry. Her reprimand to her father-in-law's sexual advances further aggravated her harassment.

(3) In-laws abused the victim psychologically for dowry and instigated the husband to use physical violence.

(4) Wife became victim of psychological abuse by in-laws immediately after her marriage. Husband started using physical violence against the wife after six months of marriage.

(5) Wife continued to suffer abusive behaviour of her husband and her parents fulfilled the dowry demands of her in-laws for one year with the hope that things would improve.

(6) Husband's drug dependency further worsened marital discord. She was forced to bring money from her parents to enable her husband to buy drugs. Her refusal to bring more money resulted in

physical abuse even though she was pregnant.

(7) The conditions became worst when allegations were made about her character and her parents were publicly insulted and threatened by her husband and his parents.

(8) Support from family of orientation helped her to come out of the abusive marital relationship.

(9) Economic independence and support from informal and formal sources have encouraged her to terminate the abusive marital relationship permanently.

CASE STUDY V : Ms. PUSHPA

Pushpa is a post-graduate in science and is 32 years old Hindu lady. At present she is working as a school teacher. She has two elder sibs, one brother and a sister. Her brother is graduate and her sister has studied upto high school. She is the youngest in the family. Her father is a landlord and her parents are neither educated nor interested in giving higher education to their daughters. Since her childhood she was very studious and always stood first in her class and was permitted to study upto Matric. Due to disencouragement from her parents, her educational career was not a smooth one, as she had to drop out for a number of times. Despite opposition she was able to complete her M.Sc from the Panjab University.

Her parents were in favour of marrying her off after her matriculation examination. Her elder siblings were also married when they were quite young. Pushpa's life is marked by many unpleasant events. Her marriage was arranged when she was 16 years old but before her marriage could take place her fiance died in a road accident. After this set back she continued her studies despite opposition from her parents, as her parents were looking for another match for her. She completed her B.Sc in first division. After her graduation, her marriage was again fixed but unfortunately her second fiance also died in a road accident before marriage. The second accident forced her parents to become ardent believers in horoscopes and on the advice of different astrologers, she was forced to keep fasts on a number of days to get rid of evil stars. In the meantime, on her persistent demand she was allowed to complete her M.Sc.

After Pushpa's M.Sc examinations were over, her parents took her to Lucknow where her paternal aunt was residing. They tried to find out some suitable match for her but her marriage could not be arranged. Her parents became very desperate and were willing to marry her to a poor person who was even less educated than her. One day a visitor to her aunt's house informed her parents about a holy person who had 'supernatural' powers. Next day, her parents visited that person and after listening to Pushpa's bad luck, he suggested that she should be married to a person who was already sitting there. He further, assured them that everything would be alright. Without any hesitation her parents agreed to marry her without caring to find out the background of the person.

Within a few days Pushpa was married at the age of 26 years. Her parents did not care to seek her consent or to enquire about boy's occupation, education or family background. After her marriage she came to stay with her husband's family at Bareilly.

It was only after her marriage that she came to know that her husband was the only son of his parents. His parents were quite old and were dependent on their son. They had a small old house. Their standard of living was very low. She also came to know that her husband was only a matriculate and working as a mechanic in the Railways. She felt angry at her parents who did not care about her feelings knowing fully well that she was a post-graduate they married her off to a matriculate. She, however, did not show her anger to anyone.

A few days after her marriage Pushpa along with her husband went to visit her aunt at Lucknow. It was at her aunt's place that Pushpa came to know that her husband lacked "basic manners" of "middle class families". Whatever eatables were offered to him he would eat them all as if he had been starving. Pushpa felt highly embarrassed by her husband's "bad manners" but refrained from showing anger and disappointment. After their return to Bareilly she gave vent to her frustrating experience and tried to teach her husband "decent manners". Instead of listening to her advice, her husband felt hurt that Pushpa, his wife who was supposed to assume a submissive position in the marital relationship, had assumed an "instrumental" role and was trying to boss over him. He became very aggressive and started shouting at her. He called her names and also slapped her. For a moment she could not understand what was going on. Later on, she felt very bad at his rude behaviour. Instead of showing her anger to him, she cursed her parents whom she held responsible for all her humiliation.

After this incident, her husband started maltreating her regularly. He would taunt her every now and then and would humiliate her in front of his parents, who did not say anything to their son. She was blamed for showing off her education and her higher family background. Pushpa continued to tolerate her husband's rude behaviour because she knew that she was trapped in marital relationship.

Pushpa's husband also started drinking which became an additional precipitating factor for marital discord. In the beginning he would drink once a while and especially whenever there would be conflict in the family. Subsequently he started drinking heavily in the company of his friends. Many a times he would bring them home and would drink till late at night. Whenever she would showed her resentment over his drinking, she was bashed by her husband in front of his friends. She felt miserable and helpless.

Her husband started criticizing the way she dressed and would accuse her of immoral character. He became strict regarding her movements. If she went to visit neighbours or to the market, he would get very angry. He would make different allegations against her and shout at her. Instead of arguing with him she would prefer to keep mum in order to stop the quarrel because she was in the family way.

Throughout her pregnancy her husband continued to harass and humiliate her. Her mother-in-law would not allow her to rest. She had to work throughout her pregnancy. She was also asked to keep fasts, as a consequence thereof she became very weak. Her husband did not show any concern for her. On the other hand, his taunts and mental and physical tortures multiplied. She suffered from malnutrition and mental agony throughout the period of pregnancy. It was under these circumstances that she gave birth to a son.

On receipt of the message her parents came to see her and their grand child. They were very happy to see that their daughter had become a mother of a male child. They, however, failed to comprehend her anguish and fears as a result of which she developed resentment against them and did not appraise them of her present miserable condition. Her husband showed great respect to her parents and behaved normally.

Because of Pushpa's under nourishment during pregnancy her child was born quite weak. Just after one week of child's birth she was asked to do all the household work hence she could not attend to her child properly. Within one month of his birth, her son suffered from pneumonia. Instead of seeking medical advice from a child specialist her in-laws and her husband treated him with home remedies. Instead of showing any improvement child's health started deteriorating. She asked her husband to take the child to a medical practitioner but he did not listen to her and went to his work. As the condition of the child was deteriorating, she begged her in-laws to have mercy on their grand child and to take him to a proper doctor. Instead of showing sympathies, they started accusing her for making mountain out of a mole hill. She felt very dejected, nevertheless, she took the child herself to the general hospital. With timely medication, the life of the child was saved. She had to stay in the hospital for the whole night. Neither her husband nor her in-laws came to the hospital to enquire about the health of the child. She kept on cursing her parents for putting her in such a situation.

Next day, when Pushpa returned home with her child she found that the house was locked from the inside. She knocked at the door but no one opened the door. She stood there for almost half an hour but got no response. Then she sought help from the neighbours. Her husband opened the door after the intervention by her neighbours. He, however, abused her for making a public issue over slight illness of the child. When the neighbours left, he locked her in the bed-room and started beating her. She was slapped, kicked, thrown against the wall and her hair were pulled. She was called a 'whore'. Her husband continued to beat her till he himself got exhausted. Her body was aching very badly. She kept on crying and cursing her fate. She developed a feeling of insecurity to her life. She even thought of committing suicide but her love for her son stopped her from taking such a drastic step. She had, however, made up her mind that she would neither stay in that abusive situation nor would go to her parents. Therefore, she decided to go to Chandigarh where her close friend was staying. Within a week's time, she was able to manage railway fare for herself and after getting suitable opportunity, she left the house of her husband along with her son where she had suffered humiliation for almost two years.

Pushpa reached her friend's place at Chandigarh and narrated her tale of woes. Her friend readily agreed to help her provided she informed her parents about her where-abouts. She informed her parents who came to take her with them but she refused to go with them. Her parents pleaded with her not to take any hasty decision but she refused to accept their advice as she held them responsible for her miseries. She also refused to take any type of financial help from them and asked them to leave her to her own fate. Pushpa started staying with her friend who took her to a family counselling centre, where she met the secretary. With her help, she was able to secure a job in a reputed school. She continued staying with her friend. Her husband came to know about her whereabouts from her parents and reached her friend's house. He tried to create a public scene outside her house. He called her names and shouted loudly. He used filthy language to embarrass her. His behaviour made her friend's landlord angry. They asked her friend to vacate their house. She, however, talked to the land lady and informed her that there was no fault of her friend. She also promised her that she would move out instead of her friend.

She shifted to one room house, her husband, however, continued humiliating her by coming to her school and abusing her in front of all the students and other teachers. She felt so embarrassed and heart broken that she started doubting her abilities to live alone. She felt very insecure and became afraid of her husband. She went to the family counselling centre and narrated her humiliation at the hands of her husband. She was consoled and assured moral support. She was given psychological counselling. Later on she was helped to get legal advice and a legal notice was sent to her husband from the family counselling centre's address.

Immediately after getting the notice, her husband came to the family counselling centre. The secretary accused him of spoiling his married life just for the sake of showing off his male chauvinism. The secretary threatened him with dire consequences if he ever tried to humiliate Pushpa again. She even warned him that a case against him will be lodged with the police for physical assaults on his wife. Her husband became scared, he agreed to mend his ways provided his wife withdrew court case and agreed to go with him. He made several assurances but Pushpa did not talk to him because she was against the compromise.

After this incident, her husband stopped harassing her. He, however, did not attend a single court hearing, as a result of which her divorce case has not been finalized. During the last four years, since she had come to Chandigarh, her brother and sister have not even tried to contact her. No doubt her parents have come twice but she did not meet them as Pushpa has developed animosity against them. Pushpa feels that she is socially isolated as she is not maintaining any link with her family of orientation as well as procreation. She has only her friend and the secretary of the family counselling who have helped her.

At the time of recording of this case study, Pushpa was teaching in a privately managed reputed school. She was also doing private tuitions and earning a handsome salary. Her son is now four years old and studying in the same school. Going through different odds she has now become economically independent but she is still afraid of her husband who might disrupt her peace of mind. She does not want his shadow to fall on her son. Although she has taken a bold step of living alone despite being married yet she wants to lead a life of anonymity because of the negative attitude of people towards a single woman and is looking forward to the day when she will get divorce from her husband and child's custody by the High Court.

Discussion :

(1) The case belongs to the working class where the wife is highly educated and the husband is only a matriculate and works as a mechanic.

(2) The main reason for violence against wife is status inconsistency between the spouses. In order to overcome his 'inferiority complex' husband used physical violence to subdue the wife.

(3) Wife abuse started within a month after marriage and wife continued to suffer abusive behaviour of her husband for two years.

(4) Unable to bear physical violence and suspicious nature of the husband, the wife after leaving her husband's home sought help from her friend and formal sources. She did not seek help from her parents because she held them responsible for her miseries.

(5) With the help of a formal source she has become economically independent.

(6) Through separation wife has got relief from psychological humiliation and physical torture.

(7) Wife wants to terminate the marital relationship permanently but reluctance on the part of the husband has prolonged the divorce case.

CASE STUDY VI : Ms. ROSY

Rosy a Christian lady, is 40 years old and a matriculate. Her father was a school teacher. She lost her mother during her early childhood. She has two brothers and two sisters. She is the eldest of all. She got married at the age of 20. Her husband is also a matriculate. He is six years elder to her. At the time of her marriage he was working with his father in their cloth shop at Jalandhar. Rosy's husband has three sisters and all of them were married before her marriage.

Rosy's married life was normal in the beginning. Within a span of four years, she gave birth to two children, a daughter and a son. Although her husband was not earning much yet they were able to meet their basic needs. After four years of her marriage her father-in-law died. Her husband was not able to manage the shop independently resulting into a great loss in the business. Her husband sold his shop and started exporting readymade garments. He started remaining very busy and could hardly get time for her and the children. He started travelling a lot and for weeks together he would remain out of station. Rosy did not like her husband's new business endeavour. Many a times she complained to him about his absence and suggested him to start his own shop once again. But her husband did not concede to her suggestion. He became self-centred and started spending a lot on his clothes, expensive cigarettes and liquor. However, he would give her a small amount for household expenses. Her children were growing and their needs were also increasing, hence she complained to her husband about her financial difficulties but failed to get a positive response. She started smelling something fishy. Twice she found a few letters of some women in her husband's pocket. When she enquired from him, he made different excuses. In this way, another two years passed by and her husband became more and more negligent towards his duty as a provider.

One day her husband informed her about his decision to go abroad. She did not agree with his decision and told him that it would be very difficult for her to live alone. He, however, assured her that he was going on a business tour. He would earn a lot so that they could have happy and peaceful life. He even promised to send her money regularly. With these promises he left for Iraq and for almost one year she continued to get money regularly. In the beginning he used to reply to her letters but later on he became quite irregular. After one year, he stopped sending her money. She wrote to him that it was difficult for her to meet the expenses but she did not get any reply. She became desperate and gave her house at Jalandhar on rent and came to Chandigarh where her sister was staying. She did not contact her brothers because after her father's death a few years back, she was not maintaining cordial relations with them.

Her sister provided shelter to her and her children. She helped her in getting a job of saleswoman. After getting the job, she took one room set on rent. Her land lady was a doctor and was very generous. She helped Rosy in getting her children admitted to a good school. She helped her in getting admission to mid-wife's course and also helped Rosy in completing the course. Later on she also helped her in getting cases. After getting training Rosy started doing private nursing service and was able to have sufficient money to look after her children. She even bought a house on instalment basis.

During a span of two years she struggled a lot, however, Rosy was able to have comfortable life subsequently. During this period there was no news from her husband. She too had stopped writing to him. After a gap of four years one day her husband came to her house at Chandigarh. He told her that he had gone to Jalandhar and from the tenants he found her new address. He had many excuses to make for his long absence and indifferent behaviour. She was very angry with him because he had left them in difficult financial conditions. Rosy did not speak to her husband properly, but her husband asked for her forgiveness. He showed her all the gifts which he had brought for the children and her. He promised to compensate for every loss. He even paid for the remaining instalments of the house which she had bought at Chandigarh. He sold his father's house at Jalandhar and invested all the money for their new house. He even asked her to stop doing the job of a nurse because he had earned a lot. She, however, refused to leave her work.

Rosy's husband did not do any work after coming to India, whenever she would go for work and children would go to school, he would sit at home. In order to pass his free time he started drinking. He even initiated drinking habit in her. Hence drinking became a routine activity of the couple. In this way time passed off peacefully.

After six months, she noticed a change in her husband. He stopped spending his free time with children. Rosy came to know from her sister that her husband was roaming about with a young woman. She enquired from her husband, but he refused to accept any of the allegations. She told him that their children had grown up and his misdemeanour would have adverse effect on them, hence he should mend his ways. Her husband did not like her sermons and this resulted in a verbal quarrel. He started shouting at her, as she could not control herself she too shouted at him. Her husband became very angry at her, he even tried to slap her but she was able to protect herself. Unable to control his anger he went out and did not return for two days. She felt quite depressed and started drinking till she became unconscious. When she came to her senses she realized her mistake. After two days when her husband returned both of them agreed to patch up and mend their behaviour for the sake of children. But they were not able to keep their promise for long. Whenever she heard anything about her husband's extra marital affairs she became furious.

In order to soothe herself, she would drink heavily, but after drinking she would loose her senses and called names to her husband who would also call her names and even tried to beat her. Thus under the influence of liquor they would fight in the presence of children and it became a routine affair. Many a times neighbours would also witness their quarrels. Their children started feeling embarrassed about their parents' daily fights. They told their father to go back to a foreign country so that they could live peacefully. She, too felt that separation was the best thing to check daily fights. She asked her husband to leave her house because she felt that it was he who was disrupting family peace. But he refused to leave the house as he had made financial investments in procuring the house. On the other hand, he asked her to leave but she refused to do so as the house was in her name. As they were unable to settle the issue, Rosy sought help from a women's organization.

Both of them were summoned by the women's organization. Instead of going for settlement, both of them accused each other and made different allegations. Members of the women's organization asked her husband to leave the house because they were not able to reconcile. Her husband agreed in front of the members but later on refused to do so. After reaching their house, they fought again. She called him names and he threw objects at her. In order to teach him a lesson she threw his belongings outside the house and when he went out to collect them, she locked the door. He kept on sitting at door for some time but left after a while.

Next day, early in the morning, he again came home but this time his children talked to him. They pleaded with him to leave the place so that they could live a peaceful life. He agreed to do so but told them he would visit them once in a month and would not provide them any financial assistance.

Her husband comes to visit them rarely. But whenever he comes, the couple quarrels on the issue of husband's relations with some other woman and his failure to give his lawful wife and children any money for maintenance. At present she is facing some financial hardship but is free from daily quarrels and fights because her husband is not staying with her. As her relations with her husband have not been legally terminated she is under constant fear that he would come to stay with them and would again disturb their peaceful life.

Discussion :

(1) This is a case of working class couple where both the spouses were evenly placed.

(2) Incapability of husband to give continued financial support to the family as well as suspicion on the part of the wife regarding her husband's moral character led to conjugal fights in which both the partners were physically violent against each other.

(3) Wife's attempt to dominate the conjugal relations because of her economic independence leads to quarrels as the husband does not accept his submissive position.

(4) After a gap of almost 11 years of her marriage discord in the marital relations started. Calling names, physical fights and throwing objects at each other have become routine with the couple after they became drunk.

(5) Intervention from the formal agency has also not helped the couple to compromise and have a peaceful life.

(6) The wife wants to get rid of the husband but the husband does not want to move out because of financial investments he has made in the house.

(7) The conjugal relationship is continuing between the periods of relative peace and conflict.

CASE STUDY VII : Ms. MALATI

Malati is 28 years old Bengali woman. She is a matriculate. Her father is a small cultivator and is living in a village near

Calcutta. Her mother expired when she was very young. She has two elder sisters and one younger brother. She was married to a shopkeeper of her own village at the age of 20. After six months of her marriage, her husband died in a road accident. She became a widow and came to stay with her father and brother.

Time passed by and she was able to adjust to the life of a widow. But her father thought of marrying her off again. Living in a traditional village community it was not possible to find a suitable match for a widow. Hence her father asked her sister who was married and living at Chandigarh to look for a match for her. Malati was sent to Chandigarh and she started staying with her sister.

It was through matrimonial advertisement that they came in contact with Vinod Prakash a Punjabi young male. He was working as a peon at Chandigarh and also was a widower. His parents had died when he was quite young. He has one elder brother and one younger sister. His elder brother looked after Vinod Prakash and his sister. Vinod Prakash was first married at the age of 25 to his brother's sister-in-law and continued staying with his brother. His wife died due to illness. He had a son from his first wife. After the death of his wife, his sister-in-law took the responsibility of looking after his son who has one son of her own and who is about 6 years older than Vinod Prakash's son.

Her sister who was living at Chandigarh contacted some person who was also working at the same place where Vinod Prakash was working. After getting all the information about Vinod Prakash, Malati was married again at the age of 27 years. Her marriage was performed according to Punjabi traditions. Her father provided her furniture and a few household items as dowry.

After her marriage she came to the house of her husband who was staying with his elder brother. Her husband's sister-in-law took control of all her wedding gifts. Even the furniture provided to her was put in her brother-in-law's room. She did not like her husband's sister-in-law's behaviour, but kept mum. She also realized that her husband was under obligation to his sister-in-law because she was looking after his son from the previous marriage. Additionally, the house in which they were staying was allotted to her brother-in-law. Under these circumstances the newly wedded couple were accorded a secondary position in the household.

After a few days of her marriage her sister came to visit her. Malati informed her sister that all her marriage gifts have been taken over by her husband's sister-in-law and she was being accorded the status of a second rate citizen in the house. She asked her to intervene and help her to get her wedding gifts back. Her sister talked to her husband who did not like intervention of Malati's sister but at that moment he kept quiet.

In the beginning she was allowed to go to her sister's place and her sister also used to come. But after one month her husband started objecting to her visits to her sister's house. He showed his displeasure whenever Malati's sister visited them. Whenever her sister came to her place she was not well received there. This constant insulting behaviour forced Malati to stop her sister from coming to her place. She did not say anything to her husband because she did not want to create unnecessary tension.

Malati had cordial relations with all the members of the household except her husband's sister-in-law. She did not like her dominating nature. Malati complained to her husband but her husband refused to listen to any of her complaints about his sister-in-law. She developed animosity towards her husband's sister-in-law. The sister-in-law would serve him food, tea, wash his clothes, in short would perform all those tasks which a wife performs in normal course, thereby relegating Malati in the background. This was done with Malati's husband's approval.

Many a times she found her husband and his sister-in-law sharing cheap jokes in the absence of her brother-in-law. She started suspecting her husband of having illicit relations with her. Her doubts became evident when three months after the marriage she caught them in the act of sexual intercourse. She felt so bad that she started wailing. He threatened her with dire consequences in case she mustered enough courage to tell anyone about the incident. She was so scared and helpless that she did not understand what to do. On the other hand, her husband and his sister-in-law behaved normally when her brother-in-law came home in the evening. Malati stopped talking to her husband's sister-in-law. She started hating her all the more. Her husband did not like it hence became strict with her and imposed restrictions on her movements. She was not allowed to visit her sister as well as neighbours. Her husband's sister-in-law would complain to her husband if she even went to the neighbours. Her husband would reprimand her for disobeying him in the presence of every one. She would feel very humiliated and would neither talk to anyone nor take food. She started feeling that the sister-in-law was poisoning her husband against her. She thought of telling everything to her brother-in-law but the sister-in-law was too clever to give her any opportunity to do so. Ultimately she dropped the idea and instead talked to her husband's sister, who was staying with them and had cordial relations with her. She listened to her but advised her to keep quiet as she felt that her silence is the only solution to the problems.

After this incident she did not find her husband indulging in illicit relation with his sister-in-law. But occasionally, difference of opinions continued to emerge between the conjugal unit because of her husband's sister-in-law. Her husband would tell everything to his sister-in-law even about their sexual relations. Malati objected to this, because the sister-in-law would then tease Malati by cracking vulgar jokes which she did not like. In this way, her husband continued to humiliate her in front of his sister-in-law.

One day, while working in the kitchen, Malati overheard her husband telling the sister-in-law about their sexual life. She could not control her anger and shouted at her husband and asked him to stop talking nonsense. Her husband shouted back and told her that he had full freedom to behave as he liked. Malati also lost her temper and called names to her husband's sister-in-law. Her husband could not tolerate her hurling insults on his sister-in-law and slapped her. She also retaliated. Her husband became annoyed at her courage to use defensive aggression against him and brought a knife from the kitchen and threatened to cut her throat. His sister-in-law stopped him and took the knife away. Her husband, however, did not stop beating her. She was kicked, slapped, punched and beaten very badly. She felt miserable and trapped. In the evening when her brother-in-law came home from the work, his wife twisted the whole incident and blamed Malati for her misbehaviour. Her brother-in-law also expressed his anger towards her. Her brother-in-law's wife also abused her and her parents. Malati realized that she would not get help from anyone at her husband's place. Looking at her fate, she continued to cry and there was no one to sympathize with her. She did not take any food for two days. She felt very lonely and miserable and then decided to seek help from her sister. She sent a message to her sister through one of the neighbours.

After receiving her message, Malati's sister came to her place. Malati told her sister about the battering given to her by her husband and asked her help. Malati asked her husband that she should be sent with her sister for a day or two. After great reluctance she was allowed to go. She went to her sister's place and continued to stay with her for a month. After a month, her husband came to take her back but she refused to go with him. Her sister also sided with her and abused Malati's husband for having illicit relations with his sister-in-law. Her husband accused her of disrespectful behaviour. He threatened to leave Malati for ever if she did not come with him. She agreed to accompany him provided he would establish an independent household away from his brother's place. He refused to accept Malati's condition and went back without her. After this incident, he did not come to see her for three months.

In the meantime, Malati's younger brother had come to Chandigarh on a job assignment and was living alone. Hence, Malati went to stay with him. She sent a message to her husband but he did not bother to visit her. For all these months, Malati remained economically dependent upon her sister and bother. Her sister suggested Malati to seek help from a women's organization located at Chandigarh. Left with no alternative Malati lodged a written complaint against her husband. Her husband was summoned to the office of the women's organization. Her husband came there but refused to accept any of the allegations made against him. He, however, made counter allegations against Malati's sister that she was responsible for his family discord. As Malati's sister never wanted Malati to live in a joint household she was instigating Malati to make wild allegations. Members of the women's organization were not able to reconcile the differences, hence they asked Malati to bring her father and the husband was asked to bring his brother and sister-in-law at the next meeting.

At the next meeting which took place after a gap of one month, Malati's father, brother-in-law, sister-in-law attended the meeting. At the intervention of the women's organization it was agreed upon that Malati would live with her husband in his brother's house for one month and during this period he would arrange to establish a separate house where the couple would shift subsequently. During this period of one month constant bickerings erupted between Malati and Vinod Prakash's sister-in-law. Malati was constantly accused for lowering the esteem of the family by allowing the intervention of the outsiders.

After a month, Malati and her husband shifted to a new house. However, her husband imposed a condition that Malati's sister would not visit them. She accepted his term but her husband refused to bring back dowry items from his brother's house. He also did not bring his son with him as he was of opinion that his brother and sister-in-law were looking after him very well. Further, he did not want to end his relations with his brother's family.

Immediately after shifting to new house, Malati and her husband did not develop good intimate relations. He did not allow her to get friendly with neighbours. She was confined to the house. Her husband would not come home for lunch at all and would come late at night. Whenever she questioned her husband he would simply say that he had gone to visit his son. She realized that her husband was still maintaining relations with his sister-in-law, whereas her own sister was not allowed to visit her. Many a times she asked her husband to bring his child, so that he would not have to visit his brother's place. Her husband did not agree. On the other hand he would accuse her of having suspicious and irritable nature. As a result frequent quarrels continued to occur between them.

Left with no alternative, Malati started threatening her husband that she would commit suicide by pouring kerosene on her and in her suicidal note she would hold her husband and his sister-in-law responsible for her death. Her husband became soared of her threats. He started coming home on time. In this way her marital relationship started improving.

In the meantime Malati conceived but developed complications. She was advised bed rest and her husband's sister-in-law refused to extend any help. As a result, her sister was called and she helped them. After sometime, she gave birth to a female child. During her pregnancy her husband took proper care of her. He became annoyed with his brother and sister-in-law who had neither extended any help during his wife's illness nor they came to see his daughter.

Malati is now happy. She has no grudge against her husband. She has no objection in keeping her husband's son with her. But her husband's sister-in-law does not want to give her husband's son back because she has brought up him up like her own child. The husband visits his son occasionally but his relations with the sister-in-law have become sour. Malati's sister visits them and he no longer object to her visits. She now feels happy that her husband has realized his mistakes and come on the right track. She is now leading a normal marital life free from tensions.

Discussion :

(1) The case belongs to the lower class where both the spouses come from different cultural backgrounds and wife is economically dependent upon her husband.
(2) The main cause of her abuse is the infidelity of the husband.
(3) The dominant position of the husband's sister-in-law precipitated the conflict in the spousal relationship.
(4) In order to check her husband's waywardness wife sought help from informal group. Such intervention worsened the relationship leading to separation.
(5) Intervention by the formal group helped them in the establishment of a separate household and for reconciliation.
(6) Husband's infidelity continued which was, however, checked by wife's threat of suicide.
(7) The wife is continuing to live with her husband as her marital relationship has improved and she now has a peaceful life.

CASE STUDY VIII : Ms SURINDER KAUR

Surinder Kaur is a 23 years old illiterate Sikh lady. Her father was a 'tandoor' owner. She lost her father five years back. She has three married sisters and one married brother who is engaged in the same profession as that of her father. After her father's death, she and her mother continued to stay with her brother. Her brother arranged her marriage at the age of 20 years to a boy of their own profession and caste at Chandigarh.

Her husband has a joint family consisting of his old parents and married brothers. Her husband is five years elder to her. A few days after her marriage she found that her husband was a drunkard. She did not like his drinking habit but tried to adjust to the circumstances. Subsequently she also came to know that her husband was not doing any work but drank all the day with his friends. She was very upset. She tried to persuade her husband in kicking this habit and leaving his friends so that he could attend to his work but he did not like her intervention. He started abusing her in front of other members of the family. Additionally, her husband criticized her on her looks. She felt humiliated. He blamed his parents for choosing an ugly girl like her for him. She silently suffered such insults. There was hardly any time when her husband treated her with love and sympathy.

From the very first day of Surinder Kaur's marriage, her husband never took her out with him, even for going to her parents. She had to go along with her in-laws. Whenever any one from her brother's family visited them, her husband was never there to greet them. Her in-laws, however, treated her relatives properly. She informed her mother and brother about her husband's humiliating behaviour, but they did not take it seriously and asked her to adjust and develop tolerance as her husband would change with time and would start liking her. After listening to her mother's advice, she tried to make her husband happy. She would do all his work and wait for him late at night. But her sacrifices yielded no result as her husband continued with his drinking and rude behaviour. He would come home late at night completely drunk. Many a time he would not turn up at all, whenever he would come he would use filthy language and call her names. He would ask her to go out of his sight as he did not like her at all. Sometimes he threw food at her or pushed her aside. Surinder Kaur continued to tolerate his rude behaviour because she felt that he was not in his senses.

One day when her husband was not drunk and sitting idle at home, Surinder Kaur asked him to go to work. Her husband became furious at her, he called her names and started beating her. He kicked, slapped and tried to strangle her. He did not like her intervention in his routine activities.

Her mother-in-law did not intervene rather asked her to stop crying which would attract the attention of the neighbours. After giving her a good thrashing her husband went out and did not return home for two days. On the third day, he came late at night and as usual was completely drunk. In the morning, she asked him to take her to her brother's place. He refused to oblige her. He even warned her from going to neighbours. She did not like her husband's restrictions on her movement. In the afternoon when no one was at home, Surinder Kaur locked the house and gave the keys to neighbours as she wanted to visit her sister who also lived in Chandigarh. As she did not have any money, she went on foot. On the way she met her brother-in-law who enquired from her as to where she was going? Instead of replying him, she ignored him and kept on walking. Her brother-in-law became angry and immediately went to call her husband. Before she could reach her sister's place, her husband was able to catch her and brought her back. On reaching home, her husband locked the room and started beating her. He beat her with anything he could get hold of. He even threatened to kill her if in future she did not obey him. No body in the family tried to intervene to save her from battering. She continued crying the whole day and did not eat anything. Next day, after finding an appropriate opportunity she ran away and went to her sister and told her the miserable tale. Her sister took her to their mother. Surinder Kaur told her mother that she does not want to get killed, therefore she should not be sent back.

In the evening her father-in-law and brother-in-law came to take her back home. They accused her of misbehaviour and disobedience. When her mother enquired about her daughter being battered by her husband there was some quarrel between the families, hot words were exchanged and they failed to reach to any compromise. Surinder Kaur continued to stay with her mother for a month.

After some time, her in-laws sent a message through a common friend and asked her to come back. She, however, did not go back. One day to her surprise her husband came to her brother's place and asked her to come with him. She did not want to go with him but her mother asked her to accompany him. Very reluctantly she went back to her husband's place. Everyone at her husband's place greeted her warmly. She found that her husband was also going to work regularly. She was happy that her husband had changed, but hardly a week had passed that he again became irregular at his work. He would come home drunk, but he did not misbehave with her.

In the meantime she became pregnant. During pregnancy she kept herself a little aloof from her husband and did not object to his not working or drinking. Her husband also did not abuse her. However, occasional quarrels did occur with regard to money matters. She continued to feel that her husband would change after the birth of the child, when additional responsibility would fall on his shoulders. When she gave birth to a female child, her husband did not express any happiness. Her mother-in-law started grudging about financial burdens after the birth of the child. Whenever Surinder Kaur would ask her husband to give some money for household expenses he would ignore her. He would say that he had nothing to spare for her and the child. He used to be rude and harsh whenever she asked him for money.

Surinder Kaur's relations with her husband further deteriorated when she came to know about her husband's extra marital relations through her brother-in-law's wife. She felt very depressed and when her husband came home, she enquired from him. Her husband told her frankly about the other woman and how much he liked her. He even told her that he could leave her but not the other woman. On hearing this, she became so angry that she started crying loudly and blaming her fate. Her husband asked her to leave him for ever otherwise he himself leave the house.

Next day she went to her brother's place and told him about her husband's infidelity. She refused to go back to her husband. Her brother's friend informed him about a women's organization at Chandigarh and told him to seek its assistance. She went with her brother to the women's organization and lodged a written complaint about ill-treatment by her husband. Her husband was summoned to the office of the women's organization. He agreed to mend his ways and promised to take full care of her and the child. She was again sent with her husband by the women's organization.

After this incident, her husband stopped talking to her. He would come home drunk late at night and sleep during the day and would not go to work. Her mother-in-law also started taunting about her idle husband. Whenever she asked for milk for the child, it would be refused and she was told to send her husband to work. She was told that she would not get any thing without making any financial contribution towards household expenses. Surinder Kaur got annoyed at her behaviour and started complaining to her husband, who asked her to stop grumbling. On her pestering he became angry and started calling her names. She also could not control herself and taunted him regarding his failure to perform the role of a provider. Her husband became angry and started beating her. He pushed her and she fell down on the floor. Surinder Kaur caught hold of her husband's legs and in order to free himself he beat her badly. He broke his empty liquor bottle on her head. She was badly hurt and started bleeding.

Her husband fled from the house. She picked up her child and went after him. Her mother-in-law tried to stop her, but she pushed her and went directly to the police station and registered a complaint against her husband. Later on, she went to her sister's place who took her to a doctor and then dropped her at their brother's place. Every one was shocked to see her in that condition. Her mother and sister-in-law tried to console her.

Next day she went to the women's organization again along with her brother and sister-in-law. Her parents-in-law were already present there. They started begging her to withdraw her complaint with police otherwise their son would be imprisoned. Her mother-in-law started crying and making promises of treating her well. Members of the women's organization told her to give one more chance to them. They got her father-in-law's thumb impression on a paper stating that he would take full responsibility of his daughter-in-law. She was asked to withdraw her complaint. Her brother also agreed to do so and she was again sent to her in-laws house.

On reaching there she was again beaten by her husband at night. She was kicked, slapped and strangled. Her husband warned her that she would not be left in a shape to lodge complaints against him. He kept on beating her very badly as to kill her but her father-in-law intervened and rescued her. He even accused her husband for making the matters worse, but he did not listen to him and left the house.

Next day Surinder Kaur's sister came to see her. She told her sister about her battering. She begged her for help. She agreed to do so provided she left the child with her husband. It was very difficult for Surinder Kaur, she started crying and asked her sister to have mercy on her. Her sister agreed to help her provided she behaved as per her advice. This time, no one from her in-law's place stopped them. Both of them went to the women's organization again and blamed them for their wrong decisions. Surinder Kaur told them that she would not go back to her husband to get killed. She would like to seek divorce. Members of the women's organization agreed to help her. Her husband and parents-in-law were asked by the women's organization to attend their office for arriving at a final decision. Only her in-laws came. At first they showed their reluctance for divorce, but when they were threatened with legal action they agreed to do so provided she would keep the child . Surinder Kaur wanted to keep the child but her brother and sister were completely against this. After great reluctance she gave the child to her in-laws and went to her brother's place.

After this incident, Surinder Kaur became so depressed that she had fever and remained bed ridden for a month. The child also continued to suffer from one ailment or the other because of lack of proper care and attention. Her husband, however, did not care to know the whereabouts of Surinder Kaur and the child. Her mother-in-law sent her a message to take the child, but her brother refused to do so. He told Surinder Kaur that in case she wanted to keep the child it would be difficult for her to get married again and in such contingency she should not expect any help from her family of orientation.

At the time of recording the case study, her divorce case was pending in the court. She is completely dependent upon her brother, hence she has to accept his advice. She feels that she has no say in her own life's decisions and like an animal she is pushed from one corner to another. She has become very pessimistic about her future life.

Discussion :

(1) The case belongs to the lower class where the wife is an illiterate and not engaged in any paid work. Her husband is also not a regular paid worker. Conjugal discord started just after marriage.

(2) Husband's failure to act as a provider and wife's resentment against her husband's drinking behaviour and his extra marital relations are the main factors of the wife abuse.

(3) Wife's attempts to seek help from informal group resulted in more severe physical violence.

(4) Formal agencies failed to put any end to wife battering. Additionally, their intervention further deteriorated marital relationship.

(5) Ultimately support from her family of orientation has helped her to come out of the present abusive relationship. After finally terminating the present marriage she is likely to go for remarriage.

Analysis

For the purpose of having an in-depth understanding of the problem of wife abuse it is desirable to make use of life cycle approach. It is for this purpose that eight case histories of the abused women belonging to different social classes have been recorded. Cases no. 1 and 2 belong to the upper class; 3 and 4 come from the middle class; 5 and 6 are of the working class and 7 and 8 represent the lower class. These case histories may not be representative of the cases discussed in earlier chapters. On the other hand, they may be unique or even unusual in a number of ways. Further, each victim may perceive her situation as unique and these victims may feel that their lives are unlike others who are supposed to have happy married life. Those cases who are still living in the abusive relationship are likely to have such a perception. However, these abused women share certain common experiences with other abused women. These common experiences are their helplessness, anguish, pain, fear, frustration, lack of alternative resources or ignorance about the steps to be taken for the termination of their abuse. It is for the purpose of finding out commonalities or distinctiveness that the developmental cycle of their married life has been taken into consideration. The subsequent analysis will highlight their socio-demographic background, the developmental cycle of their abuse, the nature of violence, the precipitating factors, their reactions and the strategies they adopt to deal with the situation.

Demographic background :

There were five cases (Cases no. 1, 3, 6, 7 and 8) who got married between the age group of 20 and 23 years and the three cases (Cases no. 2, 4 and 5) were married in the age group of 26 to 27 years. No association was noticed with regard to age at marriage and the social class background of the cases recorded. The three cases married in the age group of 26 to 27 were equally divided among the upper, middle and working classes. With regard to Case no. 7 her first marriage took place at the age of 20 years and was remarried at the age of 27 years. In her case the abuse is associated with her second marriage, hence for the purpose of analysis, her age at marriage is treated as 27 years. Thus, four cases had higher age at marriage. Keeping in view the age at marriage of the eight case histories no association was found between the age at marriage and their abuse. Additionally, no association was noticed with regard to their present age and their being victim of husband's violence. Similarly, number of children and sex of children have no bearing on their being victims of husband's violence.

The educational background of the cases indicate that five victims belonging to the upper, middle and working classes had graduated and above, two cases had educational qualification of matriculation and one case from the lower class was an illiterate. The educational background partly supports the contention that educated women are more aware about their rights in the conjugal relationship and hence may raise questions with regard to asymmetrical marital relationship resulting into use of coercive methods by their husbands to maintain their superior position. So far as their working status was concerned, irrespective of the class background all the cases were not engaged in any paid work outside their home, hence were economically dependent upon their husbands. Two cases (Cases no. economically dependent upon their husbands. With the exception of Case no. 8 the rest of the five cases have now become economically independent. Out of these five cases four cases (Cases no. 2, 3, 4 and 5) became economically independent after leaving the abusive spouse whereas Case no. 6 who is still living with her spouse became economically independent during the absence of her husband who had gone abroad and stopped extending any financial support to the family. The results of these cases do not support the contention of Hornung et al. (1981) who maintained that housewives had lower risk of violence than employed women.

The analysis of the demographic background of the cases does not indicate any clear association with violence, with the exception that educated women are at higher risk of being victims of abuse by their husbands.

Eruption of violence :
Family living brings members of the family closer to each other. This provides not only greater frequency of interaction but also better quality of interaction which implicitly implies that intimacy of family life creates not only intense awareness of the uniqueness of other members but confrontations as well. The strength of marital relationship revolves around the ability of the members to use negotiation and reasoning in situations of conflict. However, when reasoning fails and conflicting situation persists, such a situation will eventually erupt into violence.

Taking into account the time span by which violence erupted in the marital relationship, it was noted that in four cases (Cases no. 3, 5, 7 and 8) it erupted immediately following marriage. And in two cases (Cases no. 1 and 4) it erupted within one year. In Case no. 4 it started after six months of marriage and in Case no. 1, violence erupted just after one year of her marriage. On the other hand, in Case no. 2 it was after a gap of four years when her husband's waywardness were known to the informal group and when the husband failed to be a good provider, violence against wife started. In Case no. 6 violence in conjugal relationship started after a gap of 11 years after their marriage. The couple lived together peacefully for 6 years and then the husband went abroad and came back after a gap of 4 years. The couple had congenial relation for one year after the return of the husband. It was only when husband's infidelity was brought to the notice of his wife and her objections against her husband's illicit relations resulted into violence. In short, it is clear that in a majority of cases conflict and violence erupted in the marital relationship immediately after they started living together.

Nature of violence :
The most common feature of violence was a combination of verbal, psychological and physical violence. Further, Case no. 8 was also the victim of withdrawal in addition to being

victim of verbal, psychological and physical violence of her husband. It is clear that the perpetrators of violence resort to different forms of violence to subdue the victims. In response to different types of violence or combination thereof perpetuated by their husbands, most of the women victims were resorting to withdrawal or verbal or psychological or combination thereof with the exception of Cases no. 1 and 6 who were using "defensive aggression" in the physical combat between the partners. In response to the violence of their husbands 5 cases (Cases no. 2, 3, 4, 7 and 8) were taking recourse to withdrawal to check escalation. Husbands of all the cases were using verbal and psychological violence along with physical violence and in case of women victims (Cases no. 1, 4, 6, 7 and 8) belonging to different social classes were also retaliating with verbal violence. These cases disapprove the general contention that verbal violence is a common feature of the lower class.

Precipitating factors of violence :

The main precipitating factor leading to conflict and violence in the marital relationship is infidelity on the part of the husband. When the wife protests against her husband's extra marital relationship, it results into her abuse. Out of eight cases, infidelity on the part of the husbands was the main issue of conflict in five cases (Cases no. 1, 2, 6, 7 and 8). Interference in the conjugal relationship by the in-laws was another precipitating factor of wife abuse in four cases (Cases no. 3, 4, 7 and 8). Out of these two cases were from the middle class and two were from the lower class. Out of five cases living in joint households (Cases no. 3, 4, 5, 7 and 8) with the exception of Case no. 5 in the rest of the households, the in-laws did play an active role in the abuse of the wives. Additionally, Cases no. 3 and 4 belonging to the middle class were victimized for not bringing sufficient dowry. Another four cases (Cases no. 1, 4, 6 and 8) attributed their victimization to the drinking behaviour of their husbands. Overtly these cases have made consumption of alcohol on the part of their husbands as the main villain in conjugal conflict. However, the secondary conflict was over infidelity (Cases no. 1, 6, 8) and dowry (Case no. 4). There were 2 cases (Cases no. 4 and 5) in which status inconsistency was the main precipitating factor. Both these cases were better educated than their husbands and their standard of living in their family of orientation was better off than the family of procreation. These victims were critical about the 'manners' of their husbands and their parents which was resented and for the purpose of maintaining their dominance the husbands used physical violence against them. The analysis of the precipitating factors indicates that combinations of different factors resulted into wife abuse. Further, for the purpose of perpetrating violence against wives in five cases (Cases no. 2, 3, 5, 7 and 8) the husbands made the victims socially isolated, they were not allowed to have any contacts with their parents and neighbours so that they could develop a sense of loneliness and helplessness. In short, it can be concluded that no single factor can be held responsible for wife abuse, however, infidelity and drinking behaviour on the part of the husband precipitated the conflicting situation in many cases.

Reactions of the victims to abuse :

Depending upon their life situation the victims of abuse reacted differently to their respective abusive situations. In the beginning, after having been abused, six cases (Cases no. 1, 2, 3, 4, 5, and 8) felt trapped and developed a feeling of helplessness that they would not be able to negotiate any change in the behaviour pattern of their spouses. Three cases (Cases no. 1, 2 and 5) felt lonely, two cases (Cases no. 5 and 7) became fearful and one case (Case no. 6) felt ashamed of violent behaviour of her husband against her. There were, however, four cases (Cases no. 3, 4, 5 and 7) who became vengeful and developed hatred against their abusers. Keeping in view their miserable conditions four cases (Cases no. 2, 4, 5 and 7) attempted suicide or made threats of committing suicide to get rid of abusive situation. In short, the victims had a variety of reactions to their abuse.

Why did they stay? :

The sufferings of the victims ranged from six months to 20 years. There are three cases (Cases no. 1, 6 and 7) who are still continuing with the marital relationship, out of which only one case (Case no. 7) got her abuse terminated. There were four cases (Cases no. 3, 4, 7 and 8) whose sufferings did not last more than one year. Case no. 5 suffered for two years and Case no. 2 for seven years. On the other hand, Cases no. 1 and 6 are suffering for the last 18 years and 9 years respectively. As stated earlier all the cases were economically dependent upon their husbands. Additionally, Cases no. 1 and 2 could not come out of the abusive relationship for the sake of their daughters. Case no. 1 had no alternative support system. Hence these were the cases of objective dependency. Further, four cases (Cases no. 2, 4, 7 and 8) continue to suffer because of their subjective dependency. They did not want to come out of the abusive relationship because they felt that separation or divorce would result into lowering their self-esteem as well as family reputation.

Cases no. 1 and 2 are not interested to terminate the abusive relationship because they are afraid that they would not be able to get suitable partners for their daughters, once they themselves are stigmatized as divorced mothers. Case no. 4 continued to suffer with the hope that her marital relationship would improve once her parents were able to meet the dowry demands. Case no. 7 is slightly different because she got remarried as a widow and her emotional investment in the second marriage was too much in the sense that she could not visualize a third marriage after having divorced the second husband. In short, a number of conditions forced these victims to continue living in the abusive relationship though the period of their stay varied.

Intervention :

To cope with abusive behaviour of the husband each victim

sought intervention from informal and formal sources, in addition to using personal strategies. After having failed to check the abusive behaviour pattern of their spouses on their own, all the victims with exception of Case no. 5 sought intervention from the family of orientation. Cases no. 1 and 6 sought the intervention from their friends in addition to their parents and siblings. Case no. 5 who held her own parents responsible for her abuse did not seek any help from her family of orientation but from her friend. When informal sources failed to put an end to their abuse, all the eight cases had sought intervention from the formal agencies, i.e., women's organizations, family counselling centre and police to cope up with abusive situation. The intervention by the informal and formal sources failed to bring about reconciliation so that the spouses could live together peacefully. With the exception of Case no. 7, where formal sources facilitated the couple to live away from the joint household and it is in this case only that the couple has been able to have a happy married life again. In all the other cases intervention instead of checking violence in the conjugal relations further deteriorated the conditions. However, when the conditions became unbearable for the victims, the informal and formal sources came to the rescue of five Cases (2, 3, 4, 5 and 8). In three cases (Cases no. 3, 4 and 8) their family of orientation had provided shelter to the victims. In two cases (Cases no. 3 and 4) who were the victims of dowry related violence, the parents helped them to be economically independent. Hence the family of orientation by providing shelter for physical security and helping them to be economically independent helped the victims to come out of the abusive relationship. Two cases (Cases no. 2 and 5) were helped by the formal sources in the shape of helping them to become economically independent as well as providing them shelter. In this way they were able to help the victims to come out of the abusive relationship. In two cases (Cases no. 2 and 5) formal agencies intervened and in other three cases (Cases no. 3, 4 and 8) family of orientation came to the rescue of the victims.

In all these five cases intervention by the informal and formal sources have helped the victims to terminate their abuse and these are the cases who have sought legal separation or divorce from their spouses to get permanent relief from their victimization. Cases no. 1 and 6 are continuing to stay in the abusive relationship with the hope that things might improve. It is only in Case No. 7 where intervention by the formal sources have been able to restore peaceful married life to the victim.

The above analysis of the case histories facilitates in concluding that wife abuse is not limited to any age group or a social class. The victims suffer because of the objective and subjective conditions over which they do not have any control. These victims resort to seeking help from alternative resources for the sake of attaining peaceful married life. However, when such intervention fails, separation seems to be only plausible alternative to get their abuse terminated. Further, those victims whose family of orientation came to their rescue had the shortest duration of their victimization.

6

Abusive Marital Relationship : An Overview

The present study was undertaken with three main objectives :

(1) To find out the nature, extent and frequency of wife abuse,

(2) To find out the correlates of physical violence against wives, and

(3) To explicate the coping mechanisms used by wives to deal with abusive marital relationship.

The study was done at Chandigarh and 26 cases from the upper class, 74 from the middle class, 46 from the working class and 54 from the lower class were taken. In all, the study had a sample of 200 cases. An Interview Schedule was the main tool with which core data were collected. In addition, 8 case studies were also taken to explicate the developmental cycle of the marital relationship.

Violence in the present study refers to an act carried out by a spouse with an intention to inflict harm or injury to the other spouse. For the purpose of comprehension of the nature of violence and for analytical purposes, violence was further divided into four categoris: withdrawal, psychological, verbal and physical.

The subject matter of the study was very sensitive, hence, instead of asking direct questions about the presence or absence of violence in conjugal relationship, the respondents were initially asked to indicate the instances when they had difference of opinion with their spouses. When two persons interact with each other frequently, a number of issues may crop up on which they would have difference of opinion. This particular fact was admitted by the respondents and with the exception of two, all the respondents admitted that they did have difference of opinion with their spouses. A large percentage of the respondents giving a positive response can be attributed to the fact that no time span was specified. Hence the respondents might have taken into account the total period of their married life during which they had some occasion when they had difference of opinion with their spouses.

The issues on which the spouses had arguments were money matters, child care, drinking behaviour of the husband, suspicion of adultery, housekeeping, parents-in-law, friendship circle and miscellaneous. Dowry and alcohol do not emerge as the main issues which lead to conjugal discord as concluded by a number of Indian scholars (Agnes, 1989; Ahuja, 1987; Bhatti, 1989; Gautam and Trivedi, 1987; Parihar, 1989; Singh and Renuka, 1989; Shah, 1989).

Out of 200 cases under study, 187 respondents admitted that difference of opinion with their spouses had also resulted into quarrel. In 125 cases the quarrel was attributed to wives because of their (1) rude behaviour, (2) disobedience and (3) nagging. These precipitating factors identified by the respondents themselves designating a situation where the victims had assumed the responsibility of instigating the abusers. On the other hand in 144 cases husbands were held responsible for conjugal quarrel. The main precipitating factors in order of severity were their (1) rude behaviour pattern, (2) inability to act as a good provider, (3) their drinking behaviour and (4) extra marital relationships. The results indicate that husbands initiate the quarrel in most conjugal relationship.

With regard to use of different forms of violence by one spouse against the other, it was noticed that with the exception of 13 conjugal units all the other cases reported presence of one form of violence or an other in the relationship. Further, the spouses were found to be using different forms of violence or their combinations. At one period of time, the spouses resorted to one form of violence and at another time to another type or a combination of different types. It was also noted that with the exception of withdrawal more husbands used psychological, verbal and physical violence against their wives. Additionally, they resorted to these forms of violence more frequently than wives. On the other hand, more wives were found to be resorting to withdrawal. The wives who were the victims of verbal, psychological and physical violence of their husbands were found to be resorting to withdrawal. The study revealed that violence in one form or the other with the exception of physical violence was quite rampant in the conjugal relationship.

To explain the correlates of husbands' physical violence against wives, they were broadly discussed under the subheadings demographic variables, social background, class, level of traditionality, values and dependency.

The data revealed that wives of younger age and who were married at a lower age were at high risk of being physically abused in contrast to those who were of higher age group and married at later age. Women having a large number of children (5+) were at higher risk of being physically abused. Similar was the case with those who had no child. Sex of the children and composition of the household were not found to be associated with wife abuse.

The social background of women victims revealed that those wives who had no education or were highly educated were at higher risk of being battered. Similarly women engaged in paid work were at high risk of being battered than the housewives. Out of women engaged in paid work outside their homes, those engaged in occupations of lower prestige were at high risk of being abused than those engaged in occupations of higher prestige. More women belonging to the lower caste and class were found to be victims of physical violence of their husbands in contrast to those belonging to the upper caste and classes.

The correlation between level of traditional ideology and wife battering revealed that wives with low level of traditional sex role orientations were at greater risk of being abused than those with traditional sex role orientation.

The association between social values favouring use of violence and wife battering indicated that those wives who had medium score were at higher risk of being battered in contrast to those who had high or low score on values favouring use of violence to resolve family conflicts.

To find out association between dependency and wife battering, dependency was divided into objective and subjective. By combining these two aspects of dependency, its impact on wife battering was also worked out. The data of the present study revealed that wives who had higher level of objective dependency on their husband were at higher risk of being battered. Similarly with the increase in the subjective dependency of the wives their battering also increased. With regard to total dependency it was noted that wives with higher level of total dependency were at high risk of being victims of their husband's physical violence.

The study has also dealt with coping behaviour of victims of husbands' violence, i.e., what strategies the victims have adopted to deal with abusive marital relationship. The data of the present study revealed that the reactions to their abuse were self-directed. The victims developed depression, a feeling of helplessness and powerlessness. In a few cases the victims had developed negative reactions (hatred and revengefulness) against their abusers. A majority of victims did not share their victimization even with their relatives and friends. Only a one-fourth of the victims brought to the notice of their informal group about their being victimized by their husbands. The results of the study do not support the contention that more severe the violence the greater the possibility of victims seeking intervention from the formal agency because only 16 victims had sought help from the formal agencies. The data further revealed that the victims who were either less educated or highly educated sought help from formal agencies to stop their abuse. The intervention from the formal agencies could help only five cases to get their victimization terminated and this could be attained only through separation from the abusive spouse. The other cases were continuing to live in the abusive relationship because of their objective and subjective dependency. The analysis of the data has indicated that victims of husbands' violence preferred to deal with the abusive marital relationship on their own. It is only when their efforts fail and their victimization continues, they seek assistance from the family of orientation and formal agencies though their number is very less.

To get a greater insight into the developmental cycle of conjugal relationship eight case studies were also recorded. To give equal representation to all four classes, two case studies were taken from each social class. Based on the analysis of the cases, it was noticed that conjugal violence in one form or the other was present in all the eight cases. Irrespective of the class background husbands used verbal, psychological and physical violence against their wives. Additionally, one case belonging to the lower class who also used withdrawal in the shape of denying conjugal rights to his wife. In response to such victimization all the eight victims resorted to withdrawal to check escalation of the conflicting situation. However, there were two cases, one belonging to the upper class and another from the working class, who were using defensive aggression in the physical combat with their husbands. Five cases belonging to different social classes were also resorting to verbal violence against their husbands.

Infidelity on the part of the husbands emerged as the main precipitating factor for conjugal conflict. Followed by interference by in-laws, drinking behaviour of the husband, dowry related problems and status inconsistency.

No association was found between the present age of the

victim or her age at marriage and her abuse. With regard to time span in six cases, their abuse started within one year of their marriage and in one case it started after the gap of four years and in another case violence erupted after a gap of 11 years of her marriage.

Further no association was found between number of children and sex of the children and wife abuse. All the eight victims were not engaged in any paid work. Hence, the results do not support the sampled data (quantitative) of the present study and the contention that housewives are at low risk of their husbands violence than working wives (Hornung et al., 1980).

As a consequence of their victimization the reactions of all the eight victims were self-directed in the shape of being lonely or developing a feeling of depression and helplessness. In four cases when their victimization continued, they also developed a feeling of hatred and animosity against their abusers.

The cases adopted different strategies depending upon their life experiences to deal with their conflicting situations. Cases where support from family of orientation was available to the victims, their abuse from the husbands was terminated earlier than the cases where such support was not available. Out of eight cases, five cases could get rid of their husbands' abuse by terminating the conjugal relationship through legal separation, three cases are continuing with their marital relationship, it was only in one case where intervention from the formal agency helped the case to get her abuse terminated. The other two cases are continuing living in the abusive relationship for the last 16 and 20 years respectively because of dependency of Case no. 1 on her husband and in another case husband's dependency on his wife (Case no. 6).

Discussion :

In the Indian society, a majority of the marriages are still being arranged by the elders in the family. The marital partners come to know each other after marriage or using Goffman's (1961) terminology have forced 'encounter'. It is through the intimate relationship they start knowing about the likings and dislikings of each other, it is therefore quite likely that a majority of such marital partners would have difference of opinion on a number of issues. It is in this context that the responses the cases under study have to be looked into who admitted that there were a number of issues on which they had difference of opinion with their husbands and such differences led to verbal arguments between the spouses. Further, looking at the issues on which the marital partners had arguments also support the structural gender inequality. The marital partners have entered into the relationship with a preconceived gender role definitions and in case the partners fail to come up to the expectations of each other, such a situation leads to arguments between them.

Additionally, taking into account the reasons cited by respondents for marital quarrel, they also reinforce asymmetrical gender relationships. The traditional role expectation from the wife is that she has to assume a subordinate position in the marital relationship. As and when she questions the asymmetrical marital relationship and superordinate position of the husband such a situation results into conflict because the husband wants to continue with his dominant position in the marital relationship. Hence, the marital conflict can be attributed to the lack of congruence between traditional role expectation of the husband and the new role which the wife has assumed, that is, egalitarian way of life.

Violence in one form or the other was found quite widespread in the present study. However, physical violence of husbands against wives was limited to approximately one-third of the respondents. The results support the findings of Levinson (1989) who after conducting a cross cultural study came to the conclusion that out of different forms of family violence, violence against wives was most common.

Asymmetrical gender relations become very prominent even with regard to different forms of violence used by the spouses against each other. In response to husband's psychological, verbal and physical violence the wife resorts to withdrawal because this form of violence is socially accessible to women and secondly, they use it to check escalation of conjugal discard. Additionally, they treat it as an insulation mechanism to avoid the possibility of serious retaliation from their husbands.

To explicate the correlates of violence the analysis was limited to physical violence. The demographic variables of the victims such as present age, age at marriage and number of children were found to be associated with wives' battering. Younger couples face a lot of stress in making adjustments to the new role responsibilities and failure to meet new role responsibilities results into marital conflict. Almost the same trend was found in a study conducted by Straus et al. (1980) in America that all forms of marital violence occur most frequently among those under 30 years of age. Taking into account the onset of physical violence, the qualitative data (case studies) of the present study have also supported the findings of sampled data. Similarly, presence or absence of children in the family is likely to affect the quality of relationship between husband and wife. Further, presence of more children in the family would create problem of management and proper training of younger ones. Additionally, traditional role expectations hold mothers responsible for the proper upbringing of the children and for any deviance on the part of the children, the mother is blamed.

The social correlates which were found to be associated with wife battering were the education and occupational background of the victims. The quantitative data revealed a curvilinear association with wife beating. The women who were highly educated questioned the asymmetrical gender relations which was resented by the husbands and to reinforce their dominant position the husbands used physical coercion. On the other hand, those who were less educated belonged to the lower class and the men of the lower class would depend upon the use of physical force to reinforce their dominance. Further, use of physical violence is an accepted behaviour pattern in the lower class, what Oscar Lewis (1959) has called 'Culture of Poverty'. The qualitative data, however, do not support the quantitative data because with the exception of one case the rest of the cases were educated and their assertion to demand egalitarian marital relationship had resulted into physical violence against them.

With regard to economic dependency or non-dependency, the quantitative data revealed that in contrast to housewives, wives engaged in paid work outside the home were the victims of physical violence by their husbands. Looking at the nature of the paid work in which such women were engaged in, it was noticed that among the working women only those who were engaged in occupations of lower prestige were more victims of battering. These women belonged to the lower class and having attained economic independence, even though limited, they questioned the dominant position of their husbands which resulted into their battering. The case study data did not, however, support the sampled data because all the cases were not engaged in any paid work yet they were the victims of their husband's violence. Most of these cases were highly educated and their educational attainment helped them to raise objections to asymmetrical marital relations. Their efforts to have egalitarian conjugal relationship seems to have resulted into their abuse.

With regard to social class background of the victims of physical violence by their husbands, it was found that women belonging to the lower class were at a higher risk of being physically abused by their husbands. The members of the lower class are subject to a lot of economic pressures and strains and they cannot show their resentment and frustration against those who are highly placed and hence, they give vent to their frustrations on a slightest provocation by beating their wives on whom they can exert their power. Further, physical violence in the lower class families is normal, socially approved and socially inculcated behaviour as stated by Lewis (1959). The sampled data support the findings of different researchers (Ganguin, 1978; Gelles and Cornell, 1983; Saunder, 1982; Straus et al. 1980) who indicate a positive association between lower class and wife battering. The results of the qualitative data cannot be compared with quantitative data because eight cases were taken from all the four classes, representing different classes equally.

Traditional ideology promotes and serves to justify male dominance. Those wives who try to challenge or question the traditional power structure in the family are likely to be suppressed by their husbands with the use of physical force in order to maintain their dominant position. The quantitative data indicated that wives with low level of traditional sex role orientation were at higher risk of being physically abused by their husbands. The results of the study partially support the findings of Walker (1984) and Whitehurst (1974) who argue that non-traditional wives if paired with traditional husbands are at higher risk of being abused. In qualitative data almost all the cases challenged the asymmetrical role structure and as a consequence became victims of different types of violence by their husbands.

The quantitative data did not provide any clear-cut association with regard to values in favour or against the use of violence in the family and wife battering. It was noted that those respondents who had medium score on values favouring use of violence to resolve family conflict were more victims in contrast to those who had high or low score. The results do not support the contention of Levinson (1989) who maintained that physical violence against wives is more common in those societies which have value orientation in favour of force for resolving family conflicts. In the present study, I have taken into account the value orientation of the wives rather than of the husbands. It is the husbands who are the perpetrators of physical violence, had I taken the value orientation of the husbands, the results might have supported the contention of the Levinson. Hence, non-association between value orientation and wife battering might be attributed to methodology adopted in the present study.

Level of dependency of the wives was also found to be one of the correlates of wife battering. The wives who had high level of objective dependency were at higher risk of physical abuse because it was difficult for these women to think of living alone as compared with those who had low level of objective dependency. Their objective dependency was also known to their spouses who had fully exploited the situation knowing fully well that their wives would not be able to leave them. Further, family power structure is maintained through the behaviour pattern of the members involved. Those at the top end of the power structure behave in dominant ways and they do not hesitate to use coercive methods to reinforce their dominant position.

Similarly subjective dependency was also found to be related with wife battering. Even though a few women may not be objectively dependent upon their husbands yet they remain subjectively dependent upon their husbands as their social reality has not been construed outside marriages. The alternative social identity as an "earner" is not available to them. The possibility of living outside the marriage is not socially approved. Further, it is the wife's and mother's role which gives her some respect in the society. In asymmetrical gender situation the husbands use coercive methods to assert their dominant position. They use physical violence against their wives because they are confident that their violent behaviour pattern would not be challenged.

Taking into account, objective and subjective dependency of the wives together it was noticed that those women who had higher total dependency scores were at higher risk of physical abuse by their husbands. Although no clear-cut statistical correlations could be found between dependency and wife abuse yet it was found that with the increase in the level of dependency there was an increase in the percentage of victims. The results support the findings of a number of studies which have depicted association between marital dependency and wife abuse (Dobash and Dobash, 1979; Marsden, 1978; Straus, 1976; Truninger, 1971; Walker, 1978).

Taking into account both qualitative and quantitative data, dependency also acts as a condition forcing the women to continue living in the abusive marital relationship mainly because they lack alternative support systems. Even those who have alternatives also continue to suffer because of their upbringing and socialization. Women have been trained not to break up the marital relationship even under adverse conditions. Those women who had ventured to get their abuse terminated could do so only by terminating the marital relationship.

There are, however, two case studies which cannot be explained with the help of dependency framework. Case no. 2 was objectively and subjectively dependent upon her husband, hence she accepted infidelity of her husband and continued to have peaceful family life. However, when sexual waywardness of her husband became public, she started resenting her husband's extra-marital relations. The changed conditions and resentment by the wife resulted into marital conflict. Wife's persistent interference in the extra-marital relations of her husband became the main cause of her battering. Even though she remained objectively and subjectively dependent on her husband, she left her husband when conditions became intolerable. In this case it is clear that with the changed conditions and meanings, the quality of interaction between the marital partners changed to such an extent where the wife decided to come out of the marital relationship.

Case no. 6 also depicts a situation where the quality of interaction between the marital partners changes with the change in the meanings which the actors attach to the same situation. Mrs. Rosy and her husband have been living together for the last twenty years. In this case the marital discord started after gap of eleven years. After marriage they had peaceful married life for six years then the husband went abroad and remained away from the family for four years. It was during the absence of her husband, Mrs. Rosy faced financial hardships and held her husband responsible for his negligence. However, when he turned up, after initial bickerings and resentment, the wife accepted the husband when he gave her a lot of gifts and started financially supporting her. They had again peaceful and congenial relations for one year. It was only when Mrs. Rosy came to know about extra-marital relations of her husband and her objections to his infidelity, conjugal discord erupted. This is a case where the marital relationship is punctuated by relative peace and conflict. Both husband and wife, drink together and fight. As both the partners are equal participant in the physical violence against each other, this case can be explicated with the help of interactional perspective.

Traditional gender role perspective also fails to explain the onset of conflict in the conjugal relations. It is the differential perception of the conjugal roles of the husband and wife which leads to conflict. Husband expects his wife to continue with the traditional gender roles whereas the wife wants to have egalitarian role relationship. Given that men benefit from the traditional gender stratification, it is unlikely that they voluntarily give up their dominant position. Conflict in the conjugal relationship starts when wife questions asymmetrical role relationship and husband resorts to violence if the struggle for gender equality increases his wife's resource base and encourages her to question the traditional power relations. Hence, lack of consensus in the meanings of both husband and wife leads to conflict and man uses physical coercion against his wife as a last resort to reinforce his dominant position. In other words, wife abuse can also be explained with the help of interactional perspective. In the interactional situation husband and wife produce their own definitions of the situation, when the husband not only determines his own position and behaviour pattern but also of his wife who in turn does not accept the definitions of her husband, such a situation leads to marital discord.

Based on the results of the study and their discussion, it can be concluded that no single perspective can explicate wife abuse in the contemporary Indian society. As no systematic study has been conducted in the Indian setting on wife abuse our knowledge is only anecdotal. Under these circumstances it will be worth-while to use interactional perspective alongwith other perspectives to understand the phenomenon of wife abuse in future researches.

Appendix I
Social Class

In the present study more than 60 per cent (67.5) of the respondents were housewives and hence they were not engaged in any paid work outside their families nor had an independent source of income. Out of 200 respondents only 65 were working wives. Among 65 working women only 3 were engaged in occupations of high prestige, 15 belonged to middle ranked occupations and 21 to working class occupational status and 26 were engaged in occupations of lower level. Keeping in view the fact that a large number of women respondents were not working, it was decided to determine their social class background as per the achieved attributes of their husbands, viz., education, occupation and income.

For the purpose of analysis all the three variables, i.e., education, occupation and income were divided into four categories, viz., low, working, middle and high. With regard to education, husbands having education upto middle level, were put into the low category, those having education upto matric were placed into the working class category; those having education upto graduation level were placed in the middle level and professionals, post-graduates and above were placed in the high level.

For occupational prestige categories, menial occupations like sweeper, unskilled labourers were placed in the low level, followed by skilled labourers, technicians in the working class category. Those engaged in bank services and business were put in the middle level and finally professionals and administrative officers were treated as belonging to the high occupational prestige category.

The income of the husbands per month was also divided into four groups. The husbands having the income put Rs. 500 monthly occupied the lowest position, the second group consisted of those who earned between Rs. 501 to 2500 per month. In the middle level those cases were included who had income from Rs. 2501 to Rs. 5000 per month and the high group consisted to those who had income of more than Rs. 5001 per month.

After dividing the three variables into four categories, gamma test was used to find out the association between these variables, i.e., Education and Occupation; Education and Income and Occupation and Income. As the data were of ordinal level, gamma test was used.

Table I .1 : **Husband's education and occupation**

(Occupation)

Education	*Very low*	*Moderately low*	*Middle*	*High*	*Total*
Very low	47 (73.44)	8(13.79)	—	—	55(27.5)
Moderately low	16(25.00)	19(32.76)	2(4.65)	—	37(18.5)
Middle	1(1.56)	20(34.48)	14(32.56)	8(22.86)	43(21.5)
High	—	11(18.97)	27(62.79)	27(77.14)	65(32.5)
Total	64(100.00)	58(100.00)	43(100.00)	35(100.00)	200(100.00)

Gamma value = .88

TABLE I.2 **Husband's education and income**

(Income)

Education	*Very low*	*Moderately low*	*Middle*	*High*	*Total*
Very low	33(80.49)	20(33.90)	2(5.88)	0	55 (27.5)
Moderately low	8(19.51)	22(37.29)	4(11.76)	3(4.55)	37 (18.5)
Middle	0	13(22.03)	10(29.41)	20(30.30)	43 (21.5)
High	0	4(6.78)	18(52.95)	43(65.15)	65 (32.5)
Total	41(100.00)	59(100.00)	34(100.00)	66(100.00)	200 (100.00)

Gamma value = .88

TABLE 1.3 **Hosbands occupation and income**

(Income)

Education	*Very low*	*Moderately low*	*Middle*	*High*	*Total*
Very low	37(90.24)	26(44.07)	1(2.94)	0	64 (32)
Moderately low	4(9.76)	32(54.24)	18(52.94)	4(6.06)	58 (29)
Middle	0	1(1.69)	14(41.18)	28(42.42)	43(21.5)
High	0	0	1(2.94)	34(51.52)	35(17.5)
Total	41(100.00)	59(100.00)	34(100.00)	66(100.00)	200 (100.00)

Gamma = .95

With the help of gamma test it was noted that all the three variables had high positive association. The value of gamma in case of Education and Occupation was 0.88, Education and Income 0.88 and Education and Occupation 0.95.

After having established high association between these three variables one can take up the distribution of the households according to one of the variables. One can treat such distribution as constituting different social classes. However it is quite probable that there are certain discrepancies that is, persons with high income may not have high education or are engaged in occupation of high prestige. To ward off such a possibility it was decided to work out a comprehensive index for the purpose of identifying the social class. Weightages were assigned on these three variables. Individual's score could range from 3 to 12. The weightage of one was given to those persons who had low occupation, income and education, which implied that on all three variables put together, the score would be three. On the other hand, those who had high income, engaged in occupation of high prestige and with high education were given a score of four on each variable. In this way scores of such persons could go upto 12 on all the variables taken together.

TABLE I.4 **Scores taken together on all the variables**

Score	*Frequency*	*Cumulative frequency*	
3	31	31	
4	23	54	Q_1
5	18	72	
6	14	86	
7	14	100	Q_2
8	14	114	
9	15	129	
10	19	148	
11	26	174	Q_3
12	26 N-200	200	

After arranging the scores in ascending order quartiles were calculated in order to compute social class. Q_1 came out to be 50, Q_2 100 and Q_3 150 thus on the basis of distribution, Q_1 value lies on score of 4, Q_2 lies on score of 7 and Q_3 rests on the score of 11. Thus distribution is divided into four categories which became four social classes.

TABLE I.5 **Comprehensive social class**

Social class	*Score*	*Frequency*	*Percentages*
Lower	3,4	54	27
Working	5,6,7	46	23
Middle	8,9,10,11	74	37
High	12	26	13
Total		200	100

The redistributed sample according to social class background came to be 54 cases in the lower class, 46 in the working class, 74 in the middle class and 26 cases in the high class.

Appendix II

Traditional Sex Based Roles

The level of traditionality was worked out with the help of eight statements depicting traditional sex based roles. The responses to each statement preceded as agree, scmewhat agree and disagree to account for variations in the responses. To attain a cumulative position of an individual different scores were allocated to their responses. A score of three was assigned to a response indicating agreement or fully endorsing traditional sex based roles. On the other hand, those who did not agree to traditional sex based roles, that is, they disagreed with the statement they were given a score of one. Those who reacted with 'somewhat agree' responses were given the score of two. In this way total score of a respondent could range from 8 to 24.

The scores were arranged into ascending series and Quartile 3 were calculated and distribution was divided into three parts, scores ranging from 8 to 16 were labelled as having low level of traditionality; 17 to 22 as medium level of traditionality and scores ranging from 23 to 24 as high level of traditionality. In other words, those having low score were labelled as less traditional in their outlook towards gender role, those having medium score were labelled as not so traditional and those having high score were treated as highly traditional in their outlook.

TABLE II.1 **Scores regarding traditional sex based roles**

Score	*Frequency*	*Cumulative frequency*
8	1	1
9	0	1
10	4	5
11	4	9
12	7	16
13	11	27
14	10	37
15	6	43
16	18	61 Q_1
17	14	75
18	26	101
19	15	116
20	21	137
21	9	146
22	22	168 Q_3
23	11	179
24	21	200
	N-200	

Thus on the basis of distribution, 61 respondents had low level of traditionality, 107 respondents had medium level of traditional orientation and 32 respondents had high level of traditional sex role orientation.

TABLE II.2 **Traditional sex based roles**

Traditionality	*Score*	*Frequency*	*Percentages*
Low	8-16	61	30.5
Medium	17-22	107	53.5
High	23-24	32	16.0
Total		200	100.0

Appendix III

Value Orientation : Violence in the Family

The value orientation in favour or against violence was worked with the help of twelve statements. These statements were both positive and negative. Positive statements did not justify the use of physical violence in the family. Negative statements favoured the use of physical violence in the family. The statements referred to the use of physical force not only against the spouse but also the children. The responses were arranged on three-point scale ranging from 'agreement' to 'disagreement' through 'undecided.' According to the response given, each statement was coded, for every positive statement, score '1' was given for every agreement, score '2' for the response of 'undecided' and score '3' for 'disagreement' whereas for every negative statement score '1' was given for every disagreement, score '2' for undecided and score '3' for agreement. In this way, total scores could range from 12 to 26 for the total sample of 200 respondents. The distribution of scores was formed and arranged in ascending series.

Although scores could range from 12 to 36, but there was no score beyond 28, thus scores ranged from 12 to 28. On the basis of total sample, Q_1 and Q_3 were calculated from these scores and distribution was divided into three parts. Q_1 value emerged on the score of 18, thus respondents who had scores from 12 to 18 were treated on 'low level' which

TABLE III.1 **Scores on value orientation**

Score	*Frequency*	*Cumulative Frequency*	
12	3	3	
13	1	4	
14	7	11	
15	4	15	
16	18	33	
17	10	43	
18	27	70	Q_1
19	9	79	
20	33	112	
21	4	116	
22	24	140	
23	7	147	
24	32	179	Q_3
25	1	180	
26	13	193	
27	0	193	
28	7	200	
	N - 200		

means respondents who had score in this range did not fully endorsed the use of physical force in the family. Q_3 value occurred on the score of 24 which had cumulative frequency of 179. Thus respondents who had scores from 19 to 24, were labelled on 'medium level' these respondents had in between position, they neither fully endorsed use of physical force nor they fully criticized the use of physical violence in the familial relationships. The respondents who had scores from 25 to 28 were grouped under 'high level' which means that they favoured the use of violence in the familial network of relationships.

TABLE III. 2 **Value orientation and violence**

Value orientation	*Scores*	*Frequency*	*Percentages*
Low	12-18	70	35
Medium	19-24	109	54.5
High	25-28	21	10.5
Total		200	100.00

Distribution clearly indicates that 70 respondents had low level of value orientation whereas 109 respondents that is more than 50 per cent (54.5) had medium level of value orientation and only 21 respondents had high level of value orientation in favour of use of physical violence in the family.

Appendix IV

Objective Dependency

For determining the objective dependency of the respondents, six statements were used. These statements dealt mainly with factual information like, Do you have any property? Can you live alone? etc. Thus the responses were arranged at dichotomous level of 'Yes' and 'No'. Any response which depicted the objective dependency of the respondent was assigned the score of '2' and any response indicating the absence of dependency was allotted the score of '1'. The scores ranged from 6 to 12.

TABLE IV.1 **Scores on objective dependency**

Scores	*Frequency*	*Cumulative frequency*	
6	8	8	
7	37	45	
8	46	91	
			Q_1
9	53	144	
10	23	167	
			Q_3
11	24	191	
12	9	200	
	N - 200		

The scores were arranged in ascending series along with their frequencies and cumulative frequencies. Q_1 and Q_3 were calculated. Q_1 came on the score of '8' which had cumulative frequency of 91. Thus respondents who had scores from 6 to 8 were labelled as having 'low level' of objective dependency. Q_3 emerged on the score of '10' which had cumulative frequency of 167, therefore the respondents who had scores of 9 and 10 were labelled as having 'medium level' of objective dependency and the respondents with the score of 11 and 12 were labelled as having 'high level' of objective dependency. Thus with help of Q_1 and Q_3 the distribution was divided into three parts to calculate three levels of objective dependency.

TABLE IV.2. **Objective dependency of the respondents**

Objective dependency	*Scores*	*Frequency*	*Percentages*
Low	6-8	91	45.5
Medium	9-10	76	38.0
High	11-12	33	16.5
Total		200	100.0

Distribution indicates that out of 200 respondents 91 had low level of objective dependency, 76 had medium level of objective dependency and only 33 (16.5 per cent) had high level of objective dependency.

Appendix V

Subjective Dependency

In order to determine the subjective dependency of the respondents six statements were used. These statements mainly dealt with social and psychological dependency of the respondents. The responses were arranged at three-point scale because it is difficult to put attitudinal statements on a dichotomous scale, therefore three response categories were used, namely, agreement, somewhat agree and disagreement. Any response depicting subjective dependency was given the score of '3', whereas any response depicting non-dependency was given the score of '1' and partial subjective dependency was given the score of '2'. In this way the scores of the respondents could range from 6 to 18.

The scores were arranged in ascending series along with their frequencies and cumulative frequencies. There were no respondents with score of 6, 7 and 8, thus these scores were not taken. Q_1 and Q_3 were calculated from score 9 to 18. Q_1 emerged on the score of 13. Those respondents who had scores from 9 to 13 were labelled as having "low level" of subjective dependency. Q_3 emerged on the score of 17, those respondents who had scores from 14 to 17 were treated as having "medium level" of subjective dependency and respondents with score of 18 were treated as having "high level" subjective dependency.

TABLE V.1 **Scores on subjective dependency**

*Scores**	*Frequency*	*Cumulative frequency*	
9	1	1	
10	4	5	
11	10	15	
12	30	45	
13	26	71	
			Q_1
14	29	100	
15	19	119	
16	22	141	
17	21	162	
			Q_3
18	38	200	
	N - 200		

*Note** : No respondents with scores of 6, 7 and 8.

TABLE V.2 **Subjective dependency of the respondents**

Subjective dependency	*Scores*	*Frequency*	*Percentages*
Low	9-13	71	35.5
Medium	14-17	91	45.5
High	18	38	19.0
Total		200	100.0

Final distribution indicates that 71 respondents out of 200 had low level of subjective dependency, 91 respondents had medium level of subjective dependency and only 38 (19 per cent) had high level of subjective dependency.

Appendix VI

Total Dependency

It was expected that sometimes objective dependency causes subjective dependency and sometimes it is the subjective dependency which gives rise to objective dependency. Hence to see the effect of both the dependencies objective and subjective dependencies were grouped together under the broad heading of total dependency. Total dependency was calculated by taking the scores of both objective and subjective dependency and arranging them in an ascending series. The scores ranged between 12 and 30 and Quartile one and three were calculated, in order to divide the distribution into three categories—low, medium and high.

TABLE VI.1 **Score on total dependency**

*Scores**	*Frequency*	*Cumulative frequency*	
17	2	2	
18	5	7	
19	18	25	
20	19	44	
21	18	62	
			Q_1

(*Contd...*)

Scores*	Frequency	Cumulative Frequency
22	18	80
23	25	105
24	16	121
25	27	148
26	12	160
		Q_3
27	14	174
28	11	185
29	11	196
30	4	200
	N - 200	

Note :* There were no respondents with scores of 12 to 16.

Q_1 emerged on the score of 21 thus respondents who had score below 21 were treated as having low dependency. Q_3 emerged on the score of 26, thus respondents who had scores from 22 to 26 were treated as having medium level of dependency and respondents who had scores from 27 to 30 were treated as 'high level' of total dependency. In this way distribution was divided into three levels of dependency.

TABLE VI.2 **Total dependency of the respondents**

Total dependency	*Scores*	*Frequency*	*Percentages*
Low	17-21	62	31.0
Medium	22-26	98	49.0
High	27-30	40	20.0
		N 200	100.0

Distribution indicates that out of 200 respondents, 62 respondents had low level of dependency, 98 respondents had medium level of dependency and 40 respondents had high level of dependency.

Appendix VII

Interview Schedule

1.1 Address
1.2 No. of rooms -

	Wife	*Husband*
1.3	Present age	1.3.1
1.4	Age at marriage	1.4.1
1.5	Education	1.5.1
1.6	Occupation	1.6.1
1.7	Income (per month)	1.7.1
1.8	Caste	1.8.1
1.9	Religion	1.9.1

1.10 Present marital status of wife : married/divorcee/ separated

1.11 Details of persons residing with you at present

Relationship with respondent	*Age*	*Sex*	*Marital status*	*Education*	*Occupation*	*Income*

Traditional sex based roles

2.1 Do you believe that marriage is must for women?
Agreement/Somewhat Agree/Disaggrement

2.2 Are you of the opinion that wife's responsibility is to keep her husband happy?
Agreement/Somewhat Agree/Disaggrement

2.3 Do you agree with a statement that it is more important for a wife to help her husband's career even at the cost of her own?
Agreement/Somewhat Agree/Disagreement

2.4 Do you believe that it is the responsibility of the hus band to be a provider for his family?
Agreement/Somewhat Agree/Disagreement

2.5 Do you think that husband should have final say in major family decisions?
Agreement/Somewhat Agree/Disagreement

2.6 Do you believe that husbands should have more po wer in the conjugal relations?
Agreement/Somewhat Agree/Disagreement

2.7 Should a husband be an aggressive?
Agreement/Somewhat Agree/Disagreement

2.8 Do you believe that wife is expected to tolerate even the violent behaviour of her husband?
Agreement/Somewhat Agree/Disagreement

Value orientation and justification to the exercise of violence in the family.

3.1 When all the alternative means are exhausted beating a child is justified.
Agreement/Undecided/Disagreement

3.2 It is not beating but love and warmth which corrects an obstinate child.
Agreement/Undecided/Disagreement

3.3 Man who is unable to control his wife is not respected in the society.

Agreement/Undecided/Disagreement

3.4 Husband who does not beat his wife is an ideal husband.

Agreement/Undecided/Disagreement

3.5 To command obedience from wife the husband should occasionally beat his wife.

Agreement/Undecided/Disagreement

3.6 The beating husband looses respect in the eyes of his wife.

Agreement/Undecided/Disagreement

3.7 Husband who subdues his wife through beating symbolizes manliness.

Agreement/Undecided/Disagreement

3.8 A wife hates the husband who resorts to use of physical violence.

Agreement/Undecided/Disagreement

3.9 People refrain from establishing close relations in a quarrel some family.

Agreement/Undecided/Disagreement

3.10 Mutual love between husband and wife makes them an ideal couple.

Agreement/Undecided/Disagreement

3.11 The quarrelsome parents produce quarrelsome children.

Agreement/Undecided/Disagreement

3.12 Occasional beating makes the child more responsible
Agreement/Undecided/Disagreement

Objective dependency

4.1 Do you go for shopping on your own and buy articles of your choice? Yes/No

4.2 Can you go to your relatives/known persons outside your city on your own? Yes/No

4.3 If circumstances demand, can you live alone?
Yes/No

4.4 Do you work outside the home as a paid worker ?
Yes/No

4.5 Do you have any property in your own name ?
Yes/No

4.6 Do you get some financial support from your family of orientation? Yes/No

Subjective dependency

5.1 Are women in India trained not to leave their husbands' house even in adverse circumstances?
Agreement/Somewhat Agree/Disagreement

5.2 Should a woman seek divorce under adverse circumstances?
Agreement/Somewhat Agree/Disagreement

5.3 Are you of the opinion that married woman even if she is abused, has high status in contrast to divorced/separated woman.
Agreement/Somewhat Agree/Disagreement

5.4 In case you have strained relations, do your relations help you to patch up differences.
Agreement/Somewhat Agree/Disagreement

5.5 Are you of the opinion that women are more committed to marriage than men ?
Agreement/Somewhat Agree/Disagreement

5.6 In case a relationship between husband and wife is broken, do you think wife is more likely to be hurt ?
Agreement/Somewhat Agree/Disagreement

Conjugal Relations

6.1 Was there any occasion when you and your husband had difference of opinion ? Yes/No

6.2 Were there some occasion or issues on which you and your husband had an argument ? Yes/No

If yes, what were the issues ?

6.2.1 Child care Husband/Wife
6.2.2 House keeping Husband/Wife
6.2.3 Money matters Husband/Wife
6.2.4 Parents-in-law Husband/Wife
6.2.5 Drinking behaviour Husband/Wife
6.2.6 Friendship circle Husband/Wife
6.2.7 Suspicion of adultery Husband/Wife
6.2.8 Miscellaneous Husband/Wife
6.3 Were there some issues where the argument resulted into quarrel? Yes/No
6.3.1 If yes, who initiated the quarrel ? Husband/Wife/Parents-in-law
6.3.1.1 If husband initiated the quarrel what were the factors ?
6.3.1.2 Rude behaviour
6.3.1.3 Drinking behaviour
6.3.1.4 Money matters and job related problems
6.3.1.5 Extra marital relations
6.3.2.2 If wife initiated the quarrel what were the instigating factors ?
6.3.2.3 Rude behaviour
6.3.2.4 Disobedience
6.3.2.5 Taunting behaviour
6.3.2.6 Job related problems
6.3.3.3 If parents-in-law initiated the quarrel what were the instigating factors?
6.3.3.4 Dowry problem
6.3.3.5 Maladjustment
6.3.3.6 Rude behaviour
6.3.2 If yes, following quarrel how you and your husband behaved.

	Wife	*Husband*	*Rarely/ Occasionally/ Very often*
6.3.3	*Withdrawal* stopped talking Did not eat		

Went out
Started crying
Went to bed
Started drinking

6.3.4 *Psychological*
Insulted for house keeping
Insulted for the up keep of children
Demeaning while comparing with other men or women
Demeaning family background
Lacking intelligence
Denied permission to visit relatives.
Not allowed to express views.
Criticized for being outspoken.
Threatened to leave
Threatened to commit suicide.

6.3.5 *Verbal*
Shouted at each other
Called names
Verbal threat to use physical force.

6.3.6 *Physical*
Threw objects
Threw objects at the spouse.
Started beating self
Started beating children
Pushed the spouse
Kicked the spouse
Hit the spouse
Beat the spouse

6.4 Were there any instances when the quarrel occurred in front of :

6.4.1 Your children Yes/No
6.4.2 Your in-laws Yes/No
6.4.3 Outsiders Yes/No
6.4.4 No one Yes/No

6.5 What was your reactions to such quarrel?
Powerless
Humiliated

Alone
Fear
Shame
Guilty
Trapped
Depressed
Hatred against husband
Vengeful
Any other

6.6. Did you ever go to a relative or a close friend and told them about the quarrel ?

Yes/No

If yes, what was their advice ?

6.6.1 Advised to patch up
6.6.2 Advised to seek formal help
6.6.3 Advised to break off
6.6.4 Showed no interest

6.7 Who reconciles first after quarrel ?

Husband/Wife/Either Husband or Wife

6.8 Did you ever seek outside help to prevent your husband from abusing you?

Yes/No

6.8.1 If yes, from where
6.8.1.1 Women organization
6.8.1.2 Police
6.8.1.3 Legal Adviser
6.8.1.4 Other known persons
6.8.2 If yes, what type of help was extended to you.
6.8.2.1 Physical protection
6.8.2.2 Social and moral support
6.8.2.3 Financial/Job
6.8.2.4 Councilling/Psychological
6.8.2.5 Any other
6.8.3 If yes, has your husband stopped abusing you?

Yes/No

6.8.4 If no, why are you still living with him ?
6.8.4.1 No other place to go

6.8.4.2 For the sake of family reputation
6.8.4.3 For the sake of children
6.8.4.4 It is considered bad to live away from husband
6.8.4.5 Hope that things will become better
6.8.4.6 Any other.

Bibliography

Abramson, L.Y., Seligman M.E.P., and Teasdale J., 1978, "Learned helplessness in humans: Critique and Reformulation". *Journal of Abnormal Psychology*, Vol. 87, pp. 49-74.

Adams, D., 1988, "Treatment models of men who batter : A profeminist analysis" *Feminist perspectives on wife abuse.* Yllo K and Bogard M., (Eds.). Newbury Park, CA: Sage.

Adams, D.C. and McCormick A.J., 1982, "Men unlearning violence: A group approach based on collective model". *The abusive partner: An analysis of domestic battering.* Roy M. (Ed.) New York, Van Nostrand Reinhold.

Adler, E. S., 1981, "The underside of married life: Power, influence and violence". *Women and Crime in America.* Bowker L.H. (Ed.) New York, Macmillan.

Agnes, F., 1989, "Wife beating: Changes in social structure crucial to combat the problem" *Violence against women*. Sood S. (Ed.) Jaipur, Arihant Publishers.

———, 1993, "Marital Murders - The Indian Reality "*Health for the millions* 1(1), February, 1993.

Ahuja, R. 1987, *Crime against women*, Jaipur, Rawat Publications.

Allen, C. and Straus M.A., 1980, "Resources, power and husband-wife violence" *The social causes of husband-wife violence.* Straus M.A. and Hotaling G. (Eds.). Minneapolis, University of Minnesota Press.

Andersen, S.M., Boulette T.R. and Schwartz A.H., 1991, "Psychological maltreatment of spouses" *Case studies in family violence.* Ammerman, Roberts T and Hersen Michel (eds.) New York, Plenum Press.

Bach, G.R. and P. Wyden, 1974, "Why intimates must fight" in *Violence in the family*. Steinmetz S.K. and Straus M.A. (Eds.). New York, Dodd, Mead and Company.

Back, S.M., Post R.D. and Darcy G., 1982, "A study of battered women in a psychiatric setting", cited in Levinson D. Family Violence in Cross Cultural Perspective. *Frontiers of Anthropology*, Vol. I, New Delhi, Sage, 1989.

Bains, S., 1987, "Manchester's Crime Survey of Women for Women", Police Monitoring Unit, Manchester City Council, cited in Hanmer J. " Women and Policing in Britain" in Hanmer J. et al. (Eds.). *Women, Policing and Male Violence: International Perspectives*, London, Routledge, 1989.

Baldus, H., 1937, "The social position of women among the eastern Bororo" pp. 112-62, and 323-30 in *Ensaias de Ethnologia Brasileia cited in D. Levinson*, Family Violence in Cross-cultural Perspective. (New Delhi), CA: Sage, 1989.

Ball, M., 1977, "Issues of violence in family casework" Social Casework, Vol. 58, pp. 3-12 cited in Gelles R.J. and Cornell C.P., *Intimate Violence in Families*, (Second ed., New Delhi), CA: Sage.

Batra, Jagdeep, K., 1990, "Factors of divorce and problems of subsequent adjustment: A sociological study in Chandigarh", Ph.D. thesis submitted in Panjab University, Chandigarh.

Baum, F., 1987, "Preventing Family Violence: The evaluation of a group of men who are violent towards their partners". *Australian Journal of Sex, Marriage and Family*, Vol. 8(4), pp. 173-83, November, 1987, cited in Sage Family Studies Abstracts, Vol. 10(3), August, 1988.

Bergmen, B.O., Larsson G.; Brismar B. and Klang M., 1988, "Aetiological and Precipitating Factors in Wife Battering: Psychosocial Study of Battered Wives". *Acta Psychiatrica Scandinavica*, Vol. 77, (3), pp. 338-45, March, 1988, cited in Sociological Abstracts, Vol. 37(1), April 1989.

Berk, R.; Berk S.F., Loseke D.R. and Rauma D., 1983, "Mutual combat and other family violence myths" *The dark side of families: current family violence research.* Finkelhor D., Gelles R., Hotaling G. and Straus, M. (Eds.), Beverly Hills, CA: Sage.

Berkowitz, L., 1983, "Aversively stimulated aggression: Some parallels and differences in research with animals and humans". American Psychologist, Vol. 38, pp. 1135-44, cited in Andersen, S.M. et al. "Psychological maltreatment of spouses". Ammerman R.T. and Hersen Michel (Eds.). *Case Studies in Family Violence,* New York: Plenum Press, 1991.

Bernard, J.L. and Bernard M.L., 1984, "The abusive male seeking treatment: Jekyll and Hyde." Family relations, Vol. 33, pp. 543-47, cited in Stordeur R.A. and Stille R., *Ending Men's violence against their partners: One road to peace.* (New Delhi) CA: Sage, 1989.

Bersani, C.A. and Chen H., 1988, "Sociological perspectives in family violence" Van Hasselt V.B., Morrison R.L., Bellack A.S., Hersen M. (Eds.). *Handbook of Family Violence.* New York, Plenum Press.

Bhatia, H.S., 1983, "*Aging and Society : A Sociological Study of Retired Public Servants.* Udaipur, Arya's Book Centre.

Bhatti, R.S., 1985, "Family Violence — A Systematic Model" *Indian Journal of Social Psychiatry,* Vol. 2, pp. 174-85.

———, 1989, "Socio-Cultural Dynamics of Wife Beating" *Violence Against Women,* Sood, S. (Ed.), Arihant Publishers, Jaipur.

Bicchouse, Terry and Lynn Hawker (1995) Domestic Violence: Myths and Safety Issues, *Journal of Holistic Nursing,* Vol. 13(1), pp. 83-92, March 1995.

Blau, P.M., 1964, *Exchange and Power in Social Life,* New York, Wiley.

Blenkner, M., 1969, "The normal dependency of aging" *The dependencies of old people,* Richard Kalish (Ed.), Ann Arbor, University of Michigan Institute of Gerontology.

Blood, R.O. and Wolfe D.M., 1960, "Husbands and Wives: The Dynamics of Married Living. Glencoe, IL, Free Press, cited in Bersani C.A. and Chen H., "Sociological Perspectives in Family Violence" in Hasselt Van, Morrison R.L., Bellack A.S., Hersen M. (Eds.) *Handbook of Family Violence.* New York, Plenum Press, 1988.

Bordin, R., 1981, "Women and Temperance : A Quest for Power and Liberty," pp. 1873-1900, cited in Kantor G.K. and Straus M.A. in "The Drunken Bum Theory of Wife Beating" Social Problems, Vol. 34(3), June 1987.

Boulette, T.R. and Andersen S.M., 1985, "Mind Control and the battering of women", cited in Andersen S.M., Boulette T.R., and Schwartz, A.H. "Psychological maltreatment of spouses" in Ammerman R.T. and Hersen Michel (Eds.) *Case Studies in Family Violence.* New York, Plenum Press, 1991.

Bowker, L.H., 1983, "*Wife Beating*", Lexington, MA, Lexington.

———, 1988, "The effect of methodology on subjective estimates of the differential effectiveness of personal strategies and help sources used by battered women" in Hotaling G.T., Finkelhor D., Kirkpatrick J.T., Straus M.A. (Eds.); Coping with Family Violence. *Research and Policy Perspectives.* New Delhi, CA: Sage.

Boyd, V.D., 1978, "Domestic violence: Treatment alternatives for the male batterers". A paper presented at the annual meeting of the American Psychological Associates, Toronto, Canada.

Breines, W. and Gordon L., 1983, "The New Scholarship on Family Violence" Signs, Vol. 8(3), pp. 490-531, Spring, 1983, in Sociological Abstracts, Vol. 32(1), April 1984.

Brekke, J. and Saunders D., 1982, "Research on women abuse: A review of findings, needs and issues." Unpublished manuscript, cited in Gelles R.J. and Cornell C.P. (Second ed.), *Intimate Violence in Families.* New Delhi, CA: Sage, 1990.

Briere, J., 1987, "Predicting self-reported likelihood of battering: Attitudes and childhood experiences", *Journal of Research in Personality*, Vol. 21, pp. 66-69.

Brinkerhoff, M.B. and Lupri, Eugen, 1988, "Interspousal violence" *Canadian Journal of Sociology*, Vol. 13(4), pp. 407-34 fall, 1988 *Sociological Abstracts*, Vol. 37(2), June 1989.

Brockner, J. and Rubin, J. Z., 1985, "Entrapment in escalating conflicts: A social psychological analysis." New York, Springer-Verlag, cited in Andersen S.M., Boulette T.R. and Schwartz A.H. "Psychological maltreatment of spouses". In Ammerman R.T. and Hersen Michel (Eds.) *Case Studies in Family Violence*, New York, Plenum Press, 1991.

Brockner, J. Rubin J.Z. and Lang E., 1981, "Face saving and entrapment", *Journal of Experimental Social Psychology*, Vol. 17, pp. 68-79.

Brockner, J. Rubin J. Z., Fine J., Hamilton T., Thomas B. and Turestsky B., 1982, "Factors affecting entrapment in escalating conflicts: The importance of timing". *Journal of Research in Personality*, Vol. 16, pp. 247-66.

Brown, B., 1980, "Wife's employment, marital equality and husband-wife violences" in Straus M. and Hotaling G. (Eds.). *The social causes of husband-wife violence*. Minnepolis, University of Minnesota Press.

Browne, A., 1988, "Assault and homicide at home: When battered women kill", cited, Hotaling G.T., Finkelhor D., Kirkpatrick J.T., Straus M.A. (Eds.) in Family Abuse and its consequences: New Directions in Research, Beverly Hills, CA: Sage.

Browning, J.J., 1983, "Violence against intimates: Toward a profile of the wife assaulter". Unpublished Ph.D. dissertation, cited in Stordeur R.A. and Stille R., Ending men's violence against their partners: one road to peace." (New Delhi) CA: Sage, 1989.

Byles, J.A., 1982, "Family Violence in Hamilton-revisted", Canada's Mental Health, Vol. 30(4): pp. 10-11, Dec. 1982 in *Sage Family Studies Abstracts*, Vol. 5(2), May 1983.

Cantos, Arthur L., Neidig Peter H. and O'Leary K.D. "Men and women's attributions of blame for domestic violence ; *Journal of Family Violence*, Vol. 8(4), pp. 289-302, December 1993.

Carlson, B.E., 1977, "Battered women and their assailants", Social Work, Vol. 22, pp. 455-65.

Carmen, E.H., 1981, "Violence against wives: treatment dilemmas for clinicians and victims", *International Journal of Family Psychiatry*, Vol. 2(3/4), pp. 353-68, 1981 in Sage Family Studies, Abstracts Vol. 5(2), May 1983.

Casanave, N.A. and Straus M.A., 1979, "Race, class, network embeddedness and family violence: A search for potent support system". *Journal of Comparative Family Studies*, Vol. 10, pp. 281-99.

Ceaser, P. Lynn, 1988, "Exposure to Violence in the Families of Origin among Wife Abusers and Maritally Nonviolent Men" Violence and Victims, Vol. 3(1), pp. 49-63, Spring, 1988.

Chambers, G. and Tombs, J. 1984, "The British Crime Survey" Scotland, London: HMSO, cited in Hanmer J. "Women and Policing in Britain". In Hanmer J. et al. (Eds.). Women, Policing and Male Violence: *International Perspectives*. London: Routledge, 1989.

Chapman, J.R. and Gates M. (Eds.), 1978, The victimization of women. Beverly Hills. CA: Sage.

Chaudhary, J.N., 1984, The Mughal History, Vol. VII. Bharatiya Vidya Bhavan, Bombay.

———,1989, "Divorce: Socio-demographic Correlates" in Sood S. (Ed.) Violence against Women : Arihant Publishers, Jaipur.

Chawdhary, M.N. Ray, 1984, *The Statesman*, 17th December, 1984.

Clark, M., 1969, "Cultural values and dependency in later life, Richard Kalish (Ed.) *The Dependencies of Old People*. Ann Arbor. Institute of Gerontology, University of Michigan.

Coleman, D.H. and Straus M.A., 1983, "Alcohol abuse and family violence" in Edward Gottheil et al. (Eds.). Alcohol, Drug Abuse and Aggression. Springfield, IL: Charles C. Thomas. cited in Kantor G.K. and Straus M.A. in "The Drunken Bum Theory of Wife Beating". *Social Problems*, Vol. 34(3), June 1987.

———, 1986, "Marital Power, Conflict and Violence in a Nationally Representative Sample of American Couples. *Violence and Victims*, Vol. 1(2) 1986.

Coleman, K.H., 1980, "Conjugal violence: What 33 men report". *Journal of Marital and Family Therapy*, Vol. 6, pp. 207-13.

Collman, K.H., Weinman L.M. and Hsi B.P., 1980, "Factors affecting conjugal violence." *The Journal of Psychology*, Vol. 105(2), pp. 197-202, July 1980 and in *Sociological Abstracts*, Vol. 30(2), June 1982.

Counts, D.A., 1988, "Female suicide and wife abuse: A crosscultural perspective" cited in Levinson D., *Family Violence in Cross-cultural Perspective: Frontiers of Anthropology*, Vol. I, New Delhi, Sage, 1989.

Daly, M., Wilson M. and Weghorst S.J., 1982, "Male sexual jealousy" Ethology and Sociobiology, Vol. 3, pp. 11-27, cited in Dutton D.G. and Browning J.J. in "Concern for Power, Fear of Intimacy and Aversive Stimuli for Wife Assault" in Hotaling G.T., Finkelher D., Kirkpatrick J.T., Straus M.A. (Eds.). *Family Abuse and its consequences*, Beverly Hills, CA: Sage.

Dasgupta, S. and Banerjee M., 1984, "A study of dowry system in West Bengal". Unpublished manuscript, *Jaya Prakash Institute of Social Change*, Calcutta.

Davis, N.J., 1980, "Sociological constructions of deviance" Dubuque, I A: Brown, cited in Bersani C.A. and Chen H. "Sociological Perspectives in Family Violence", in Hasselt V.B. Van et. al. (Eds.). *Handbook of Family Violence*, New York, Plenum Press, 1988.

Davis, W.A., 1963, "Child rearing in the class structure of American society, *Source book of Marriage and the family*, Sussman M.B. (Ed.), Boston, Houghton, Muffin.

Demaris, A., 1987, "The efficacy of a spouse abuse model in accounting for courtship violence", *Journal of Family Issues*, Vol. 8(3), pp. 291-305, September 1987.

Denzin, N., 1989, *The Research Act: A theoretical introduction to sociological methods*," (2nd ed.), New Jersey, Prentice Hall, Englewood.

Desai, K.G. and Naik R.D., 1971, *Problems of the Retired People in Greater Bombay* (Mimco) Bombay, The Institute of Social Sciences.

Dobash, R.E. and Dobash, R., 1979, *Violence Against Wives: A case against the patriarchy*, New York, Free Press.

Dollard, J., Doob L.W., Miller N.E., Mowrer O.H. and Sears R.R., 1939, *Frustration and Aggression*. New Haven, CT, Yale University Press.

Downes, D., 1982, "The Language of Violence: Sociological Perspectives on Adolescent Aggression" *Aggression and Violence.* Marsh P. and Campbell A. (Eds.). Oxford Basil Blackwell.

Dutton, D.G., 1983, "A nested ecological theory of male violence towards intimates", *Feminist psychology in transition,* Caplan P. (Ed.), Montreal, Eden, cited in Stordeur R.A. and Stille R. *Ending men's violence against their partners.* New Delhi, CA: Sage, 1989.

———, 1988, "Profiling of wife assaulters: Preliminary evidence for a trimodal analysis". *Violence and Victims,* Vol. 3(1), pp. 5-29, 1988.

Dutton, D.G., and Browning J.J, 1988, "Concern for power, fear of intimacy and aversive stimuli for wife assault" *Family abuse and consequences,* Hotaling G.T., Finkelhor D., Kirkpatrick J.T. and Straus M.A. (Eds.), Beverly Hills, CA: Sage.

Dutton, D.G. and Painter S.L., 1981, "Traumatic bonding: The development of emotional attachments in battered women and other relationships of intermittent abuse" *Victimology,* an international journal, Vol. 1, pp. 139-55.

Dvoskin, J.A., 1981, "Battered Women — An epidemiological study of spousal violence". Unpublished Ph. D. dissertation. cited in Stark E. and Flitcraft A. "Violence Among Intimates" in Hasselt V.B. Van et. al. (Eds.). *Handbook of Family Violence,* New York, Plenum Press, 1988.

Edelson, J.L., 1984, "Working with men who batter" *Social Work,* Vol. 29, pp. 237-42, cited in Stordeur R.A. and Stille R., Ending men's violence against their partners: one road to peace, New Delhi, CA: Sage, 1989.

Edgell, S., 1980, *Middle Class Couples.* London, Allen and Unwin, cited in Graham Allan-Family Life: Domestic Roles and Social Organization, Oxford, Basil Blackwell.

Elbow, M., 1977, "Theoretical considerations of violent marriages" *Social Casework,* Vol. 58, pp. 515-26, cited in Stordeur R.A. and Stille R., Ending men's violence against their partners: One road to peace, New Delhi, CA: Sage, 1989.

Elliot, F.A., 1977, "The neurology of explosive rage: The dyscontrol syndrome", Roy M. (Ed.), *Battered Women: A psychosociological study of domestic violence.* New York, Van Nostrand.

Eme, R.F., 1979, "Sex differences in childhood psychopathology: a review". *Psychological Bulletin*, Vol. 86, pp. 574-95.

Emery, R.E., 1989, "Family Violence" American Psychologists, Vol., 44, pp. 321-28, cited in Andersen S.M., Bouletle T.R., Schwartz, A.H., "Psychological maltreatment of spouses". Ammerman Roberts T. and Hersen Michel (Eds.). *Case Studies in Family Violence,* New York, Plenum Press, 1991.

Erchak, G.M., 1984, "Cultural anthropology and spouse abuse", *Current Anthropology*, Vol. 25: pp. 331-32, cited in Levinson D., Family Violence in cross-cultural perspective, New Delhi, CA: Sage, 1989.

Erlanger, H.S., 1979, "Childhood punishment experience and adult violence". Children and Youth Services Review, Vol. 1(1), pp. 75-86, Spring, 1979.

Erlich, V. St., 1966, Family in Transition: A Study of 300 Yugoslav Villages, Princeton, Princeton University Press, cited in Levinson *D. Family Violence in Cross-cultural Perspective.* New Delhi, CA: Sage, 1989.

Etzioni, A., 1971, "Violence" in Merton R.L. and Nisbet R. (Eds.). *Contemporary social problems.* New York, Harcourt Brace Jovanovich.

Evans-Pritchard, E.E., 1937, Witchcraft, Oracles and Magic among the Azande, Oxford: Clarendon, cited in D. Levinson Family Violence in cross-cultural perspective, New Delhi, CA: Sage, 1989.

Fagen, J., D. Stewart and Hansen K., 1983, "Violent men or violent husbands? Background factors and situational correlates" in Finkelhor D., Gelles R., Hotaling G., and Straus M. (Eds.) *The Dark Side of Families: Current Family Violence Research*, Beverly Hills, Sage.

Faulk, M., 1977, "Men who assault their wives", *Battered Women: A psychosocial study of domestic violence.* Roy M. (Ed.), New York, Van Nostrand Reinhold.

Fergusson, David M., Horwood L.J., Kershaw K.L. and Shanon T.F., 1986, "Factors in association with reports of wife assault in New

Zealand". *Journal of Marriage and the Family,* Vol. 48(2), pp. 407-12, May 1986.

Ferraro, K.J. and Johnson J.M., 1983, "How Women experience battering? The Process of Victimization" *Social Problems,* Vol. 30: pp. 325-39.

Finch, J., 1983, Married to the Job, London, Allen and Unwin, cited in Graham Allan, *Family Life: Domestic Roles and Social Organization.* Oxford, Basil Blackwell.

Finkelhor,D., 1981, "Sexual abuse : A sociological perspective", cited in Susan V. Mcleer "Psychoanalytic perspective on family violence" in Hasselt V.B. Van, Morrison R.L., Bellack A.S., Hersen M. (Eds.). *Handbook of Family Violence,* New York, Plenum Press, 1988.

———, 1983, "Common features of family abuse" in Finkelhor D., Gelles R., Hotaling G. and Straus M. (Eds.). *The dark side of families: Current family violence research.* Beverly Hills, CA: Sage.

———, Gelles R., Hotaling G. and Straus M. (Eds.), 1983, *The dark side of families,* Beverly Hills, CA: Sage.

Fitch, F.J. and Papantonia A., 1983, "Men who batter: Some pertinent characteristics", *Journal of Nervous and Mental Disorders,* Vol. 171(3), pp. 190-2, cited in Margolin G., Sibner L.G. and Gleberman L., "Wife Battering" in Hasselt V.B. Van, et. al. (Eds.). *Handbook of Family Violence,* New York, Plenum Press, 1988.

Flemons, D.G., 1989, "An ecosystem view of family violence", *Family Therapy,* Vol. 16(1) pp. 1-10, 1989, in Sage Family Studies Abstracts, Vol. 11(4), November, 1989.

Foss, J.E., 1980, "The paradoxical nature of family relationships and family conflict" in Straus M.A. and Hotaling G. (Eds.). *The social causes of husband-wife violence,* Minnepolis, MN: University of Minnesota Press.

Foulke, S.R., 1980, "Caring for the parental generation: an analysis of family resources and support", Master's Thesis. University of Delaware, cited in Steinmetz S.K. *Duty Bound: Elder abuse and family care,* Beverly Hills, CA: Sage.

Freeman, M.D.A., 1979, *Violence in the home*, Westmer UK, Saxon House.

Frieze, I. H., 1976, "Research on psychological factors in battered women", cited in Moore Donna M. (Ed.), *Battered Women*, Beverly Hills, Sage, 1979.

Frieze, I., J. Knoble, Washburn C. and Zomnir G., 1980, "Characteristics of battered women and their marriages" Cited in Bowker L.H., "The effect of methodology on subjective estimates of differential effectiveness of personal strategies and help sources used by battered women", in Hotaling G.T. et. al. (Eds.). *Coping with family violence*, New Delhi, CA: Sage.

Gaguin, D.A., 1978, "Spouse abuse: Data from National Crime Survey", *Victimology*, Vol. 2, pp. 632-43.

Ganguli, S. N., 1980, "Violence: A reflective note" in Bhuvan Chandel (Ed.), *Nature of Violence*, Chandigarh, P.U. Publication Bureau.

Ganker, V.D., 1993, Women and Social evils" Ashok Kumar (Ed.) *Women in Contemporary Indian Society*, Vol 2, New Delhi, Anmol Publications.

Ganley, A.L., 1981, "Resource Paper: Causes and characteristics of battering men", in Ganley A.L. (Ed.) *Participants' manual for workshop to train mental health professionals to counsel court mandated batterers*. Washington, D.C., Centre for Women Policy Studies.

Ganley, A.L. and Harris L., 1978, "Domestic Violence: Issues in designing and implementing programs for male batterers". Paper presented at the annual meeting of the American Psychological Association. Toronto, cited in Stordeur R.A. and Stille R. *Ending Men's violence against their partners: One road to peace*, (New Delhi) CA: Sage, 1989.

Garbarino, J. and Gilliam G., 1980, *Understanding abusive families*. Lexington, MA: Lexington Books.

Gautam, D.N., and Trivedi B.V., 1987, "Unnatural deaths of married women with special reference to dowry deaths : A sample study of Delhi". *Police, Research and Development* (January-March) cited in *The Indian Journal of Social Work*, Vol. XLIX, No. 3, July, pp. 271-79.

Gayford, J.J., 1975, Wife battering: A preliminary survey of 100 cases. British Medical Journal, Vol. 1, pp. 194-97.

Gelles, R.J., 1972, *The Violent Home: A Study of Physical Aggression between Husbands and Wives*, Beverly Hills: Sage.

———, 1974, *The Violent Home: A Study of Physical Aggression between Husbands and Wives*, (2nd ed.), Beverly Hills: Sage.

———, 1976, "Abused Wives: Why do they stay?" *Journal of Marriage and the Family*, Vol. 38, November, pp. 659-68.

———, 1979, *Family Violence*, Beverly Hills: Sage.

———, 1980, "Violence in the family: A review of research in the seventies". *Journal of Marriage and the Family*, Vol. 42, pp. 873-85.

———, 1983, "An exchange social theory" in Finkelhor D., Gelles R.J., Hotaling G.T. and Straus M.A. (Eds.). *The dark side of families*, Current Family Violence Research, Beverly Hills, CA: Sage.

———, 1988, "Violence and Pregnancy: Are pregnant women at greater risk of abuse?" *Journal of Marriage and the Family*, Vol. 50(3), pp. 841-47, August, 1988.

———, and Cornell C.P. (Eds.)., 1983, *International perspectives on family violence*, Lexington, MA : Lexington.

———, 1990, *Intimate Violence in Families*, (Second ed.), New Delhi, CA: Sage.

———, J.W. Harrop, 1989, "Psychological distress and violence". *Journal of Interpersonal Violence*, Vol. 4, (4) December, pp. 400-20.

———, Straus, M.A., 1979a, "Determinants of Violence in the family : Toward a theoretical integration", pp. 549-89, *Contemporary Theories about the Family*, Burr W.R, Hill R., Nye, F.I. and Reiss I.L. (Eds.), Vol. 1, New York, Free Press.

———, 1979b, "Violence in the American family", *Journal of Social Issues*, Vol. 35, pp. 15-39.

———, 1987, "Is violence towards children increasing? A comparison of 1975 and 1985 national survey rates", *Journal of Interpersonal Violence*, Vol. 2, pp. 212-22.

Gelles, R.J. and Strauss M.A., 1988, *Intimate Violence*, New York, Simon and Schuster.

Genteman, K.M., 1980, "Attitudes of North Carolina women toward the acceptance and causes of wife beating", paper presented at the meeting of Southeastern women's studies association, cited in Stark E. and Flitcraft A. "Violence among intimates" in Van Hasselt V.B. et al. (Eds.). *Handbook of Family Violence*, New York, Plenum Press, 1988.

Ghosh, S.K., 1984, *Women in a changing society*, New Delhi, Ashish Publishing House.

Gil, D.G., 1979, "Societal violence and violence in families," *Sage Family Studies Abstracts*, Vol. 2(1), February 1980.

Giles-Sims, J., 1983, *Wife Battering : A system theory approach.* New York, Guilford.

Gleason, Walter, J., 1993, Mental disorders in battered women : An empirical study" *Violence and victims*, Vol. 8(1): pp. 353-68, Spring, 1993.

Goel, R.P., 1988, *Marriage age in India*, New Delhi: B.R. Publishing Corporation.

Goffman, E., 1961, *Encounters*, Indianapolis, Bobbs-Merrill.

Gondolf, E.W., 1985, "Men who batter: An integrated approach to stopping wife abuse." Holmes Beach, F.L.: Learning Publications cited in Stordeur R.A. and Stille R, Ending men's violence against their partners, New Delhi, CA: Sage, 1989.

———, 1987, "Evaluating programs for men who batter: Problems and Prospects", *Journal of Family Violence*, Vol. 2, pp. 95-108.

Gondolf, E.W. and Russell D.E.H., 1986, "The case against anger control treatment programs for batterers" *Community Mental Health Journal*, Vol. 21, pp. 109-17, cited in Stordeur R.A. and Stille R. in Ending men's violence against their partners, New Delhi, CA: Sage, 1989.

Gondolf, E.W., and Fisher E.R., 1988, *Battered women as survivors: An alternative to treating learned helplessness*, Lexington, M.A.: Lexington.

———, 1991, "Wife Battering" In Roberts Ammerman T. and Hersen Michel (Eds.). *Case studies in family violence*, New York, Plenum Press.

Gondolf, E.W. and Hennekin J., 1987, "The gender warrior : Reformed batterers on abusers, treatment and change". *Journal of Family Violence*, Vol. 2, pp. 177-91.

Goode, W., 1971, "Force and violence in the family", *Journal of Marriage and the Family*, Vol. 33: pp. 614-36.

Gregory, M., 1976, "Battered Wives", Borland M. (Ed.), *Violence in the family*. Atlantic Highlands, NJ: Humanities Press.

Grewal, B., 1982, "Family Violence: A case study of slum dwellers of Chandigarh" A dissertation submitted for M. Phil degree, Dept. of Sociology, Panjab University, Chandigarh.

Gursharan, 1964, "Problems of aged women in Batala: An Industrial town". M.A dissertation submitted to the Panjab University, Chandigarh.

Hall, Ruth, 1986, "Ask any woman: A London Inquiry into Rape and Sexual Assault", Bristol : Falling Wall Press, cited in Hanmer J., "Women and Policing in Britain" in Hanmer J. et al. (Eds.). *Women, Policing and Male Violence: International Perspectives*. London, Routledge, 1989.

Hammond, P.B., 1964, "Mossi joking". Ethnology, Vol. 3, pp. 259-67, cited in Levinson D. Family Violence in cross cultural perspective, New Delhi, CA: Sage, 1989.

Hanmer, J., 1989, "Women and Policing in Britain" in Hanmer J., Radford J. and Stanko E.A. (Eds.). *Women, Policing and Male Violence: International Perspectives*. London, Routledge.

Hanmer, J., and Saunders, S. 1984, Well Founded Fear, London: Hutchinson cited in Hanmer J. "Women and Policing in Britain", Hanmer J. et al. (Eds.). *Women, Policing and Male Violence: International Perspectives*, London: Routledge.

Harris, L. and Associates, 1979, "A survey of spousal violence against women in Kentucky" report prepared for the Kentucky commission on women, cited in Andersen S.M., et al. "Psychological maltreatment of spouses" Ammerman Robert T. and Hersen Michel (Eds.). *Case Studies in Family Violence*, New York, Plenum Press, 1991.

Hastings, J.E. and Hamberger L.K., 1988, "Personality Characteristics of spouse abusers: A controlled comparison". *Violence and Victims*, Vol. 3(1), pp. 31-48, 1988.

Hatty, S.E., 1989, "Policing and Male Violence in Australia" Hanmer J, Radford J. and Stanko E.A. (Eds.) *Women , Policing and Male Violence: International Perspectives*, London, Routledge.

Hatty, S.E. and Sutton J.E., 1986, "Policing violence against women", in Hatty S.E. (Ed.) National Conference on Domestic Violence, Canberra: Australian Institute of Criminology in Hatty S.E., "Policing and Male Violence in Australia" Hanmer J. et al. (Eds.). *Women, Policing and Male Violence : International Perspective*, London, Routledge, 1989.

Hauser, W.J., 1982, *Differences in relative resources familial power and spouse abuse*, Palo Atto, CA: R & E, Research Associates.

Helton, A.S., 1985, "Battering during pregnancy: A prevalence study in a metropolitan area" cited in Stark E. and Flitcraft A. in "Violence Among Intimates" in Hasselt V., Morrison R.L., Bellack A.S. and Hersen M. (Eds.). *Handbook of Family Violence*, New York, Plenum Press.

Heppner, P., 1981, " A holistic approach to the treatment of violent families". *Social casework*, Vol. 62, pp. 594-600.

Hilberman, E., 1980, Overview: The "Wife-beater's Wife" reconsidered *American Journal of Psychiatry*, Vol. 137, pp. 1336-47.

----, Munson K., 1977-81, "Sixty battered women", *Victimology*, Vol. 2, pp. 460-70.

Hill and Hausen, 1960, "The identification of conceptual framework utilized in family studies", *Marriage and Family Living*, Vol. XXII, pp. 299-311.

Hoffman, Kristi L., Demo D.H. and Edwards J.N, 1994, "Physical wife abuse in a non-western society : An integrated theoretical approach" *Journal of Marriage Family*, Vol. 56(1), February 1994.

Homans, G.C., 1961, *Social Behaviour : Its elementary forms.* New York, Harcount, Brace Jovanovich.

Hotaling, G.T., Finkelhor D., Kirkpatrick J.T., Straus M.A. (Eds.). 1988, *Coping with Family Violence, Research and Policy Perspectives.* Beverly Hills, CA: Sage.

Hotaling, G.T. and Sugarman D.B., 1986, "An analysis of risk markers in husband to wife violence. The current state of knowledge", *Violence and Victims,* Vol. 1(2): pp. 101-24.

Hornung, C.A., McCullough B.C. and Sugimoto T., 1981, "Status Relationships in Marriage : Risk Factors in Spouse Abuse", *Journal of Marriage and the Family,* Vol. 43, pp. 675-92, August 1981.

Hough, M. and Mathew P., 1983, cited in Hanmer J. "Women and Policing in Britain". Hanmer J. et. al. (Eds.) "Women, Policing and Male Violence: International Perspectives." London: Routledge, 1989, *The British Crime Survey, Research Study,* Vol. 76, London: HMSO.

----, 1985 "Taking account of Crime: Key Findings from the 1984 British Crime Survey", Research Study 85, London: HMSO in Hanmer J. et al. (Eds.). *Women, Policing and Male Violence: International Perspectives.* London: Routledge, 1989.

Iwarimie, Jaja, Darlington, 1989, "Physically abused women: An empirical study" *Philosophy and Social Action,* Vol. 15(1-2) Jan-June, pp. 7-16 cited in Sociological Abstracts, Vol. 38, No. 2, June 1990.

Jain, R. 1992, *Family Violence in India.* New Delhi, Radiant Publications.

Johnson, N. (Ed.), 1985, *Marital Violence.* London. Routledge and Kegan Paul.

Johnston, M.E., 1988, "Correlates of early violence experience among men who are abusive toward female mates." Hotaling G.T., Finkelhor D., Kirkpatrick J.T. and Straus M.A. (Eds.). *Family abuse and its consequences,* Beverly Hills, CA: Sage.

Joshi, S., 1993, "Focus on Violence against Women". *The Times of India,* December 1993.

Kalmuss, D., 1984, "The intergenerational transmission of marital aggression". *Journal of Marriage and the Family*, Vol. 46, pp. 11-19.

Kalmuss, D.S., and Straus M.A., 1982, "Wife marital dependency and wife abuse". *Journal of Marriage and the Family*, Vol. 44, pp. 277-86.

Kane, P.V., 1940, *History of Dharmsastra*. Vols. 1-4. Poona: Bhandarkar Research Institute.

Kantor, G.K. and Straus M.A., 1987, "The Drunken Bum Theory of Wife Beating" *Social Problems*, Vol. 34(3), June 1987.

Kaplan, H.B., 1972, "Toward a general theory of psycho-social deviance: The case of aggressive behaviour". Social Science and Medicine, Vol. 6, pp. 593-617.

Karp, Leonard and Karp Chery L., 1994, "Beyond the normal ebb and flow-infliction of emotional distress in domestic violence cases. *Sage Family Studies Abstracts*, Vol. 17(3), August 1994.

Kaushik, S., 1989, "Social and treatment issues in wife battering: A reconsideration" in Sood S. (Ed.) *Violence Against Women*. Jaipur, Arihant Publishers.

Kertzman, D., 1980, "Dependency, frustration, tolerance and impulse control in child abusers". Saratoga. CA: Century Twenty one Publishing in *Sage Family Studies Abstracts*, Vol. 3(1), February, 1981.

Khan, M.Z., and Ray R., 1984, "Dowry Death", *The Indian Journal of Social Work*, Vol. XLV(3) pp. 303-15.

Khotkina, Zoya, 1995, "Raging Crime hits Russian Women" *The Times of India*, March 11, 1995.

Kipnis, D., 1976, The power holders. Chicago: University of Chicago Press, cited in Andersen S.M., Boulette T.R., Schwartz A.H., "Psychological maltreatment of spouses", in Ammerman R.T. and Hersen M. (Eds.). *Case Studies in Family Violence*, New York, Plenum Press, 1991.

Kishwar, M. and Vanita R. (Eds.), 1984, *In search of answers: Indian women's voices from Manushi*, London, Zed Books.

Knopf, O., 1975, Successful Aging, the Facts and Fallacies of Growing

Old. New York Viking, cited in Steinmetz S.K. *Duty Bound Elder, Abuse and Family Care.*, Beverly Hills, Sage.

Knox, D. and Wilson K., 1978, "The difference between having one and two children." The family coordinator. Vol. 27., Jan. 23-26.

Kratcoski, P.C., 1984, "Perspectives on Intra Family Violence" *Human Relations*, Vol. 37(6) June, pp. 443-53, *Sociological Abstracts*, Vol. 33(1), April 1985.

Kulkarni, M.G., 1982, "Family Research in India" Nayar P.K.B. (Ed.), *Sociology in India: Retrospect and Prospect*, New Delhi, B.R. Publishing Corporation.

Kumagai, F., 1979, "Social Class, power and husband-wife violence in Japan", *Journal of Comparative Family Studies*, Vol. 10(1), pp. 91-106, Spring, cited in Sage Family Studies Abstracts, Vol. 2(1), February 1980.

Labell, L.S., 1979, "Wife abuse: A sociological study of battered women and their mates". *Victimology*, Vol. 4, pp. 258-67.

Landes, R., 1937, *Ojibwa Sociology*, New York, Columbia University Press, cited in Levinson D., Family Violence in cross cultural perspective, New Delhi, CA: Sage, 1989.

Lata, P.M., 1989, "Violence within Family: Experiences of a feminist support group" in Sood S. (Ed.) *Violence against women*. Jaipur, Arihant Publishers.

Leghorn, L., 1977, "Social Responses to Battered Women" Parts 1 and 2, cited in Moore Donna M. (Ed.) Battered Women. Beverly Hills, Sage, 1979.

Leonard, K.E. and Jacob T., 1988, "Alcohol, Alcoholism and Family Violence", In Van Hasselt V.B., Morrison R.L., Bellack A.S. and Hersen M. (Eds.) *Handbook of Family Violence*, New York, Plenum Press.

Levinson, D., 1989, Family Violence in Cross-cultural Perspective, *Frontiers of Anthropology*, Vol. 1., New Delhi, Sage.

Lewis, B.Y., 1987, "Psycho-social factors related to wife abuse", *Journal of Family Violence*, Vol 2(1), pp. 1-10.

Lewis, I.M., 1962, Marriage and the family in Northern Somaliland. *Kampala: East African Institute of Social Research*, cited in Levinson D., Family Violence in cross-cultural perspective, New Delhi, CA: Sage, 1989.

Lewis, Oscar, 1959, *Five families: Mexican case studies in the culture of poverty*, New York, Basic Books, Inc, Publishers.

Linnel, T., Zieman G.L. and Romano P.A., 1984, "Treating abusive families in heterogeneous parent groups". *Family Therapy*, Vol. 11(1), pp. 79-86, 1984, cited in Sage Family Studies Abstracts, Vol. 6(4), November 1984.

Lips, H.M., 1991, *Women, men and power*. Mountainview, California, Mayfield.

Lockhart, L.L., 1987, "A re-examination of the effects of race and social class on the incidence of marital violence: A search for reliable differences". *Journal of Marriage and the Family*, Vol. 49(3), pp. 603-10, August 1987.

Lupri, E., 1991, "Harmony and Aggression" *The dialectics of conjugal violence*, Vol. 42(3), September, pp. 474-501 cited in Sociological Abstracts, Vol. 39(1), April 1991.

Lystad, M., 1982, "Violence in the home: A major public problem", The Urban and Social Change Review, Vol. 15(2), pp. 21-25, Summer, 1982 in *Sage Family Studies Abstracts*, Vol. 5(2), May 1983.

Mahajan, A., 1986, "Wife beating as instrumental violence" *NIPCCD Newsletter*, Nov-Dec. 1986.

———, 1987, *Problems of the Aged in an Unorganized Sector*. New Delhi: Mittal Publication.

———, 1989a, "Instigators of Wife Battering" Sood Sushma (Ed.) *Family Violence in India*. Jaipur: Arihant Publishers.

———, 1989b, "State, Family and Child Development" Pimpley P.N., Singh K.P., and Mahajan A. (Eds.) *Social Development: Processes and Consequences*. Jaipur: Rawat Publications.

Mahajan, A. and Madhurima, 1995, *Family Violence and Abuse in India*., New Delhi, Deep and Deep Publications.

Mahajan, M., 1989, "Institutional care of the elderly: A study of inmates of an old age home at Chandigarh. M.A dissertation submitted to the Panjab University, Chandigarh.

Maidment, S., 1985, "Domestic violence and the law: The 1976 act and its aftermath". Johnson N. (Ed.) *Marital Violence*, London, Routledge and Kegan Paul.

Mair, L.P., 1940, *Native Marriage in Buganda*. London: Oxford University Press, cited in Levinson D., Family Violence in Cross Cultural Perspective, New Delhi, CA: Sage 1989.

Majumdar, R.C. (Ed.), 1980, *The Age of Imperial Unity*, Vol. II, Bombay, Bharatiya Vidya Bhavan.

Malone, J., Tyree A. and O'Leary K.D., 1989, "Generalization and Containment: Different effects of past aggression for wives and husbands", *Journal of Marriage and the Family*, Vol. 51, pp. 687-91, August 1989.

Mane, Purnima N., 1991, "Socialization of Hindu women in childhood: An analysis of literature". *The Indian Journal of Social Work*, Jan., Vol. LII(1).

Margolin, G., Sibner L.G. and Gleberman L., 1988, "Wife Battering", Van Hasselt, V.B.; Morrison R.L.; Bellack A.S. and Hersen M. (Eds.) *Handbook of family violence*, New York: Plenum Press.

Marsden, D., 1978, "Sociological Perspectives on Family Violence", Martin J.P. (Ed.), *Violence and the Family*, New York: Wiley.

Marsden, D., and Owens D., 1975 "The Jekyll and Hyde Marriages", *The New Society*, Vol. 32, pp. 333-35.

Martin, D., 1976, *Battered Wives*. San Francisco: Glide Publications.

———, 1979, "What keeps a woman captive in a violent relationship? The Social Content of Battering" in Moore D.M. (Ed.), *Battered Women.*, Beverly Hills, Sage.

Martin, M.J.; Schumm W.R.; Bugaighis M.A.; Jurich A.P.; Bellman S.R., 1987, "Family violence and adolescents' perceptions of outcomes of family conflict". *Journal of Marriage and the Family*, Vol. 49, pp. 165-71, February 1987.

Mathur, G., 1978, "Introduction to Violence" Udayan Sharma (Ed.) *Violence Erupts*. New Delhi, Radhakrishna Prakashan.

Maydeo, Anjali, 1989, "Domestic violence: The perspective and experiences of an activist group". Sood S. (Ed.) *Violence against Women*. Jaipur: Arihant Publishers.

Mc Adoo, H. 1981, "Patterns of Upward mobility in black families" *Black Families*. Beverly Hills, Sage.

Mc Farlane, J.W., Allen L. and Honzig P., 1954, "A Developmental study of behaviour problems of normal children between 21 months and 14 years". Univ. of California Publications in *Child Development*, Vol. II., Berkeley and Los Angeles: Univ. of California Press.

Meiselman, K., 1978, Incest. San Francisco: Jossey-Bass, cited in Finkelhor D., Gelles R.J., Hotaling G.T. and Straus M.A. (Eds.) The Dark Side of Families. *Current Family Violence Research*, Beverly Hills, CA: Sage, 1983.

Miller, T.D. and Carol P.A., 1983, "Self blame in victims of violence". *Journal of Social Issues*, Vol. 39(2), pp. 139-52.

Miller, W., 1976, "Youth gangs in the urban crisis era" cited in Downes D., "The language of violence: Sociological perspective on Adolescent Aggression" in Harsh P. and Campbell A. (Eds.) *Aggression and Violence*. Oxford Basil Blackwell.

Misra, A., 1994, "Atrocities against women increasing". *The Times of India*, February 11, 1994.

Mitchell, R.E. and Hodson C.A., 1983, "Coping with domestic violence: Social support and psychological health among battered women". American Journal of Community Psychology, Vol. 11, pp. 629-54, cited in Andersen S.M., Boulette T.R., Schwartz A.H., "Psychological maltreatment of spouses" in case studies in Family Violence (Eds.) Ammerman R.T. and Hersen M., New York, Plenum Press, 1991.

Mitchell, William E., 1990, "Why Wape men do not beat their wives: Constraints towards domestic tranquillity in a New Guinea Society". *Pacific Studies*, Vol. 13(3), July, pp. 141-50 cited in Sociological Abstracts, Vol., 39(2), June 1991.

Mohan, K., 1989, "The negative attitude of society towards women victims of family violence" Sood S. (Ed.) *Violence against women*. Jaipur: Arihant Publishers.

Mookerji, R.K., 1980, "Ashoka, the Great" Majumdar R.C. (Ed.) *The Age of Imperial Unity*. Bombay : Bharatiya Vidya Bhawan.

Moore, M.D. (Eds.), 1979, *Battered Women*. Beverly Hills: Sage Publications Inc.

Munshi, D, 1994, "Emotional Aggression. Plea to halt violence against women". *The Times of India*, June 7, 1994.

Muratoria, B., 1981, "Protestantism, ethnicity and class in Chimboraza", in Whitten N.E. (Ed.) *Cultural transformations and ethnicity in modern Ecuador*. Urbana: University of Illinois, cited in Levinson D. Family violence in cross cultural perspective, New Delhi, CA: Sage 1989.

Muzumdar, K., 1992, "Women and Violence" Perspectives in Social Work, Vol., 7(2), July-December 1992.

Naik, R.D., 1984, "A study of dowry practices in Greater Bombay". Unpublished manuscript, *Tata Institute of Social Sciences*, Bombay.

Nair, T. Krishnan, 1980, *Older people in rural Tamil Nadu* : Madras: Madras School of Social Work.

Neidig, P.M. and Friedman D.H., 1984, "Spouse Abuse: A treatment program for couples" *Champaign*, IL: Research Press cited in Stordeur R.A. and Stille R., Ending men's violence against their partners: One road to peace. New Delhi, CA: Sage, 1989.

Nicarty, G., 1982, Getting Free. cited in Hotaling G.T., Finkelhor D., Kirkpatrick J.T., Straus M.A. (Eds.) in Family Abuse and its Consequences: New Directions in Research. Beverly Hills. CA: Sage.

Nisonoff, L. and Bitman I., 1979, "Spouse abuse: Incidence and relationship to selected demographic variables. *Victimology*: An international journal, Vol. 4(1), pp. 131-39.

Norman, J., (Ed.), 1985, *Marital Violence*. London: Routledge and Kegan Paul.

Nye, F.I., (Ed.), 1982, Family relationships, *Rewards and Costs*, New Delhi: CA: Sage.

O'Brien, J., 1971, "Violence in divorce prone families", *Journal of Marriage and the Family,* Vol. 33, pp. 692-98.

Okun, L., 1988, "Termination or resumption of cohabitation in woman battering relationships : A statistical study" in Hotaling G.T., Finkelhor D., Krikpatrick J.T. and Straus M.A. (Eds.). *Coping with Family Violence. Research and Policy Perspectives.* Beverly Hills. CA: Sage.

O'Leary, K.D., Arias I., Rosenbaum A., Barling J., 1988, "Premarital physical aggression". Unpublished manuscript cited in O'Leary K.D. "Physical aggression between spouses" in Van Hasselt V.B. et al. (Eds.) *Handbook of Family Violence.* New York: Plenum Press, 1988.

O' Leary, K.D., 1988, "Physical aggression between spouses: A social learning perspective". Van Hasselt V.B., Morrison R.L., Bellack A.S. and Hersen M. (Eds.) *Handbook of Family Violence.* New York: Plenum Press.

Otten, J. and Shelley F.C., 1977, *When your parents grow old.* New York: Crowell, cited in Steinmetz S.K. *Duty Bound* Elder Abuse and Family Care, Beverly Hills, Sage.

Pagelow, M., 1978, "Need assessment of victims of domestic violence". Research into violent behaviour: Domestic violence, cited in Sedlak A.J. "Prevention of wife abuse" in Van Hasselt et al. (Eds.) *Handbook of Family Violence.* New York: Plenum Press, 1988.

Pagelow, M.D., 1981a, Woman battering: Victims and their experience, Beverly Hills, CA: Sage.

Pagelow, M., 1981b, "Secondary battering and alternatives of female victims to spouse abuse" cited in Bowker L.H. "The effects of methodology in subjective estimates of differential effectiveness of personal strategies and help sources used by battered women" Hotaling G.T., Finkelhor D., Kirkpatrick J.T., Straus M.A. (Eds.), Coping with family violence research and policy perspectives, Beverly Hills, CA: Sage, 1988.

Pagelow, M.D., 1984, Family Violence. New York: Praeger.

Parihar, L., 1988, "Wife beating: A prerogative of male Chauvinism." A paper presented at *National Workshop on Family Violence against Women*, New Delhi, February 15-18, 1988.

———, 1989, "Battered wife syndrome: Some socio-legal aspects" in Sood S. (Ed.) *Violence against women*. Jaipur: Arihant Publishers.

Parsons, T. and Bales R.F., 1955, *Family, Socialization and interaction process*, Glencoe, IL: Free Press.

Paul, M.C., 1992, "Dowry related Crimes against women: A study of Delhi metropolis" Social Change, Vol. 22(4), December 1992.

Pillemer, K., 1985, "The dangers of dependency. New findings on domestic violence against the elderly". *Social Problems*, Vol. 33(2), Dec. 1985.

Pleck, E., 1987, *Domestic Tyranny*, New York: Oxford University Press.

Post, R.D.; Willett A.B.; Franks R.D.; House R.M.; Beck S. and Weissberg M.P., 1980, "A preliminary report on the prevalence of domestic violence among psychiatric impatients. *American Journal of Psychiatry*, Vol. 137, pp. 974-75.

Ponzetti, J.J.; Cate R.M. and Koval J.E., 1982, "Violence between couples: Profiling the male abuser". Personnel and Guidance Journal, Vol. 61, pp. 222-4 cited in Andersen S.M., Boulette T.R., Schwartz A.H. "Psychological maltreatment of spouses" Ammerman R.T. and Hersen Michel (Eds.) *Case studies in Family Violence*, New York: Plenum Press, 1991.

Prasad, B.D., 1989, "Dowry related violence towards women: A sociological perspective". Sood S. (Ed.) *Violence against Women*. Jaipur: Arihant Publishers.

Prasad, B.D. and Vijaylakshmi B., 1988, "Dowry related violence towards women — Some issues". *The Indian Journal of Social Work*, Vol. 49(3), July, pp. 271-80.

Prescott, S. and Letko C., 1977, "Battered women: A social psychological perspective". Roy M. (Ed.), *"Battered women: A psycho-sociological study of domestic violence*. London: Van Nastrand.

Ptacek, J., 1988, "The clinical literature on men who batter: A review and critique" in Hotaling G.T., Finkelhor D., Kirkpatrick J.T. and Straus M.A. (Eds.) *Family abuse and its consequences,* Beverly Hills, CA: Sage.

Purdy, F. and Nickle N., 1981, "Practice principles for working with groups of men who batter" Social work with Groups, Vol. 4, pp. 111-12. cited in Stordeur R.A. and Stille R., *Ending men's violence against their partners: One road to peace,* New Delhi, CA: Sage 1988.

Radford, L., 1987, "Legalising Women Abuse", Hanmer J. and Maynard M. (Eds.) *Women, Violence and Social Control,* London: Routledge.

Rajender, Indra, 1963, "Problems of old women in village". M.A.,dissertation submitted to Panjab University, Chandigarh.

Randawa, M. and Bhatnagar G.S., 1985, "Changing attitudes and beliefs of the retired people". *The Journal of Sociological Studies,* Vol. 4, Jan, pp. 120-27.

Rai, U., 1994, "Calm balm for battered women". *The Indian Express,* August 10,1994.

Ridington, J., 1977-78, "The transition process: A feminist environment as reconstitutive milieu". *Victimology,* Vol. 2, pp. 563-75.

Rieker, P. and Carmen E.M., 1986, "The Victim-to-patient process: The disconfirmation and transformation of abuse". *American Journal of Ortho-psychiatry,* Vol. 56, pp. 360-70 cited in Andersen S.M., Boulette T.R. and Schwartz A.H. "Psychological maltreatment of spouses" in Ammerman R.T. and Michel Hersen (Eds.) *Case studies in Family Violence.* New York: Plenum Press, 1991.

Roberts, A.R., 1984, "Intervention with the abusive partner" Roberts A.R. (Ed.) *Battered women and their families.* New York: Springer.

Rollins, B.C. and Foldman H., 1970, "Marital satisfaction over the family life cycle". *Journal of Marriage and the Family,* Vol. 32, February, pp. 20-28.

Rosenbaum, A., 1986, "Group treatment for abusive men: Process and outcome". *Psychotherapy,* Vol. 23(4), pp. 607-12 cited in Stordeur R.A. and Stille R., Ending men's violence against their partners: One road to peace. New Delhi: CA: Sage, 1989.

Rosenbaum, A. and O'Leary K.D., 1981a, "Marital violence: Characteristics of abusive couples". *Journal of Consulting and Clinical Psychology,* Vol. 49, pp. 63-71.

———, 1981b, "Children: The unintended victims of marital violence". *American Journal of Ortho-psychiatry,* Vol. 51(4): pp. 692-99, October 1981.

Rounsaville, B., 1978, "Theories in marital violence: Evidence from a study of battered women". *Victimology,* Vol. 3(1-2), pp. 11 and 31.

———, and Weissman M.H., 1978, "Battered Women": A medical problem requiring detection". *International Journal of Psychiatry in Medicine,* Vol. 8, pp. 191-201 cited in Gelles R.J. and Harrop J.W. "Psychological distress and violence". Journal of Interpersonal Violence, Vol. 4(4), pp. 400-20, December, 1989.

Roy, M., 1977, *Battered Women: A psycho-social study of domestic violence.* New York: Van Nostrand Reinhold.

-----, 1982, *The abusive partner: An analysis of domestic battering.* New York: Van Nostrand.

Russell, D.E.H. and Nicole Van de Ven (Eds.), 1976, *International Tribunal on Crimes against Women,* cited in Moore D.M. (Ed.) Battered Women, Beverly Hills, CA: Sage 1979.

Ryckman, R.M., 1978, *Theories of Personality.* New York: D. Van Nostrand Co.

Saheli, 1986, "Wife Battering: Issues facing the women's movement". A paper presented at the *Third National Conference on Women Studies,* October, 1-4, 1986 at Panjab University, Chandigarh.

Sanders, I.T., 1962, *Rainbow on the Rock: The people of rural Greece.* Cambridge. Harvard University Press, cited in Levinson D. Family, Violence in cross-cultural perspective. New Delhi: CA: Sage, 1989.

Saunders, D.G., 1982, "Counselling the violent husband" Keller P.A. and Ritt L.G. (Eds.) *Innovations in clinical practice,* Vol. 1, Sarasota: Professional resource exchange, cited in Stordeur R.A. and Stille R., Ending men's Violence against their partners: One road to peace, New Delhi, CA: Sage, 1989.

Saunders, D.G., 1984, "Helping husbands who batter" *Social Casework,* Vol. 65(6), pp. 347-53, cited in Stordeur R.A. and Stille R., Ending men's violence against their partners: One road to peace, New Delhi, CA: Sage, 1989.

Savishinsky, J.S., 1976, Stress and mobility in an arctic community: *The Hare Indians of Colville Lake, Northwest Territories,* Ann Arbor: University Microfilms International cited in Levinson D., Family Violence in cross cultural perspective. New Delhi, CA: Sage, 1989.

Schauss, A.G., 1982, "Effects of environmental and nutritional factors on potential and actual batterers". Roy M. (Ed.) *The abusive partner: An analysis of domestic battering.* New York: Van Nostrand.

Schechter, S., 1982, Women and male violence. Boston, M.A.: South End Press, cited in Gondolf E. W., and Fisher E.R., "Wife Battering" in Ammerman R.T. and Hersen M. (Eds.) *Case Studies in Family Violence.* New York: Plenum Press, 1991.

Schulman, M.A., 1979, Survey of spousal violence against women in Kentucky" conducted for Kentucky Commission on Women, cited in Stark E. and Flitcraft A. "Violence among intimates" in Van Hasselt V.B. et al. (Eds.) *Handbook of Family Violence.* New York: Plenum Press, 1987.

Schwartz, Martin D., 1990, "Work Status, resource equality, injury and wife battering: The National Crime Survey data" *Free Enquiry in Creative Sociology,* Vol. 18(1), May, pp. 37-67 cited in Sociological Abstracts, Vol. 38(5), Dec. 1990.

Seager, J. and Olson A., 1986, *Women in the World: An International Atlas.* New York. Simon and Schuster, Inc.

Sears, R.R., 1961, "Relation of early socialization experiences to aggression in middle childhood". *Journal of Abnormal and Social Psychology,* Vol. 63, pp. 466-92.

Sedlak, A.J., 1988, "The effect of personal experiences with couple violence on calling it battering and allocating blame". In Hotaling G.T., Finkelhor D., Kirkpatrick J.T., Straus M.A. (Eds.) *Coping with Family Violence: Research and Policy Perspectives.* New Delhi. CA: Sage.

Shaffer, D.; Meyer-Bahlburg H.F.L. and Stokman C.L.J., 1980, "The development of aggression" in Rutter M. (Ed.) *Scientific Foundations of Developmental Psychiatry.* London: Heineman Medical, 358-68.

Shah, G., 1989, "Crime against women: Dowry, divorce and bride burning" in Sood S. (Ed.) *Violence against women.* Jaipur: Arihant Publishers.

Shainess, N., 1977, "Psychological aspects of wife battering" in Roy M. (Ed.) *Battered women: A psycho-sociological study of domestic violence.* New York: Van Nostrand.

———, 1979, "Vulnerability to violence: Masochism as process" American Journal of Psychotherapy, 33, 174-189 cited in Gelles R.J. and Harrop J.W. "Psychological distress and violence". *Journal of interpersonal violence,* Vol. 1, No. 4, pp. 400-20, Dec. 1989.

Sharma, Raka, 1985, "Socio-psychological problems of the aged". M.A dissertation submitted to the Panjab University

Sharma, M.L.; Salitesh, Darshan; L. Abrol and Neerja Sharma, 1986, "Aging, health status and health care in rural Haryana". Paper presented in *XI World Congress of Sociology* held at New Delhi from August 18-22.

Sharma, S.S., 1992, "Case Study of Battered Women" in Mishra R.P. and Singh C. (Eds.) Indian Women: Challenges and Change. New Delhi, Common-wealth Publications.

Shupe, A., W.A. Stacey and L.R. Hazlewood, 1987, *Violent Men, Violent Couples.* Lexington, M.A.: D.C. Health.

Singh, D., 1985, "Family Violence: A case study of a village preponderated by scheduled castes". A dissertation submitted for M.Phil degree, Dept. of Sociology, Panjab University, Chandigarh.

Singh, I.P. and Renuka, 1989, "Dowry: How many more deaths to its end?" in Sood S. (Ed.) *Violence against women.* Jaipur: Arihant Publishers.

Singh, S., 1991, "Violence against Women in Indian Society." *Indian Journal of Social Research,* Vol. 32(1), March 1991.

Singhal, Sujata, 1988, "Aged Women: Work participation and problems". M.A. dissertation submitted to Panjab University, Chandigarh.

Smith, Michael, D., 1990, "Patriarchal ideology and wife beating: A test of a feminist hypothesis". *Violence and Victims* 5(4), Winter, pp. 257-73.

Snell, J.E.; Rosenwald R.J. and Robey A., 1964, "The wife beater's wife: A study of family interaction" *Archives of General Psychiatry*, Vol. 11, pp. 107-12. Cited in Stark E. and Flitcraft A. in "Violence among intimates" in Van Hasselt V.B. et al. (Eds.) *Handbook of Family Violence.* New York: Plenum Press, 1988.

Sonkin, D.L.; Martin D. and Walker L., 1985, The male batterers: A treatment approach. New York: Springer, cited in Stordeur R.A. and Stille R., Ending men's violence against their partners: one road to peace. New Delhi: CA: Sage, 1989.

Sood, S. (Ed.), 1989, *Violence against Women*. Jaipur: Arihant Publishers.

Sprey, J., 1974, "On management of conflict in families". In Steinmetz S.K. and Straus M.A. (Eds.) *Violence in the family*. New York: Harper and Row.

Srivastava, S.L., 1974, *Folk Culture and Oral Tradition*. New Delhi: Abhinav Publications.

Stacey, W. and Shupe A., 1983, *The family secret*. Boston: Beacon.

Star, B., 1980, "Patterns of Family Violence". Social Casework, Vol. 61, pp. 339-46 Quoted by Finkelhor D., Gelles R.J., Hotaling G.T. and Straus M.A. (Eds.) *The Dark Side of Families*. Current Family Violence Research, Beverly Hills, CA: Sage, 1983.

-----, 1983, Helping the abuser: Intervening effectively in family violence. New York: Family Service Association of America, cited in Stordeur R.A. and Stille R., Ending men's violence against their partners: One road to peace. New Delhi, CA: Sage, 1989.

Star, B., Clark C.G.; Goetz K.M. and O'Malia L., 1979, "Psychological aspects of wife battering" Social Casework, Vol. 60; pp. 479-87, cited in Stordeur R.A. and Stille R., *Ending men's violence against their partners*. New Delhi. CA: Sage, 1989.

Stark, E. and Flitcraft A.H., 1985, *Spouse Abuse*. Atlanta: Centres for Disease Control, Violence Epidemiology branch, quoted by Levinson D. in Family Violence in cross cultural perspective. *Frontiers of Anthropology*, Vol. I, New Delhi: Sage.

-----,1988, "Violence among intimates" In Van Hasselt V.B., Morrison R.L., Bellack A.S., Hersen M. (Eds.) *Handbook of Family Violence*. New York: Plenum Press.

Stark, E. Flitcraft A.; Zuckerman D.; Grey A.; Robinson J. and Frazier W., 1981, "Wife Abuse in medical setting: An introduction for health personnel", cited in Stark E. and Flitcraft A. in "Violence among intimates" Van Hasselt V.B., Morrison R.L., Bellack A.S. and Hersen M. (Eds.) *Handbook of Family Violence*. New York: Plenum Press.

Stark, R. and McEvoy I.J., 1970, "Middle class Violence" *Psychology Today*, Vol. 4, pp. 52-4 cited in Margolin G., Sibner L.G. and Gleberman L. "Wife Battering" in Van Hasselt V.B. et al. (Eds.) *Handbook of Family Violence*. New York: Plenum Press, 1988.

Steinmetz, S.K., 1977, *The cycle of violence: Assertive, aggressive and abusive family interaction*. New York: Praeger.

----, 1978, "Violence between family members" *Marriage and Family Review*, Vol. 1, pp. 1-16.

Steinmetz, S.K. and Straus M.A., 1974, *Violence in the family*. New York, Dodd, Head and Company.

Stich, S.M. and Farley S.C., 1993, "A predictive model of male spousal abuse." *Journal of Family Violence*, Vol. 8(2), pp. 183-201, June 1993.

Stolen, Kristi Anne, 1990, "Dangerous women, violent men: A socio-cultural analysis of wife abuse in Caipi Ecuador". Tidsskrift for Samfemns-forsking, Vol. 31(5), pp. 441-59, cited in Sociological Abstracts, Vol. 39(4), Oct. 1991.

Stordeur, R.A. and Stille, R. 1989, Ending men's violence against their partners: One road to peace. New Delhi. CA: Sage.

Straus, M.A., 1973, "A general systems theory approach to a theory of violence between family members". *Social Science Information*, Vol. 12, p. 105.

———, 1976, "Sexual inequality, cultural norms and wife beating". *Victimology*, Vol. 1, pp. 54-76.

———, 1978, "Wife beating: How common and why?" *Victimology:* An International Journal, Vol. 1: pp. 54-76.

———, 1979, "Measuring intra-family conflict and violence: The conflict tactics scales". *Journal of Marriage and the Family*, Vol. 41, pp. 75-88.

------, 1980a, "A Sociological perspectives on the causes of family violence" in Green M.R. (Ed.) *Violence and the family*. Boulder Co: Westview.

———, 1980b "Sexual inequality and wife beating" in Straus M.A. and Hotaling G.T. (Eds.) The social causes of husband-wife violence. Minnepolis, MN: University of Minnesota Press.

———, 1980c, "Social stress and marital violence in a national sample of American families" Symposium on Forensic Psychology and Psychiatry, New York, cited in O'Leary L.D. "Physical aggression between spouses" in Van Hasselt V.B. et al. (Eds.) Handbook of Family Violence. New York: Plenum Press, 1988.

———, and Gelles R.J., 1986, "Societal changes and family violence from 1975 to 1985 as revealed by two national surveys". *Journal of Marriage and the Family*, Vol. 48, pp. 465-79.

Straus, M., Gelles R. and Steinmetz S., 1980, *Behind closed doors : Violence in the American family*. New York: Anchor.

Strube, M.J., 1988, "The decision to leave an abusive relationship" in Hotaling G.T., Finkelhor D., Krikpatrick J.T. and Straus M.A. (Eds.) *Coping with family violence: Research and policy perspectives*. Beverly Hills: CA: Sage.

Strube, M.J. and Barbour L.S., 1983, "The decision to leave an abusive relationship: Economic dependence and psychological commitment". *Journal of Marriage and the Family*, Vol. 45, pp. 785-93.

Stryker, S., 1967, "Symbolic interaction as an approach to family research" in Marris J.G. and Meltzer B.N. (Eds.) *Symbolic interaction.* Boston, MA: Allyn and Bacon.

Sugumar, M., 1989, "The relationships to psycho-social distress: A study to predict dowry-psychological violence on working women" in Sood S., (Ed.) *Violence against Women.* Jaipur : Arihant Publishers.

Sundaram, M., 1981, "The bridal torture chamber" *Imprint* 21(3) June, pp. 6-10.

Szinovacz, M.E., 1983, "Using couple data as a methodological tool: The case of marital violence". *Journal of Marriage and the Family,* Vol. 45, pp. 633-44.

Teger, A.I., 1980, *Too much invested to quit.* New York: Pergamon.

Telch, C.F. and Lindquist C.V., 1984, "Violent versus non-violent couples" A comparison of patterns, Psychotherapy, Vol. 21, pp. 242-48 cited in Margolin G., Sibner L.G. and Gleberman L. "Wife battering" in Van Hasselt V.B. et al. (Eds.) Handbook of Family Violence. New York: Plenum Press, 1988.

Teske, R.H.C. and Parker M.L., 1983, "Spouse abuse in Texas : A study of women's attitudes and experiences", cited in E. Stark and Flitcraft A. in "Violence among intimates" in Hasselt V., Morrison R.L., Bellack A.S. and Hersen M. (Eds.) Handbook of Family Violence. New York: Plenum Press, 1988. *The Times of India* (1995) Gender bias against females at every stage. Survey, March 8, 1995.

Truninger, E., 1971, "Marital violence: the legal solutions" Hastings Law Review, Vol. 13: pp. 159-176 cited in Kalmuss D.S. and Straus M.A. in "Wife's Marital Dependency and Wife Abuse". *Journal of Marriage and the Family.* Vol. 44, May, 1982.

The Tribune, 1994, "Wife beating on the rise" August 1st, 1994; "Sharp rise in crime against women, August 21st, 1995.

Turner, W. and Shapiro C.H., 1986, "Battered Women: Mourning the death of a relationship" Social Work, Vol. 31, pp. 372-76 cited in Andersen S.M., Boulette T.R., Schwartz A.H. "Psychological maltreatment of spouses". Ammerman Roberts T. and Hersen

Michel (Eds.) *Case Studies in Family Violence.* New York: Plenum Press: 1991.

Ulbrich, P. and Huber J., 1981, "Observing parental violence: Distribution and effects". *Journal of Marriage and the Family,* Vol. 43(3), pp. 623-31, August, 1981.

Verghese, J., 1980, *Her gold and her body.* Sahibabad (Uttar Pradesh): Vikas Publishing House.

Vaugan, S.R., 1979, "The last refuge: Shelter for battered women" *Victimology,* Vol. 4, pp. 113-50.

Walker, L.E., 1978, "Treatment alternatives for battered women" cited in Kalmuss D.S. and Straus M.A. "Wife's marital dependency and wife abuse" in *Journal of Marriage and the Family,* Vol. 44, May 1982.

Walker, L.E., 1979, *The battered woman.* New York: Harper and Row.

Walker, L.E., 1981, "Battered Women: Sex roles and clinical issues". *Professional Psychology,* Vol. 12, pp. 81-91.

———, 1983, "Battered women in the correctional system". Paper presented at the American correctional association annual congress, Chicago, cited in Andersen S.M., Boulette T.R., Schwartz A.H. "Psychological maltreatment of spouses" in Ammerman R.J. and Hersen M. (Eds.) Case Studies in Family Violence. New York: Plenum Press, 1991.

———, 1984, The Battered women syndrome, New York : Springer,

———, 1988, "The battered woman syndrome" in Hotaling G.T., Finkelhor D., Kirkpatrick J.T. and Straus M.A. (Eds.) *Family abuse and Its Consequences.* Beverly Hills, CA: Sage.

Weitzman, J. and Dreen K., 1982, "Wife beating: A review of the marital dyad". Social Casework, Vol. 63, pp. 259-65, cited in Stark E. and Flitcraft A. "Violence among Intimates" in Van Hasselt V.B. et al. (Eds.) *Handbook of Family Violence.* New York: Plenum Press, 1988.

Whitehurst, 1971, "Violence potential in extramarital sexual responses". *Journal of Marriage and Family* , Vol. 33, pp. 683-91.

Whitehurst, R.N., 1974, "Violence in husband-wife interaction" Steinmetz S.K. and Straus M.A. (Eds.) *Violence in the Family*. New York: Dodd, Mead and Company.

Willie, C., 1981, A new look at Black families. New York: General Hall, cited in Lockhart L.L. in "A Re-examination of the effects of Race and Social class on the incidence of marital violence : A research for reliable differences". *Journal of Marriage and the Family*, Vol. 49(3), pp. 603-10, August 1987.

Wolfgang, M.E. and Ferracuti F., 1982, *The sub culture of violence*. Beverly Hills: CA: Sage.

Yllo, Kersti, 1983, "Sexual equality and violence against wives in American States". *Journal of Comparative Family Studies*, Vol. 14(1), pp. 67-86, Spring 1983 in *Sociological Abstracts*, Vol. 31(4), Oct. 1983.

Young, L.R., 1963, "The behaviour syndromes of parents who neglect and abuse their children", cited in Noel A. Cazenave and Straus M.A. in "Race, class, network embeddedness and family violence: A search for potent support system". *Journal of Comparative Family Studies*, Vol. 10(3), Autumn, 1979.

Zoomer, Olga J., 1983, "On the social causes on a function of violence against women". *International Journal of offenders therapy and comparative Criminology*, Vol. 27(2), September, pp. 173-83 cited in *Sociological Abstracts*, Vol. 33(2), August 1985.

Index

Abuse, 17
Adultry, 186
Age at marriage, 80, 178
Agnes, 27, 66
Ahuja, 27, 32-33, 65, 81
Alcohol, 32, 65, 180, 186
Allen, 94
Asymmetric gender relations, 20, 192

Bersani, 47
Bhatti, 27, 32-33, 65
Blenkner, 50
Bowker, 35, 110

Case studies, 129
Caste, 94-96
Chen, 47
Coleman, 35, 37, 47, 51, 65
Conflict perspective, 46-47
Conjugal violence, 18, 190
Coping behaviour, 39-40, 109, 189
Cornell, 29-30, 33, 36, 110
Culture of poverty, 46, 93

Davis, 33, 47
Denzin, 45
Dependency, 37-38, 56, 101-4
  Economic, 183, 195
  Framework, 49-52
  Objective, 51, 57, 103-4, 196, 213-14
  Subjective, 51, 57, 104-6, 196, 215-17
  Total, 57, 106-7, 217-18
Dobash, 16, 33, 92, 98
Dowry, 33, 66, 180, 186

Education, 21, 87-88, 178, 187
Employment status, 34-35
Exchange/Social control theory, 44

Ferracuti, 46
Finkelhor, 47, 98
Flitcraft, 28, 87

Gelles, 15-17, 33, 44, 89, 110, 113-15
General systems theory, 48-49
Goode, 15, 44, 100
Gondolf, 40-41, 110

Hornung, 34, 89

Jealousy, 31

Kalmuss, 29, 52, 89
Knopf, 50

Learned helplessness, 39, 114, 123
Levinson, 16-17, 24, 35, 42, 100
Lewis, 33, 46, 93

Madhurima, 33, 51, 60
Mahajan, 30, 33, 51, 60, 102
Majumdar, 20
Mane, 19
Marital satisfaction, 31
Martin, 31, 51, 128

National movement, 20
Number of children, 83-84

Occupation, 89-90, 193
Occupational prestige, 91, 187
O' Leary, 29, 30, 35-36, 98

Pagelow, 17, 36, 41, 113, 116
Parihar, 32, 60, 65, 127
Patriarchal perspective, 47-48
Personality disorder, 28-29
Pillemer, 50
Power dynamics, 17
Pregnancy, 31
Psychological entrapment, 39

Race, 32-33
Reconciliatory approach, 122
Reform movement, 20
Resource theory, 44
Rosenbaum, 29, 36, 98, 110
Roy, 31, 51, 128

Self-blame, 30, 64
Self-esteem, 29, 39
Sex of children, 22, 84-85, 178
Sexual jealousy, 31
Shah, 27, 32, 85
Shainess, 28-29
Shupe, 31, 81, 89
Singh, 27, 32, 60, 85
Social class, 33-34, 92-94, 125, 177, 201
Social learning, 36-37
Social trap, 123
Stark, 87
Status inconsistency, 37
Steinmetz, 15, 23, 33, 92
Stordeur, 38, 111
Straus, 15, 17, 23, 33, 35, 98-100, 102, 113
Stress, 30
Strube, 40, 51, 121
Sub-culture of violence, 46
Symbolic interaction, 45-46

Traditional sex role orientation, 35-36, 55, 97, 99, 188, 207
Treatment, 40-41, 110
Truninger, 37, 51, 102, 121, 126
Tulsidas, 19

Value orientation, 35, 99, 101, 188, 211
Victims reactions, 113-17, 181-82
Violence, 16-17, 53, 60, 130, 185
  incidence of, 23-27, 59
  family, 16-18
  withdrawal, 53, 60, 66, 73-77, 187
  psychological, 41, 53, 60, 68-69 73-77, 187
  verbal, 53, 60, 70, 73-77, 185
  physical, 41, 53-54, 60, 70-77, 79-82 185

Walker, 16, 29, 33, 38, 41, 92, 98-99, 102
Whitehurst, 31, 33, 35, 99
Wife abuse, 60, 111, 113
Wife battering, 48, 92, 94
Wife beating, 39, 47, 59
Wolfgang, 46
Women organisations, 124

Yllo, 36